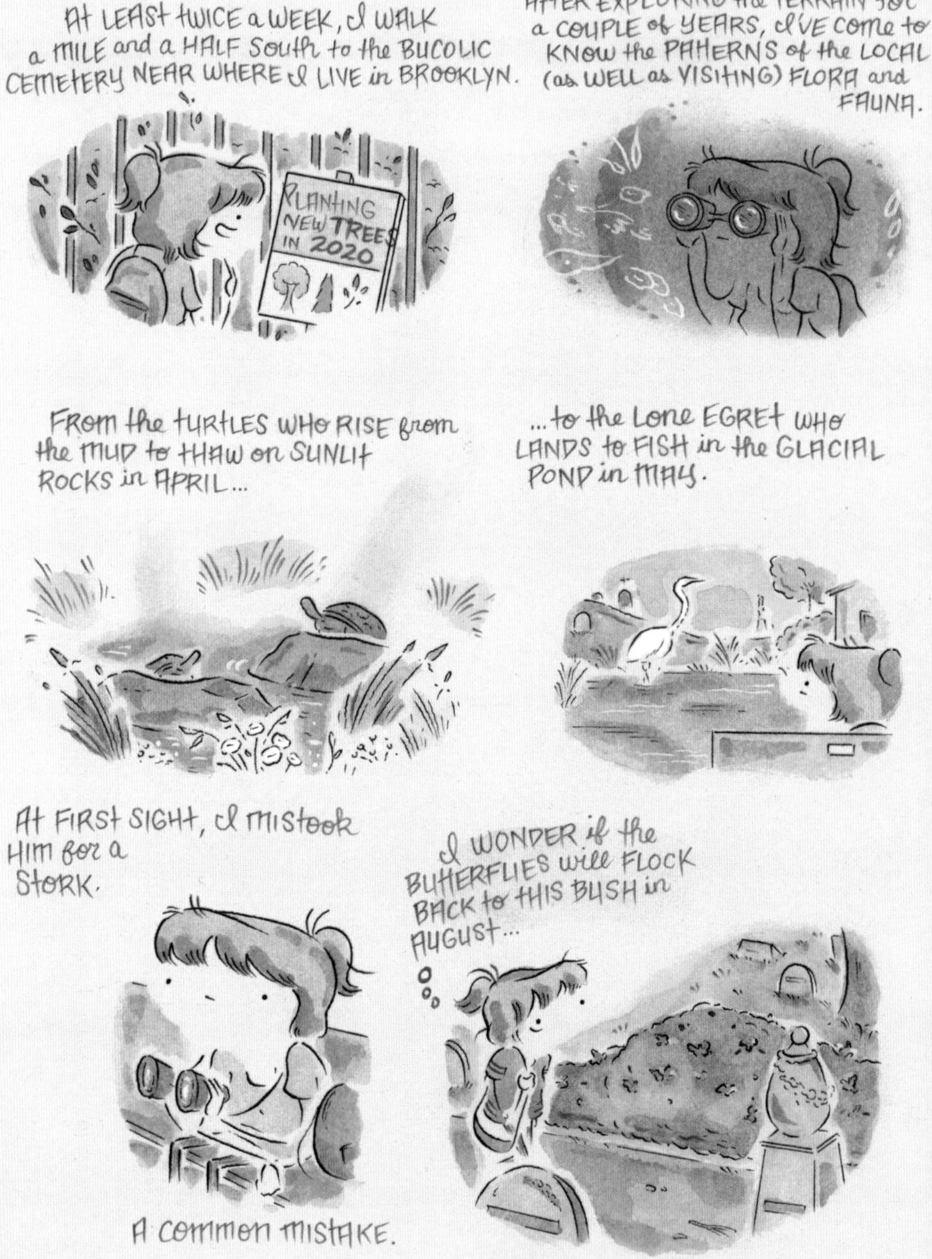
AT LEAST TWICE A WEEK, I WALK A MILE AND A HALF SOUTH TO THE BUCOLIC CEMETERY NEAR WHERE I LIVE IN BROOKLYN.
PLANTING NEW TREES IN 2020
AFTER EXPLORING THE TERRAIN FOR A COUPLE OF YEARS, I'VE COME TO KNOW THE PATTERNS OF THE LOCAL (AS WELL AS VISITING) FLORA AND FAUNA.
FROM THE TURTLES WHO RISE FROM THE MUD TO THAW ON SUNLIT ROCKS IN APRIL...
...TO THE LONE EGRET WHO LANDS TO FISH IN THE GLACIAL POND IN MAY.
AT FIRST SIGHT, I MISTOOK HIM FOR A STORK.
A COMMON MISTAKE.
I WONDER IF THE BUTTERFLIES WILL FLOCK BACK TO THIS BUSH IN AUGUST...

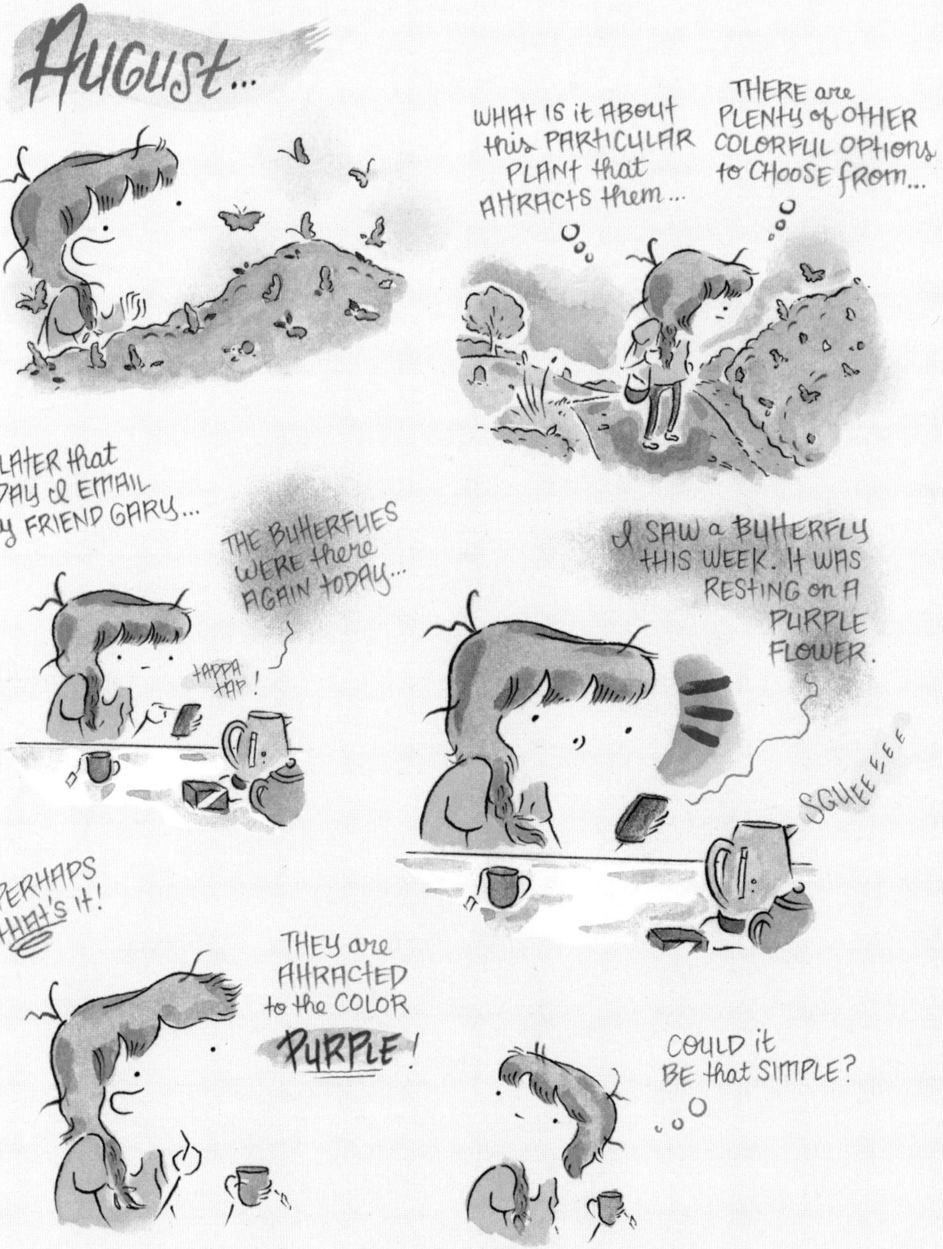
August...
WHAT IS it ABOUT this PARTICULAR PLANT that ATTRACTS them...
THERE are PLENTY of OTHER COLORFUL OPTIONS to CHOOSE from...
LATER that DAY I EMAIL my FRIEND GARY...
THE BUTTERFLIES WERE there AGAIN TODAY...
TAPPA TAP!
I SAW a BUTTERFLY THIS WEEK. IT WAS RESTING on A PURPLE FLOWER.
SQUEEEEEE
PERHAPS THAT'S it!
THEY are ATTRACTED to the COLOR PURPLE!
COULD it BE that SIMPLE?

*Thank you: Everyone at Drawn and Quarterly,
my friends, my family.*

drawnandquarterly.com

First edition: May 2020 | Printed in China | 10 9 8 7 6 5 4 3 2 1

Cataloguing data available from Library and Archives Canada.

Published in the USA by Drawn & Quarterly, a client publisher of Farrar, Straus and Giroux. Published in Canada by Drawn & Quarterly, a client publisher of Raincoast Books. Published in the United Kingdom by Drawn & Quarterly, a client publisher of Publishers Group UK.

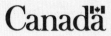 Drawn & Quarterly acknowledges the support of the Government of Canada and the Canada Council for the Arts for our publishing program.

I Know You Rider

a memoir

Leslie Stein

Drawn & Quarterly

December

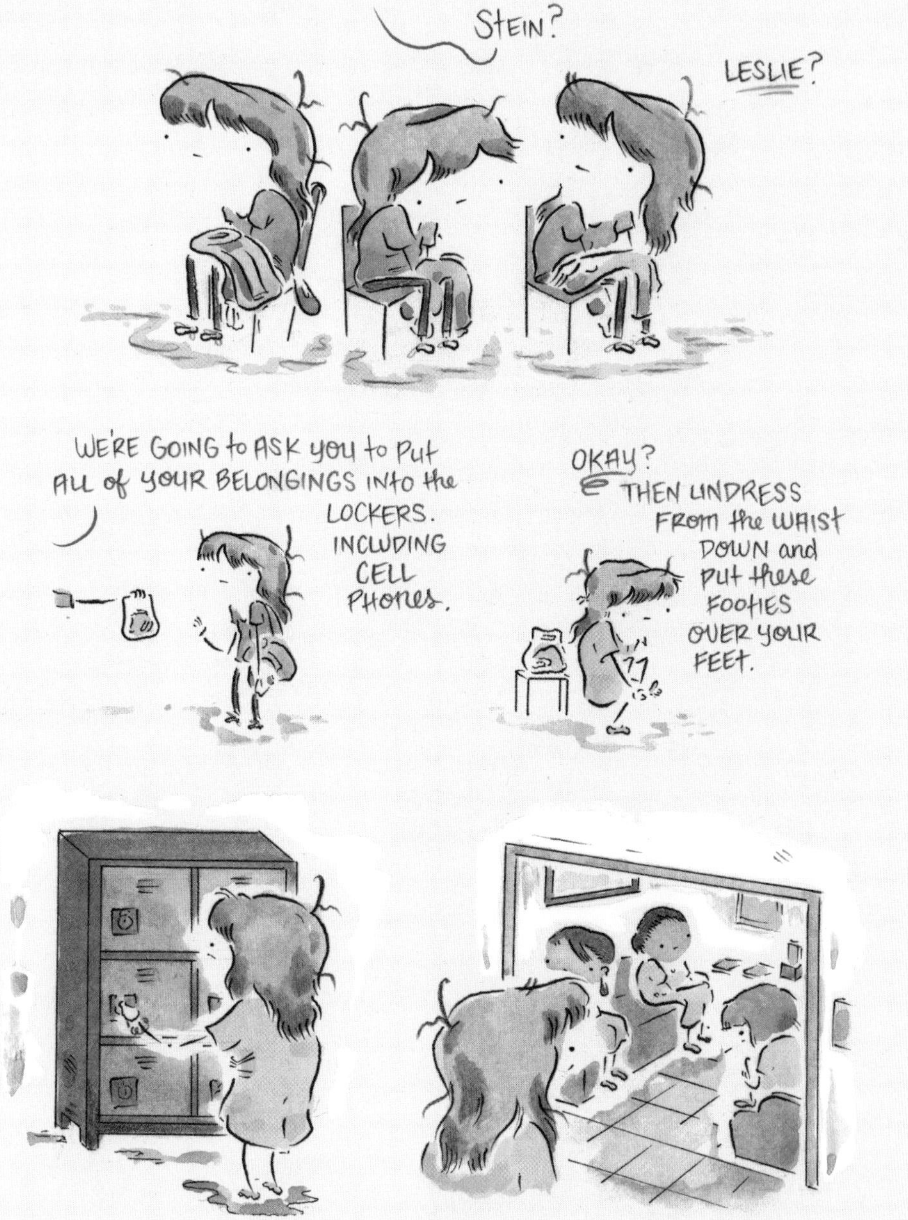
STEIN?
LESLIE?
WE'RE GOING to ASK you to Put ALL of YOUR BELONGINGS into the LOCKERS. INCLUDING CELL PHONES.
OKAY?
THEN UNDRESS FROM the WAIST DOWN and put these FOOTIES OVER YOUR FEET.

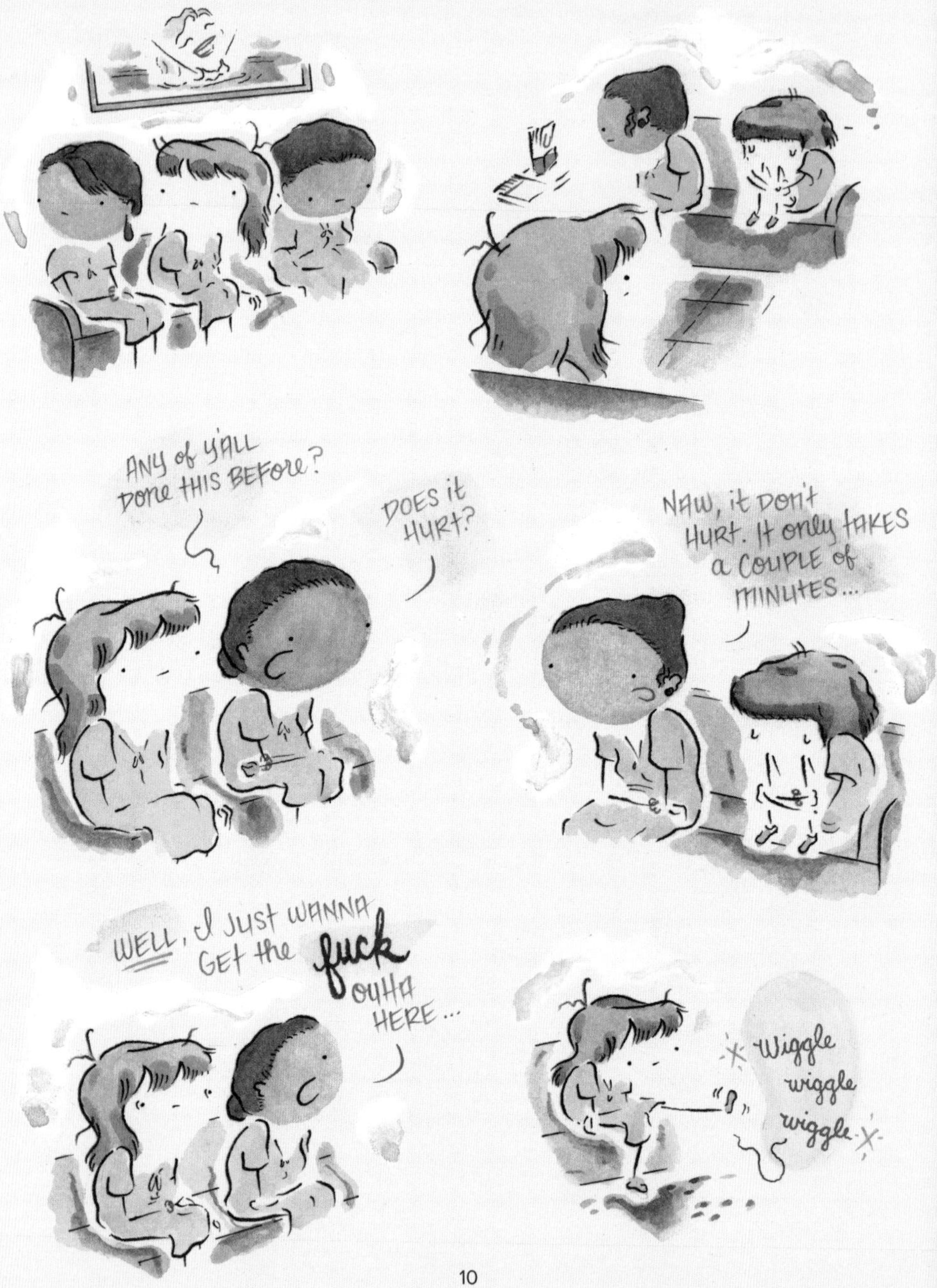
ANY of Y'ALL DONE THIS BEFORE?
DOES it HURT?
NAW, it DON'T HURT. It only TAKES a COUPLE of MINUTES...
WELL, I JUST WANNA GET the fuck OUTTA HERE...
wiggle wiggle wiggle

November

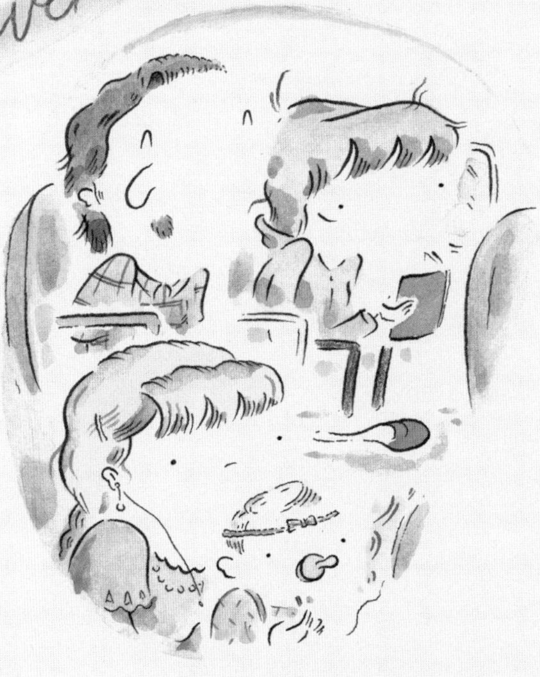

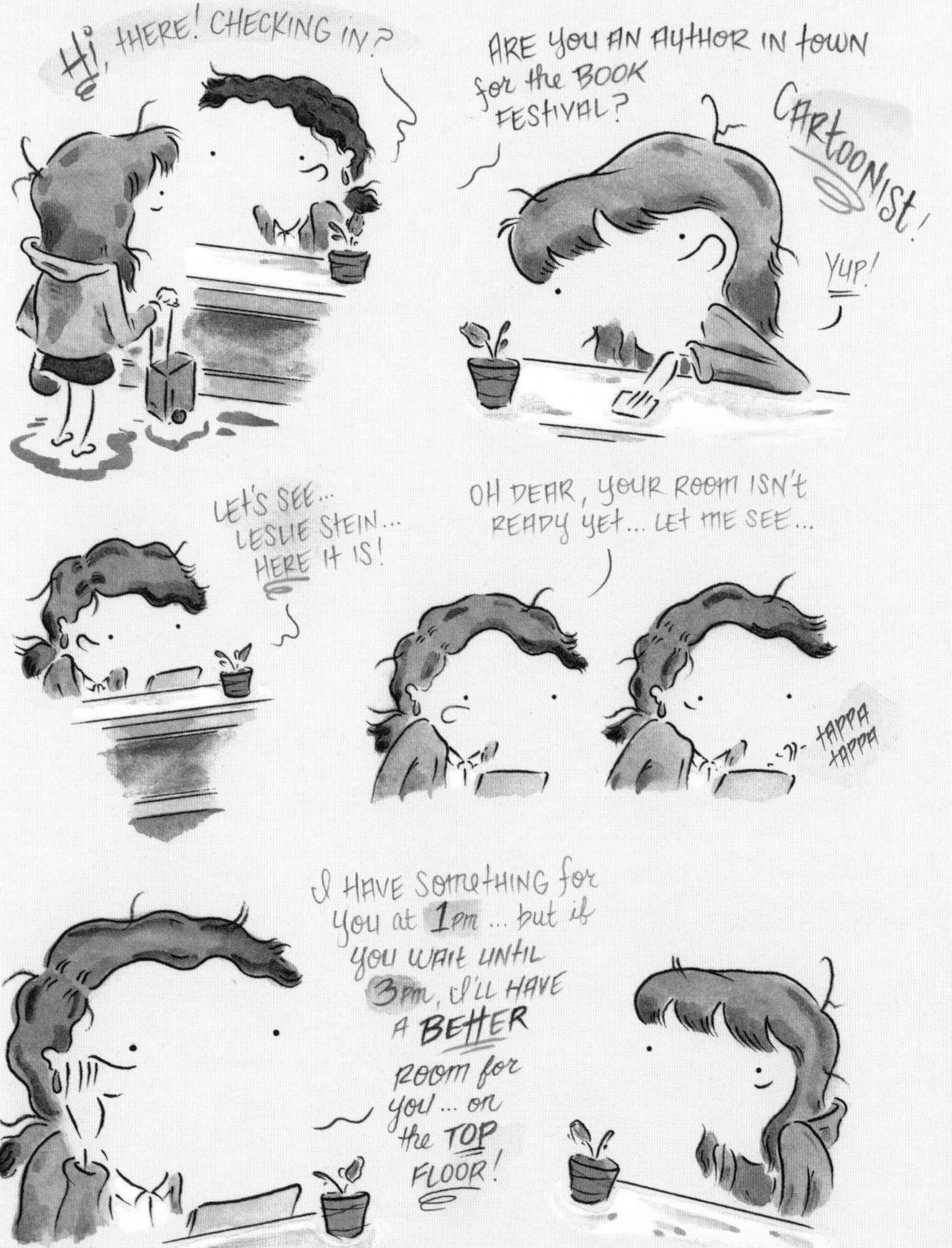

Hi, THERE! CHECKING IN?
ARE YOU AN AUTHOR IN TOWN for the BOOK FESTIVAL?
CARTOONIST!
YUP!
LET'S SEE... LESLIE STEIN... HERE IT IS!
OH DEAR, YOUR ROOM ISN'T READY YET... LET ME SEE...
TAPPA TAPPA
I HAVE SOMETHING FOR YOU AT 1PM ... BUT IF YOU WAIT UNTIL 3PM, I'LL HAVE A BETTER ROOM FOR YOU... ON THE TOP FLOOR!

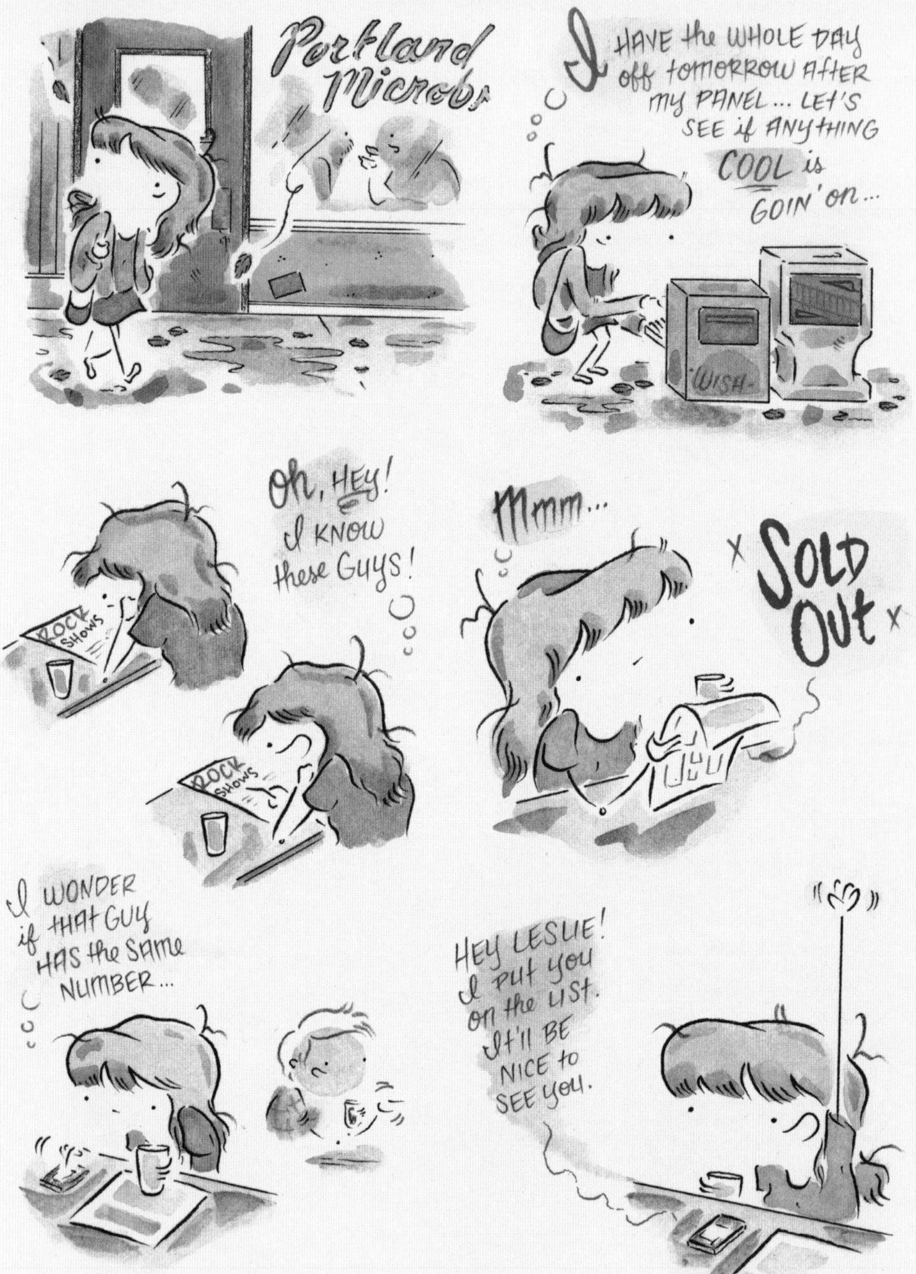
Portland Microbr
I HAVE the WHOLE DAY off tomorrow After my PANEL ... LET'S SEE if ANYTHING COOL is GOIN' on...
WISH
Oh, HEY! I KNOW these GUYS!
ROCK SHOWS
ROCK SHOWS
Mmm...
SOLD OUT
I WONDER if THAT GUY HAS the SAME NUMBER...
HEY LESLIE! I PUT YOU ON the LIST. It'll BE NICE to SEE YOU.

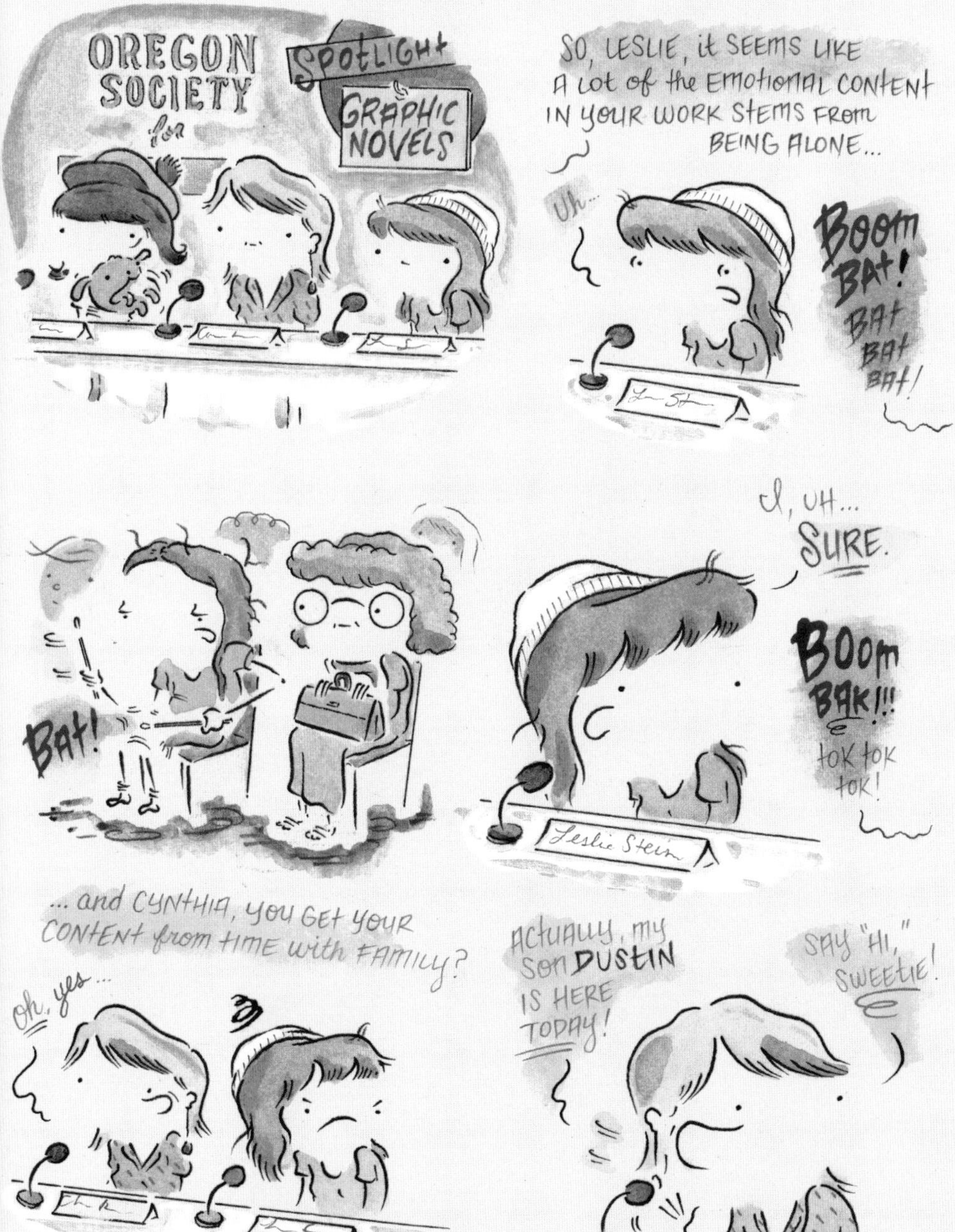
OREGON SOCIETY for
SPOTLIGHT ON GRAPHIC NOVELS
SO, LESLIE, it SEEMS LIKE A LOT of the EMOTIONAL CONTENT IN YOUR WORK STEMS FROM BEING ALONE...
Uh...
BOOM BAT! BAT BAT BAT!
BAT!
I, UH... SURE.
BOOM BAK!!! tok tok tok!
Leslie Stein
... and CYNTHIA, you GET YOUR CONTENT from time with FAMILY?
Oh, yes...
ActuALLY, my Son DUSTIN IS HERE TODAY!
SAY "HI," SWEETIE!

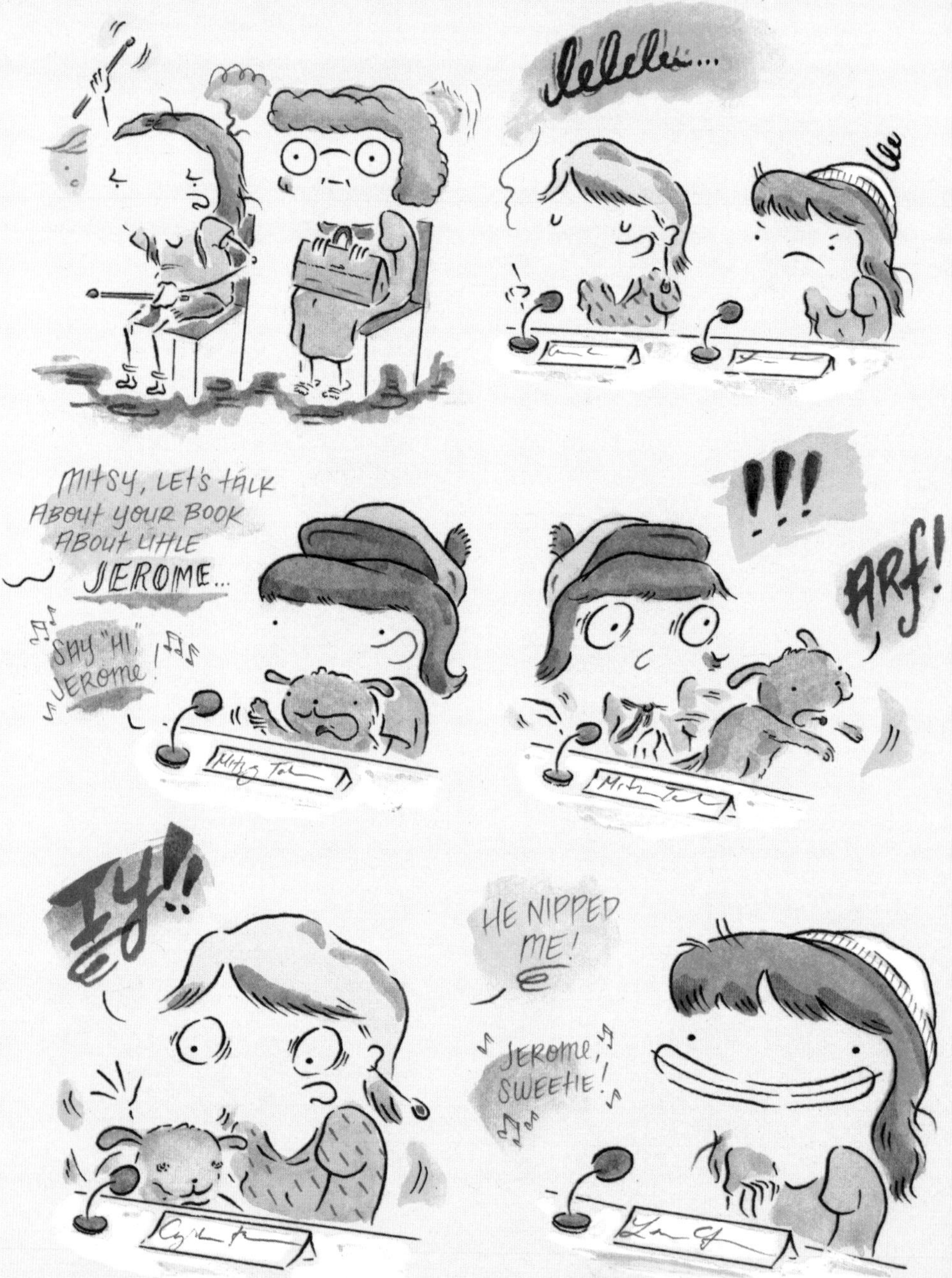
Lelelee...
Lee
Mitsy, let's talk about your book about little JEROME...
Say "Hi," Jerome!
!!!
Arf!
Iy!!
He nipped me!
Jerome, sweetie!

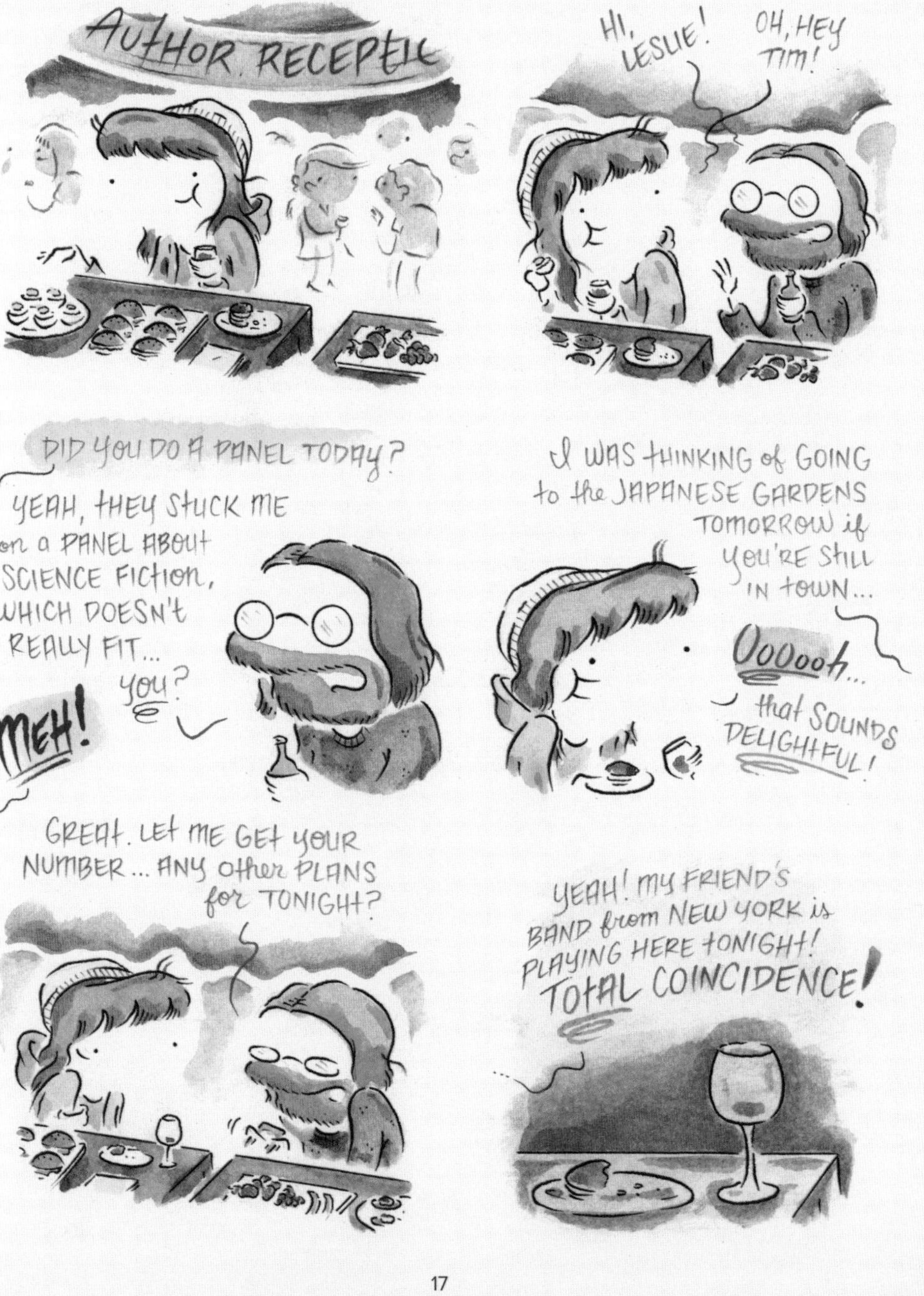
AUTHOR RECEPTI
HI, LESLIE!
OH, HEY TIM!
DID YOU DO A PANEL TODAY?
YEAH, THEY STUCK ME on a PANEL ABOUT SCIENCE FICTION, WHICH DOESN'T REALLY FIT... YOU?
MEH!
I WAS THINKING OF GOING to the JAPANESE GARDENS TOMORROW if YOU'RE STILL IN TOWN...
Ooooooh... that SOUNDS DELIGHTFUL!
GREAT. LET ME GET YOUR NUMBER... ANY OTHER PLANS for TONIGHT?
YEAH! MY FRIEND'S BAND from NEW YORK is PLAYING HERE TONIGHT! TOTAL COINCIDENCE!

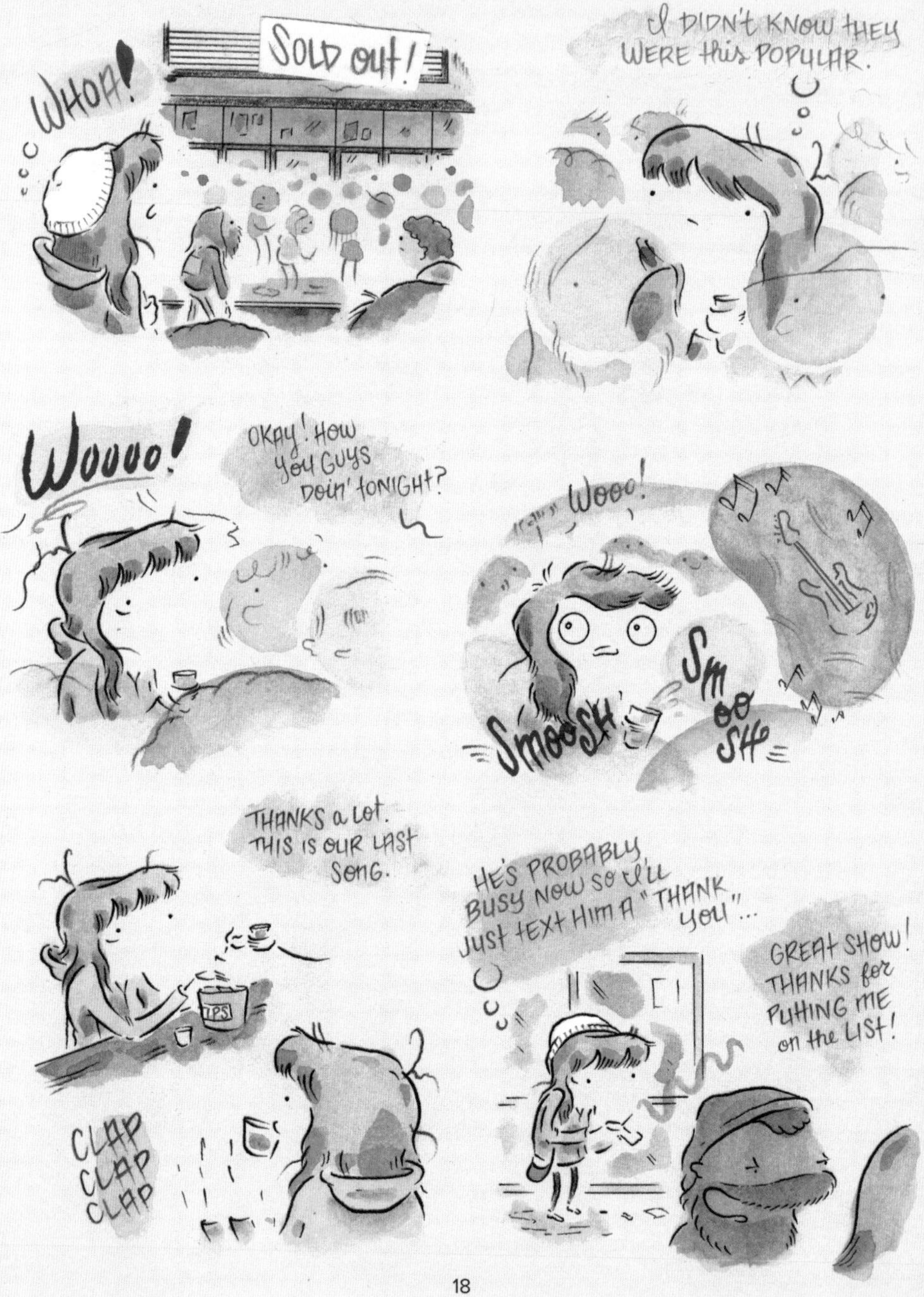
WHOA!
SOLD OUT!
I DIDN'T KNOW THEY WERE THIS POPULAR.
WOOOO!
OKAY! HOW YOU GUYS DOIN' TONIGHT?
WOOO!
SMOOSH
SMOOSH
THANKS A LOT. THIS IS OUR LAST SONG.
TIPS
CLAP CLAP CLAP
HE'S PROBABLY BUSY NOW SO I'LL JUST TEXT HIM A "THANK YOU"...
GREAT SHOW! THANKS FOR PUTTING ME ON THE LIST!

WHERE
ARE YOU?

IN FRONT
SMOKING.

COME
TO THE
BACK.

IT'S OKAY, SHE'S
WITH ME...

HOW ARE YOU?

I'M OKAY, HOW
ARE YOU?

OKAY. DO YOU
WANT TO COME
DOWNSTAIRS? DO
YOU WANT SOME
BEER?

HEY MAN, CAN YOU
BRING US DOWN A CASE
OF BEER? SO WHAT
BRINGS YOU
TO TOWN?

BOOK
FESTIVAL!

HEY GUYS, THIS IS
MY FRIEND
LESLIE...

DRINK
DRINK
DRINK

YADA
YADA

YADA
...

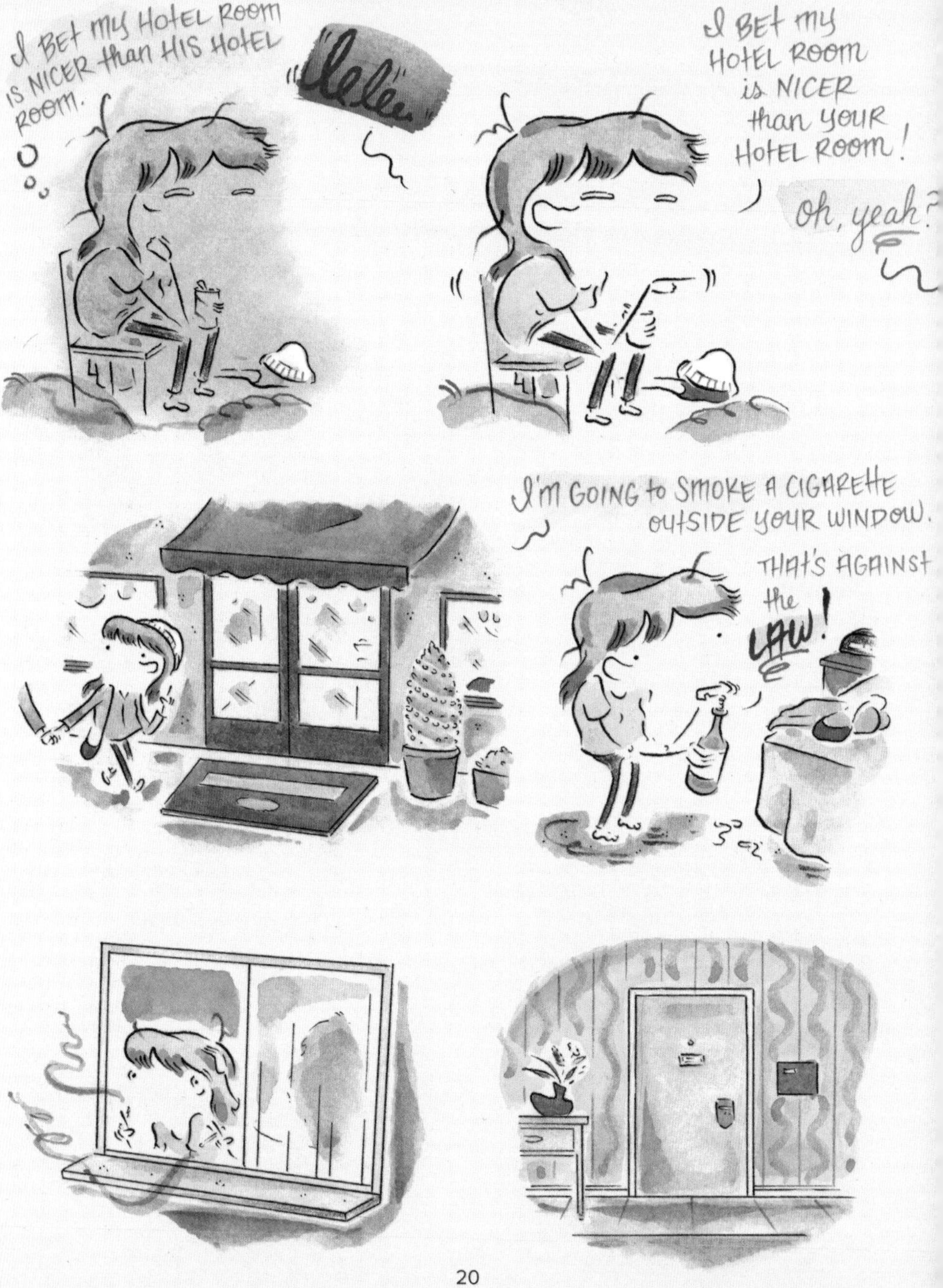
I BET my HOTEL ROOM IS NICER than HIS HOTEL ROOM.
I BET my HOTEL ROOM is NICER than YOUR HOTEL ROOM!
Oh, yeah?
I'M GOING to SMOKE A CIGARETTE OUTSIDE YOUR WINDOW.
THAT'S AGAINST the LAW!

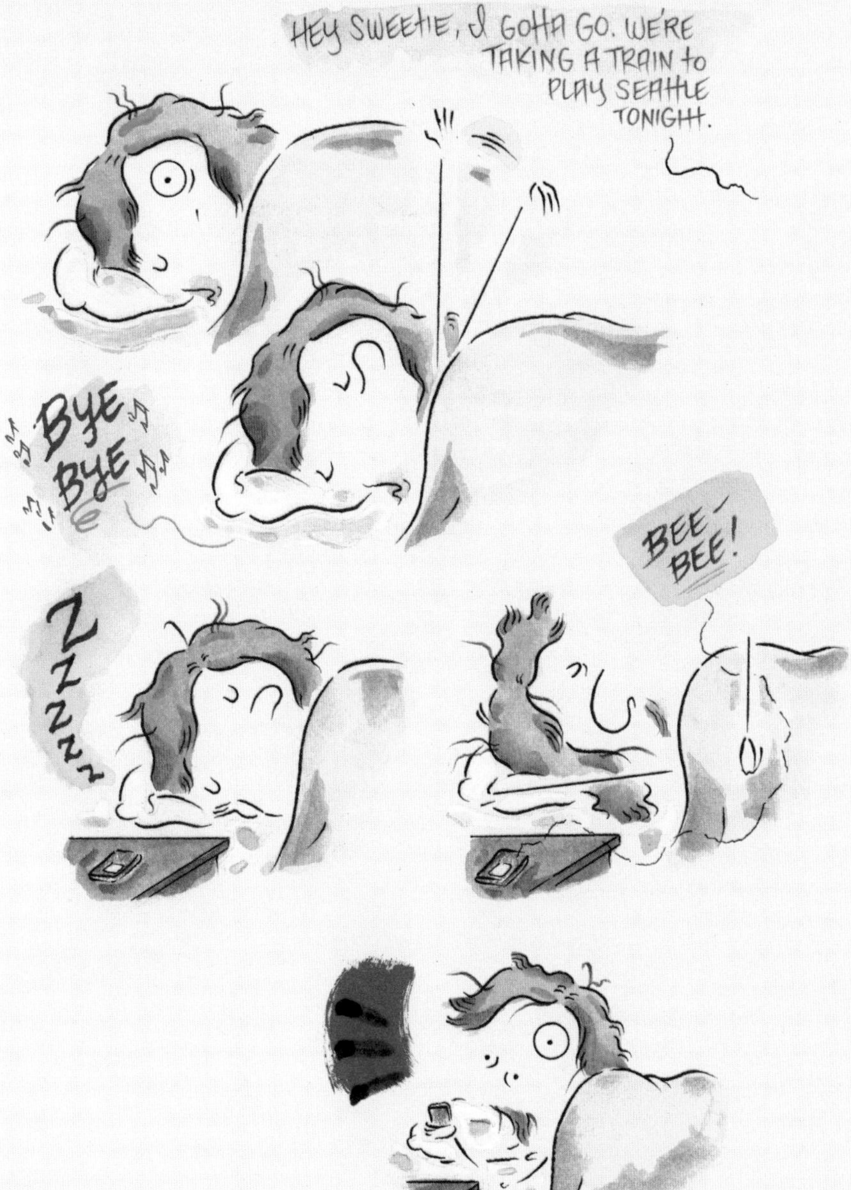
HEY SWEETIE, I GOTTA GO. WE'RE TAKING A TRAIN TO PLAY SEATTLE TONIGHT.
BYE BYE
ZZZZZZ
BEE-BEE!

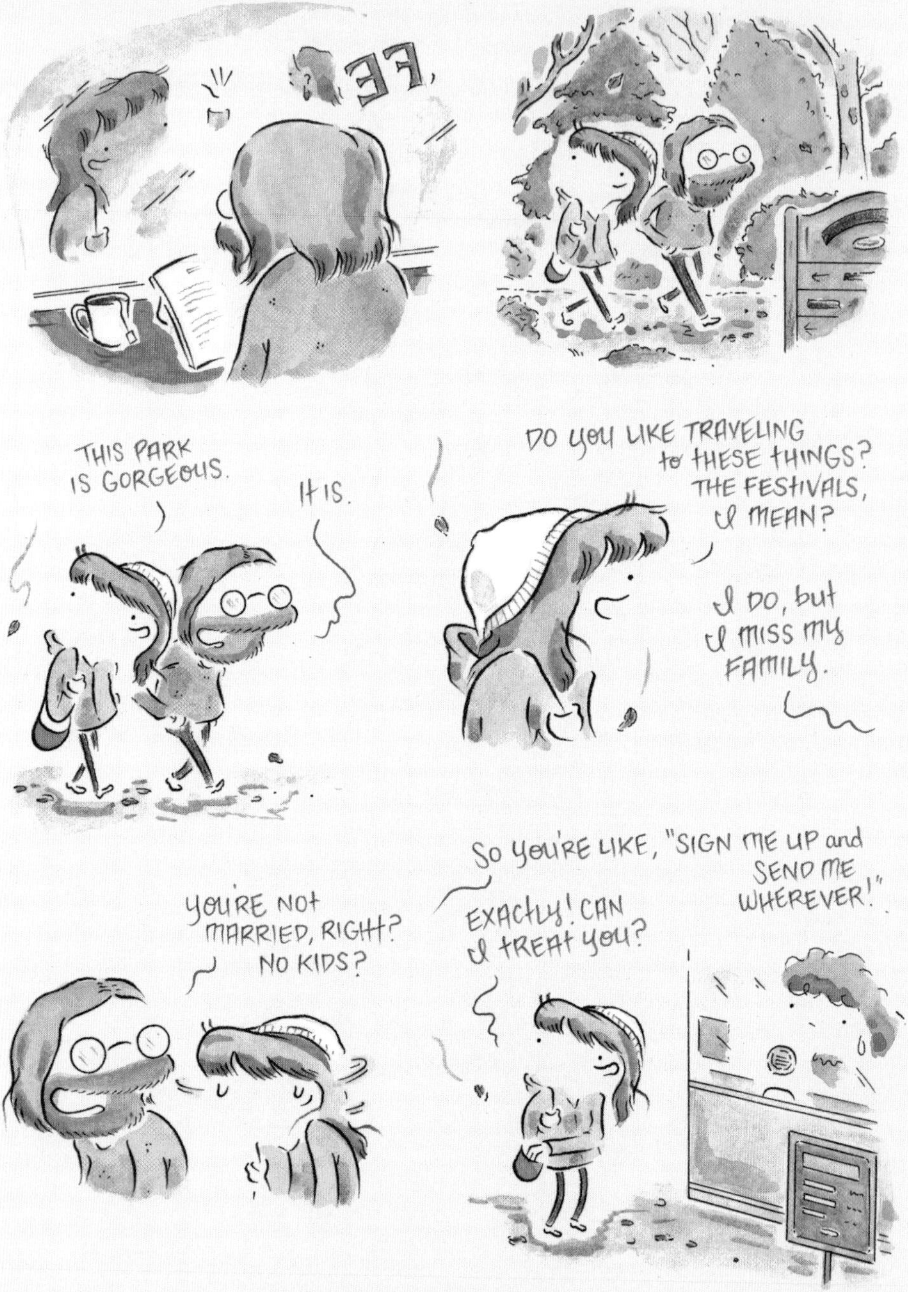
THIS PARK IS GORGEOUS.
IT IS.
DO YOU LIKE TRAVELING TO THESE THINGS? THE FESTIVALS, I MEAN?
I DO, BUT I MISS MY FAMILY.
YOU'RE NOT MARRIED, RIGHT? NO KIDS?
SO YOU'RE LIKE, "SIGN ME UP AND SEND ME WHEREVER!"
EXACTLY! CAN I TREAT YOU?

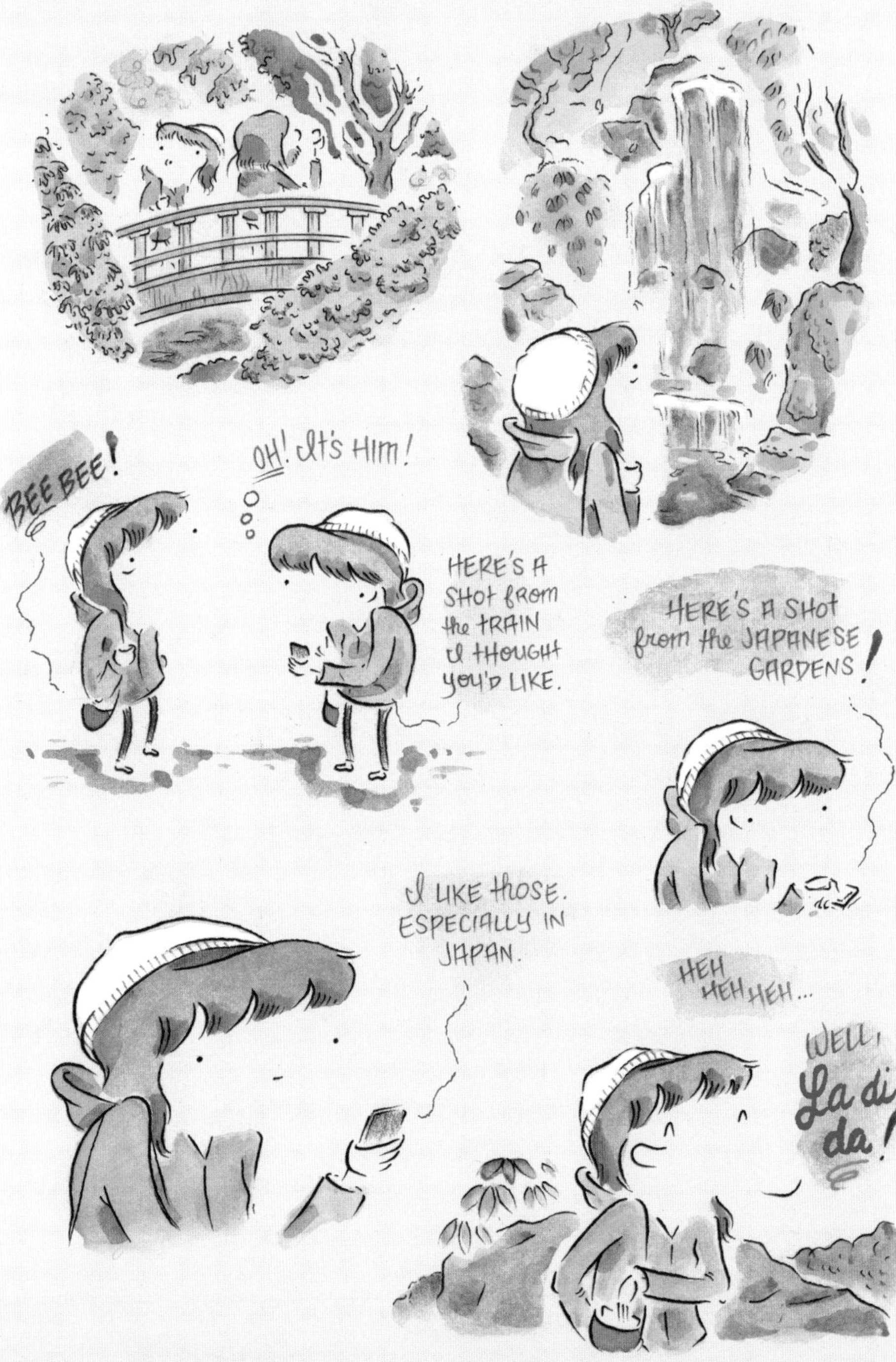
BEE BEE!
OH! It's HIM!
HERE'S A SHOT from the TRAIN I THOUGHT YOU'D LIKE.
HERE'S A SHOT from the JAPANESE GARDENS!
I LIKE THOSE. ESPECIALLY IN JAPAN.
HEH HEH HEH...
WELL, La di da!

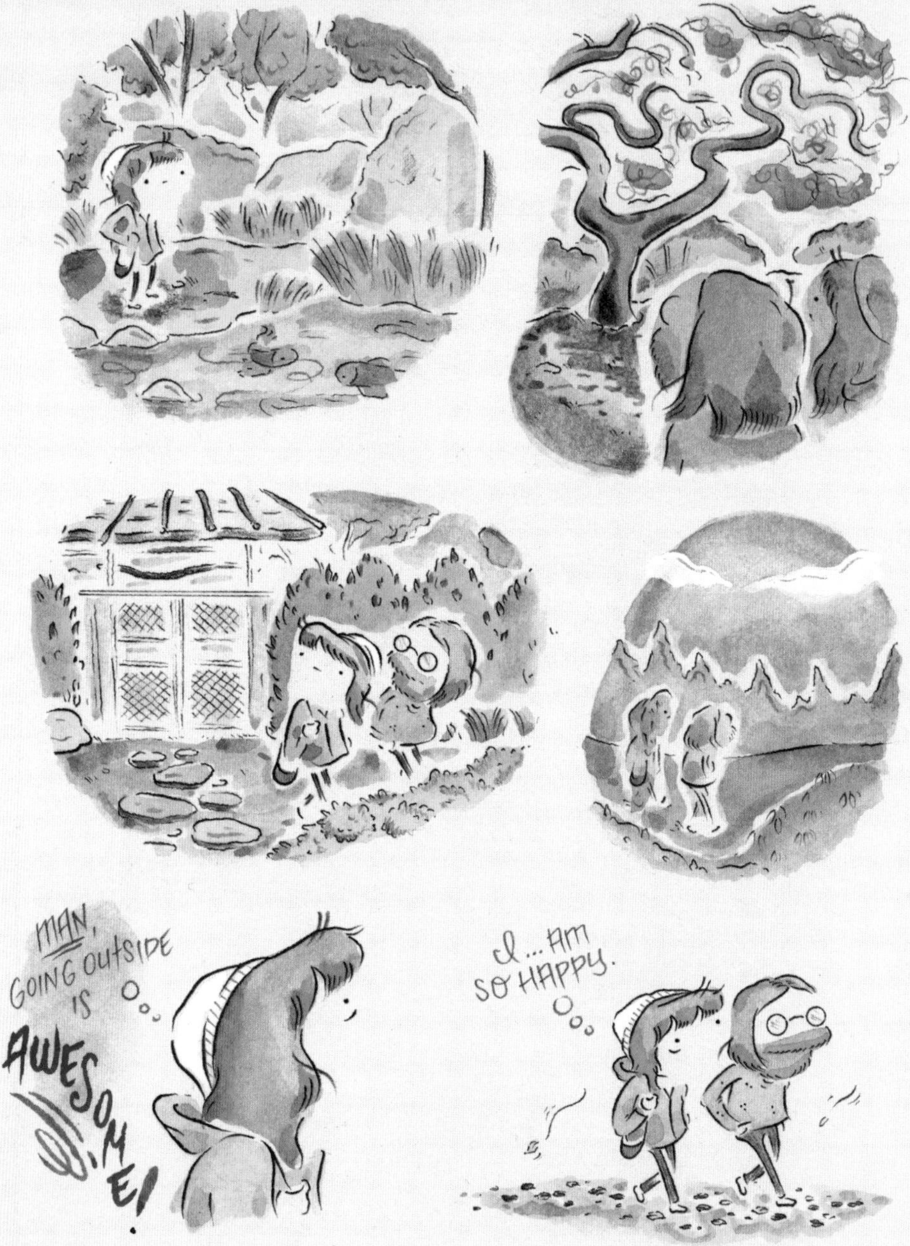
MAN, GOING OUTSIDE IS AWESOME!
I... AM SO HAPPY.

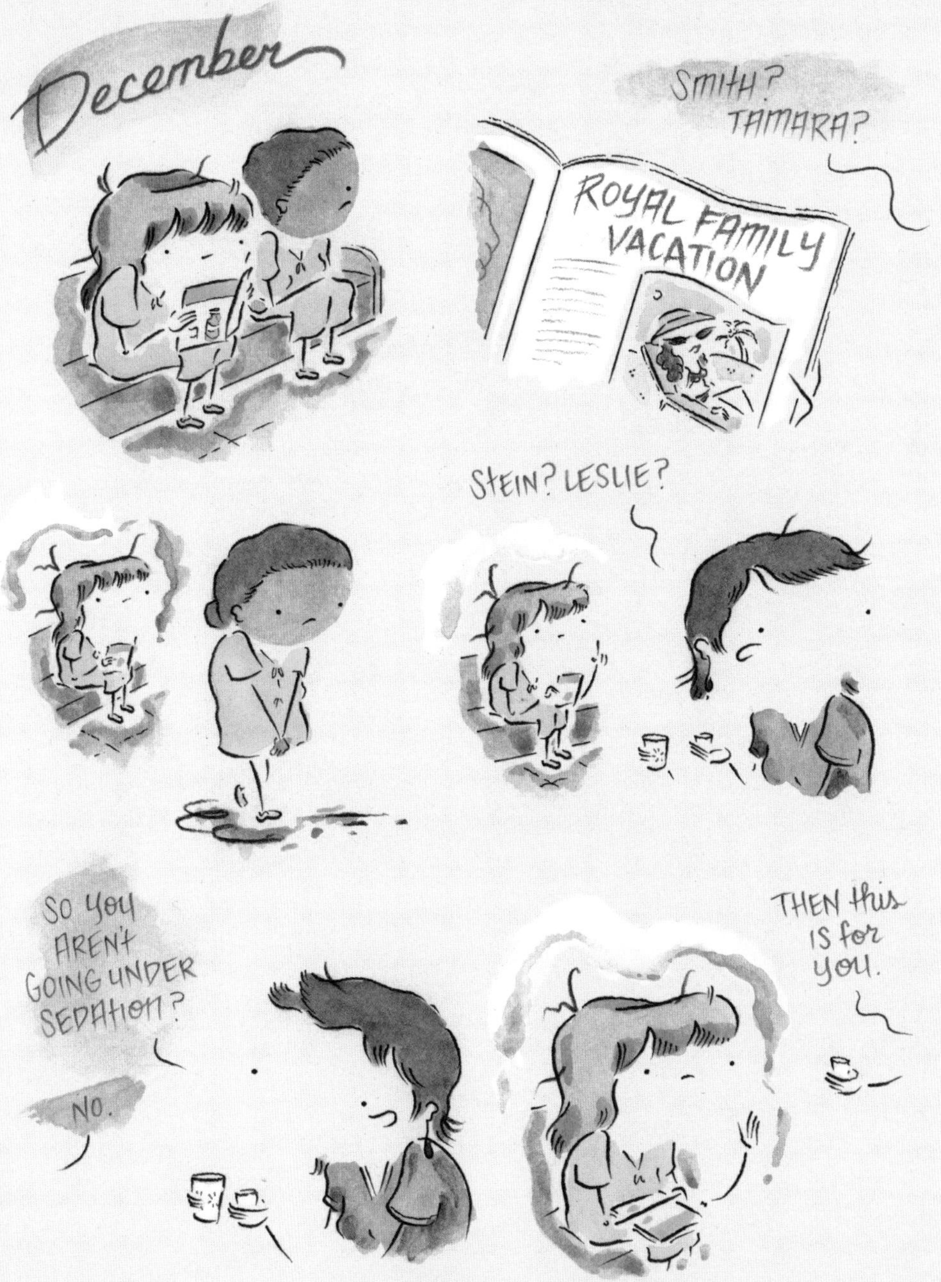
December
SMITH? TAMARA?
ROYAL FAMILY VACATION
STEIN? LESLIE?
SO YOU AREN'T GOING UNDER SEDATION?
NO.
THEN this IS for YOU.

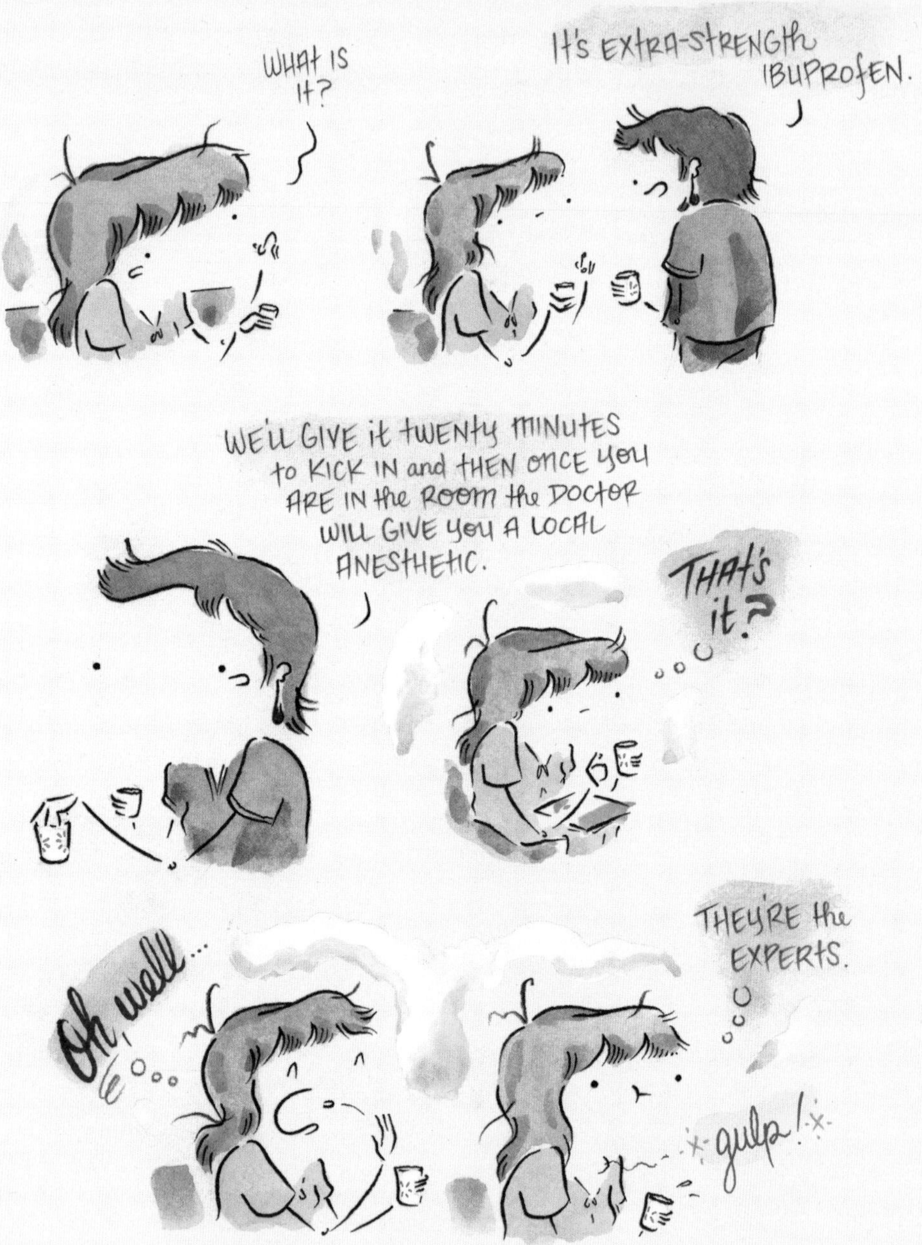
WHAT IS IT?
IT'S EXTRA-STRENGTH IBUPROFEN.
WE'LL GIVE IT TWENTY MINUTES TO KICK IN AND THEN ONCE YOU ARE IN THE ROOM THE DOCTOR WILL GIVE YOU A LOCAL ANESTHETIC.
THAT'S IT?
Oh, well...
THEY'RE THE EXPERTS.
gulp!

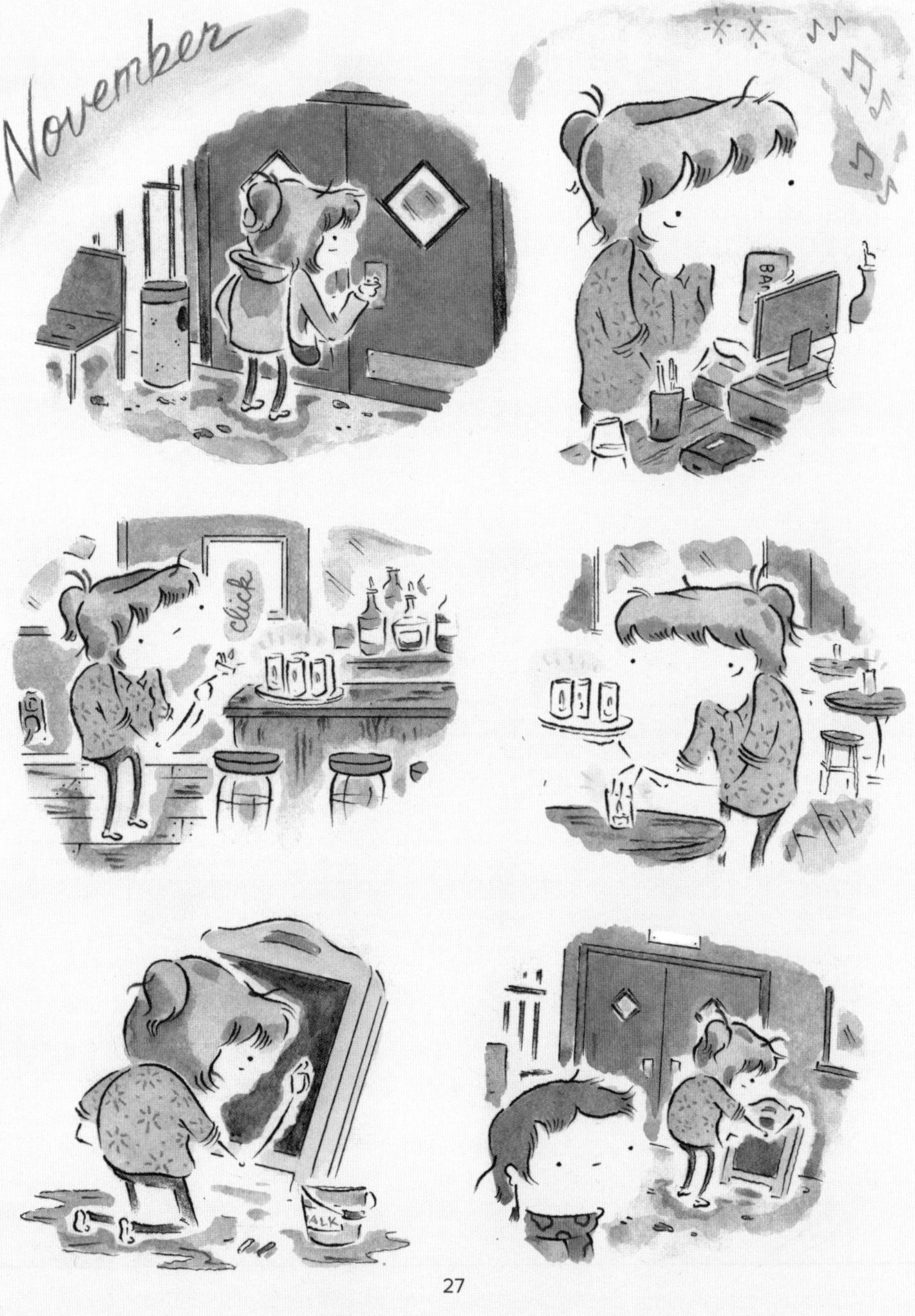
November
click

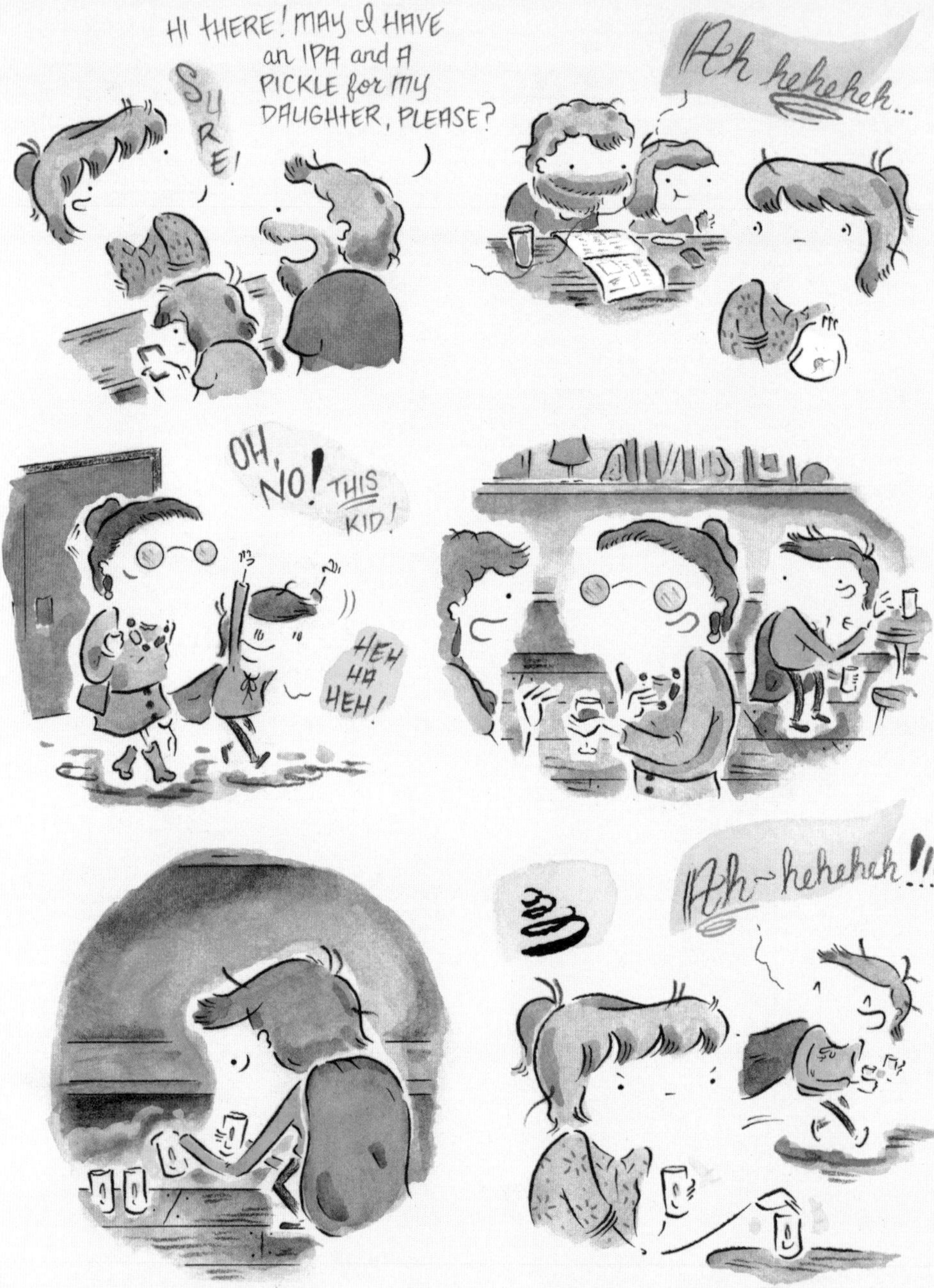

HI THERE! MAY I HAVE an IPA and A PICKLE for MY DAUGHTER, PLEASE?
SURE!
Ah hehehe...
OH, NO! THIS KID!
HEH HA HEH!
Ah-hehehah!!!

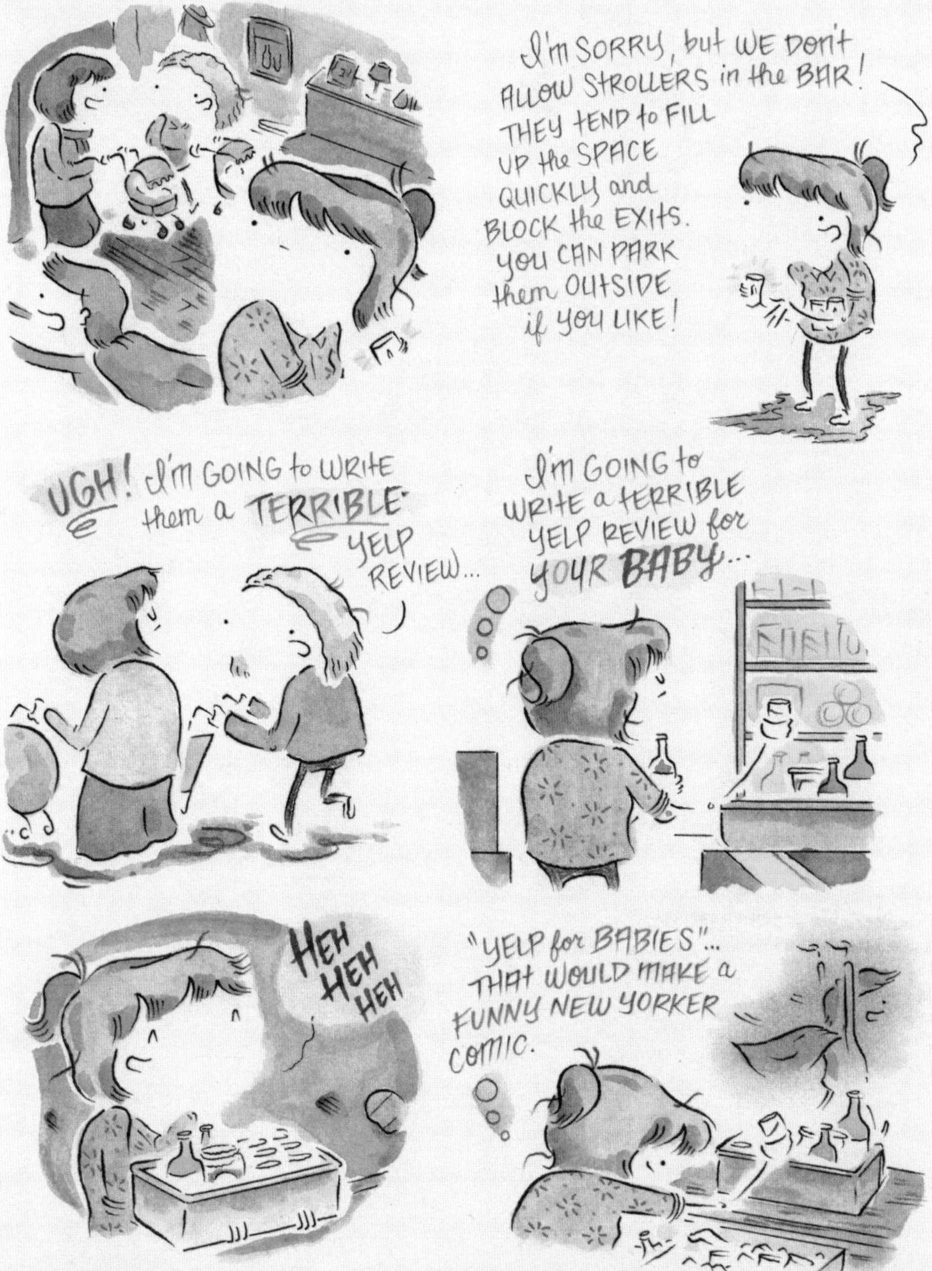
I'm SORRY, but WE DON'T ALLOW STROLLERS in the BAR! THEY TEND to FILL UP the SPACE QUICKLY and BLOCK the EXITS. YOU CAN PARK them OUTSIDE if YOU LIKE!
UGH! I'm GOING to WRITE them a TERRIBLE YELP REVIEW...
I'm GOING to WRITE a TERRIBLE YELP REVIEW for YOUR BABY...
HEH HEH HEH
"YELP for BABIES"... THAT WOULD MAKE a FUNNY NEW YORKER COMIC.

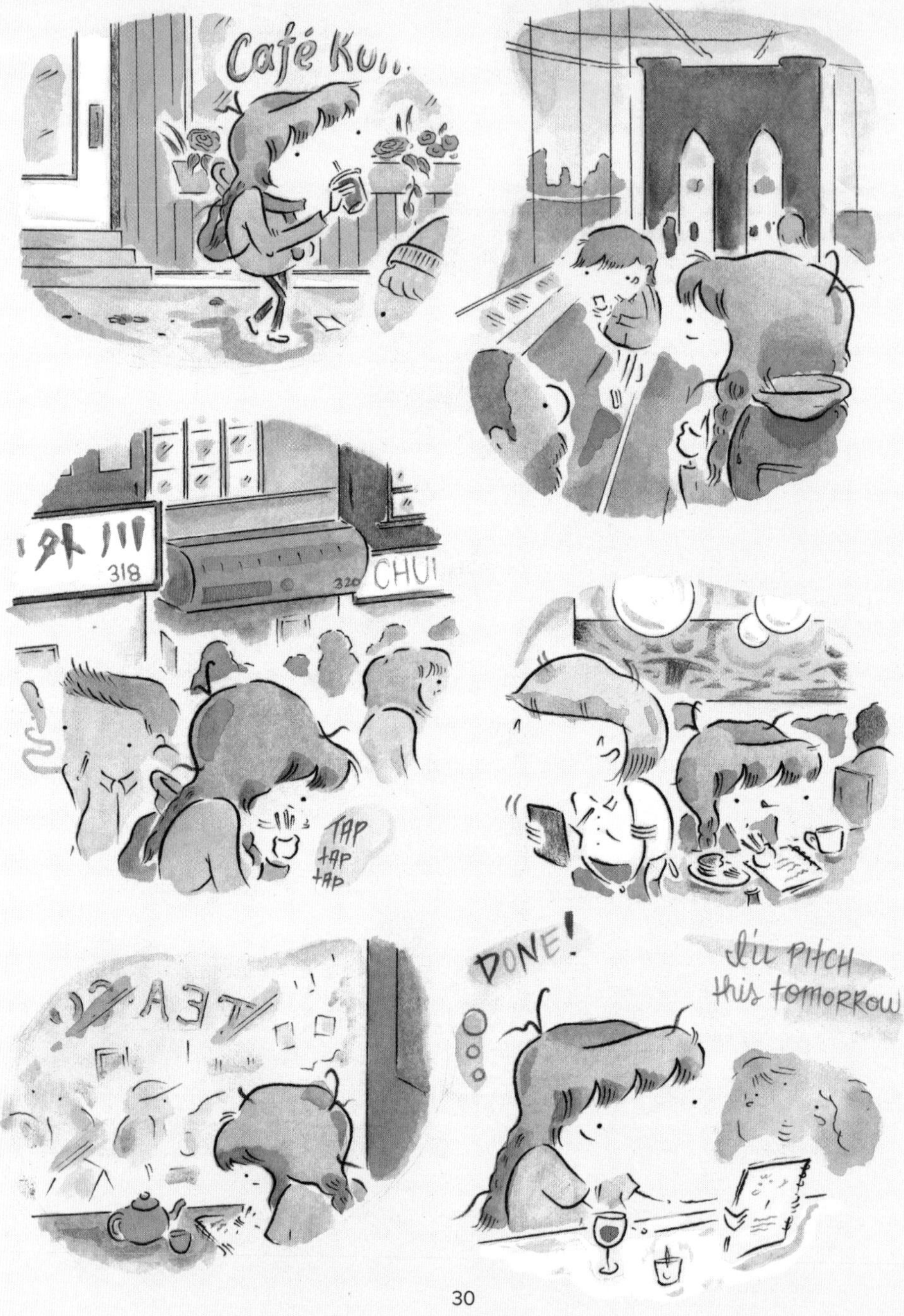

Café Ku
318
320
CHU
TAP
tap
tap
DONE!
I'll PITCH
this tomorrow!

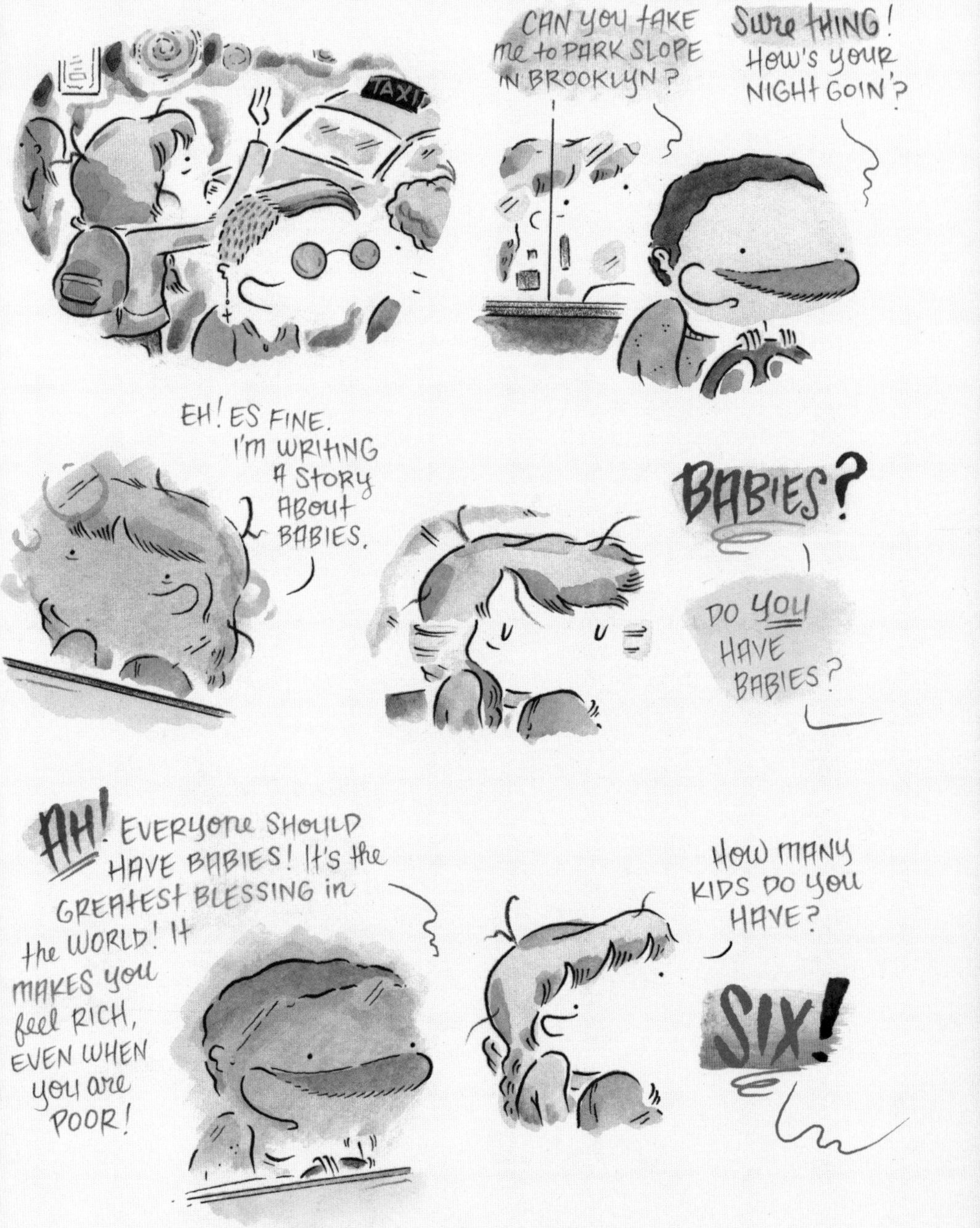
TAXI
CAN YOU TAKE me to PARK SLOPE IN BROOKLYN?
Sure THING! How's your NIGHT GOIN'?
EH! ES FINE. I'M WRITING A STORY ABOUT BABIES.
BABIES?
DO YOU HAVE BABIES?
AH! EVERYONE SHOULD HAVE BABIES! It's the GREATEST BLESSING in the WORLD! It MAKES you feel RICH, EVEN WHEN you are POOR!
HOW MANY KIDS DO YOU HAVE?
SIX!

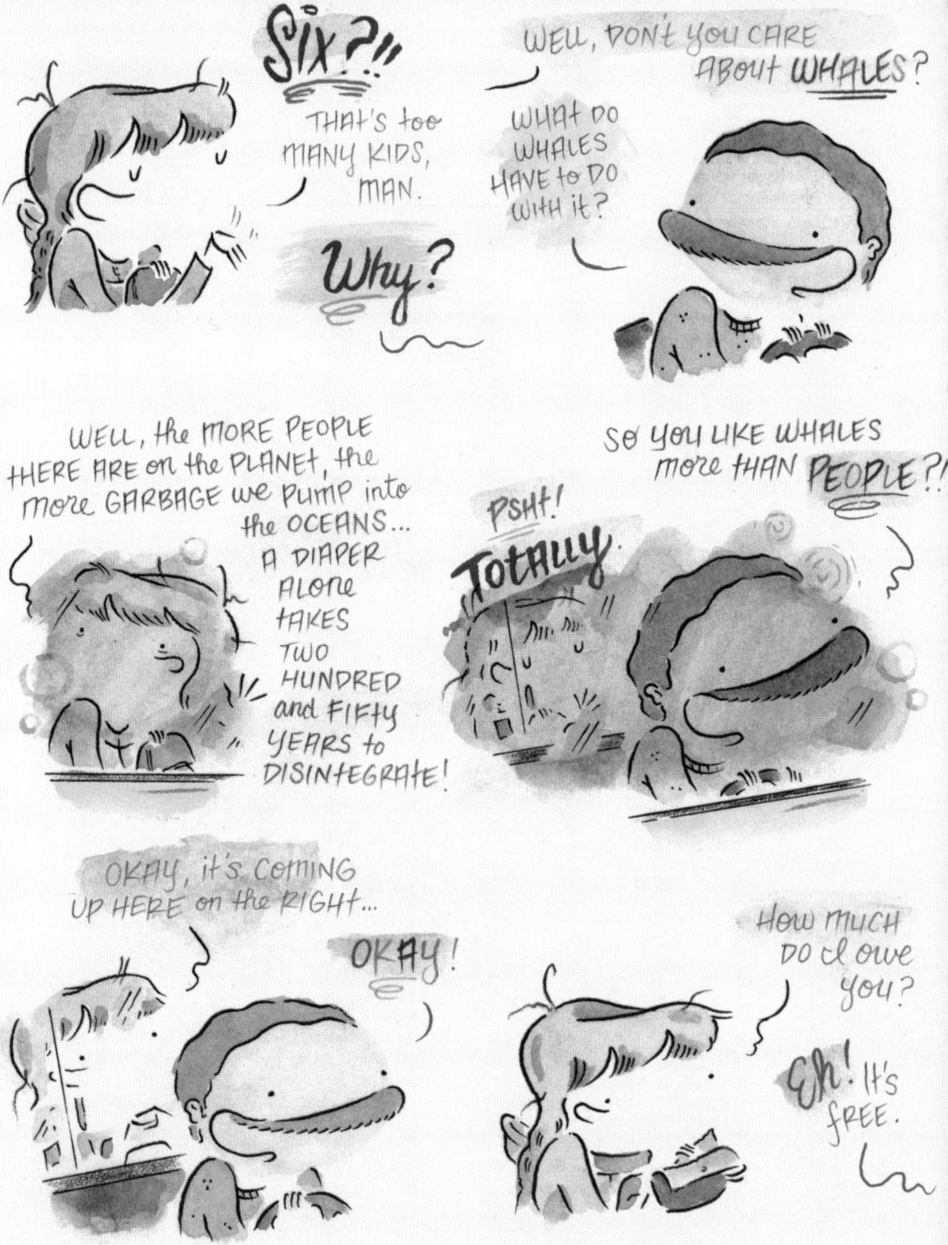
SIX?!!
THAT'S too MANY KIDS, MAN.
Why?
WELL, DON'T YOU CARE ABOUT WHALES?
WHAT DO WHALES HAVE TO DO WITH IT?
WELL, the MORE PEOPLE THERE ARE ON the PLANET, the MORE GARBAGE WE PUMP into the OCEANS... A DIAPER ALONE TAKES TWO HUNDRED and FIFTY YEARS to DISINTEGRATE!
SO YOU LIKE WHALES MORE THAN PEOPLE?!
PSHT!
TOTALLY.
OKAY, it's COMING UP HERE on the RIGHT...
OKAY!
HOW MUCH DO I OWE YOU?
Eh! It's FREE.

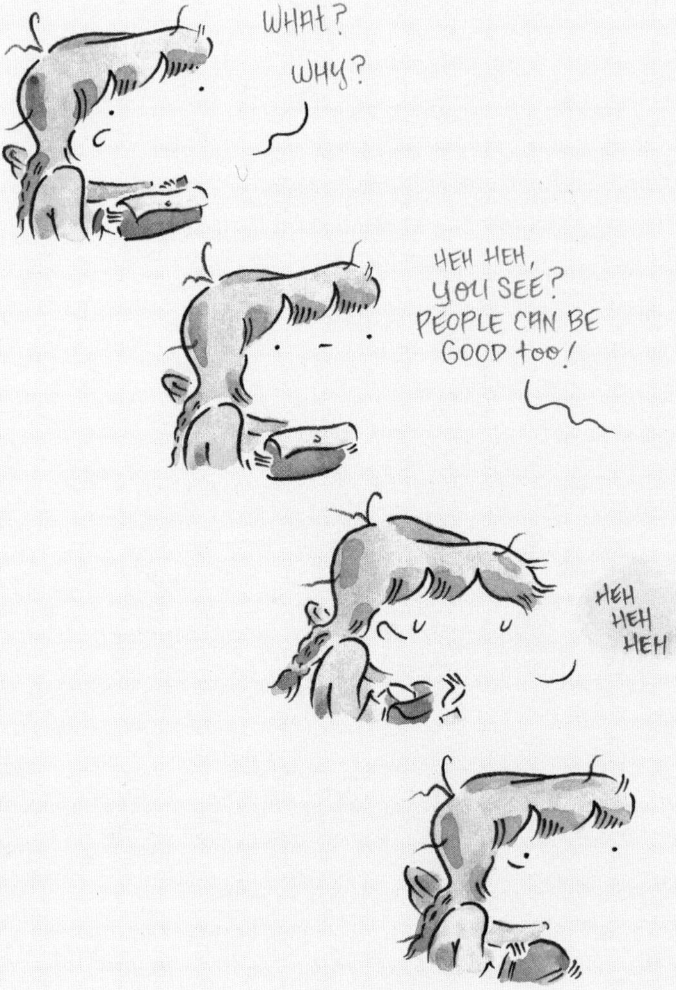
WHAt?
WHY?
HEH HEH,
YOU SEE?
PEOPLE CAN BE
GOOD too!
HEH
HEH
HEH

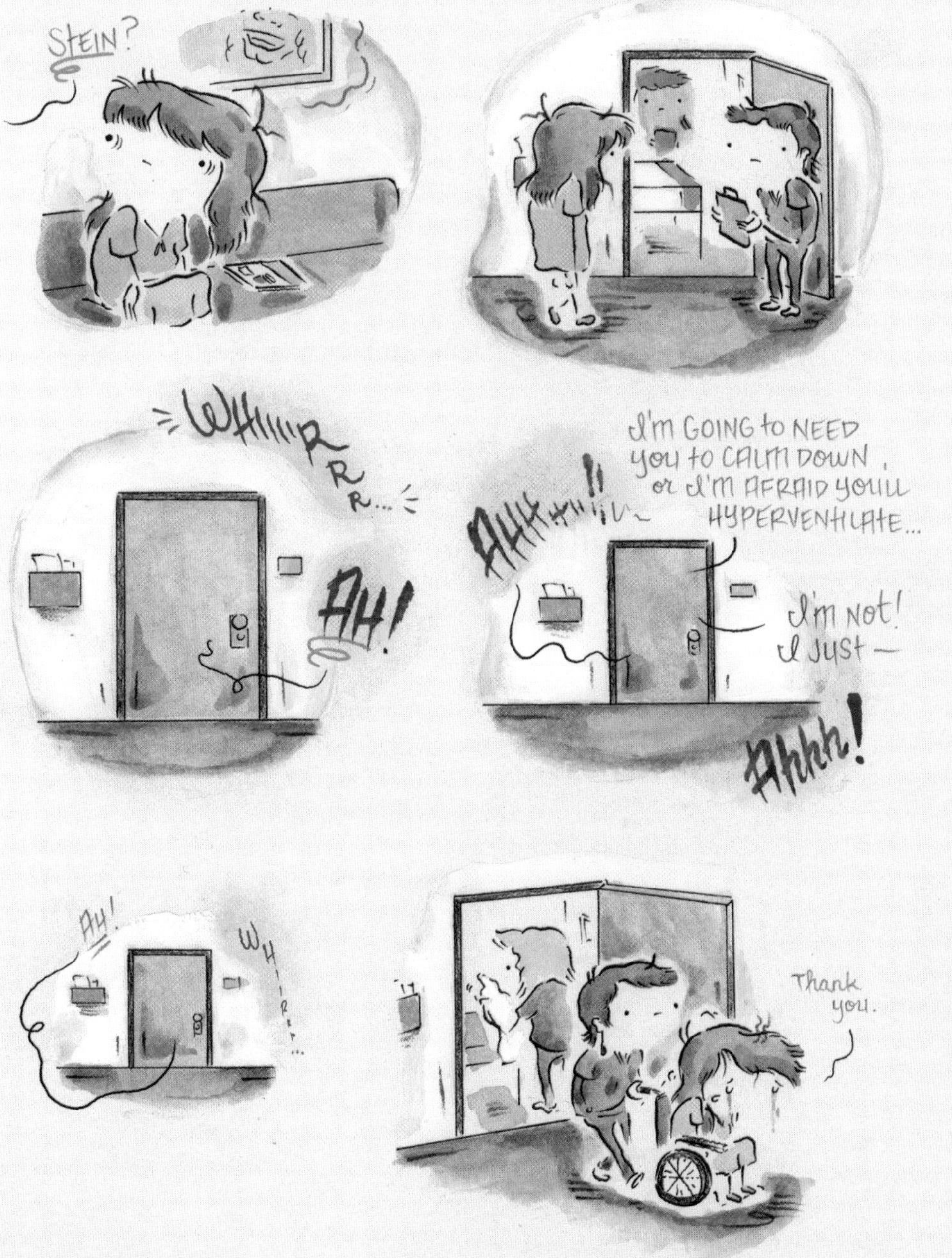
STEIN?
WH R R R...
AH!
AHH...!!
I'm GOING to NEED you to CALM DOWN, or I'm AFRAID you'll HYPERVENTILATE...
I'm NOT! I JUST—
Ahhh!
AH!
WH R R R...
Thank you.

YOU CAN SIT HERE to RECUPERATE. I'LL CHECK on YOU IN A BIT.

SEDATION. MAYBE that WAS the WAY to GO...

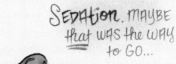

I CAN'T WAIT to GET OUT of HERE TODAY.

UGH!

ME too...

...LAST SHIFT BEFORE CHRISTMAS!

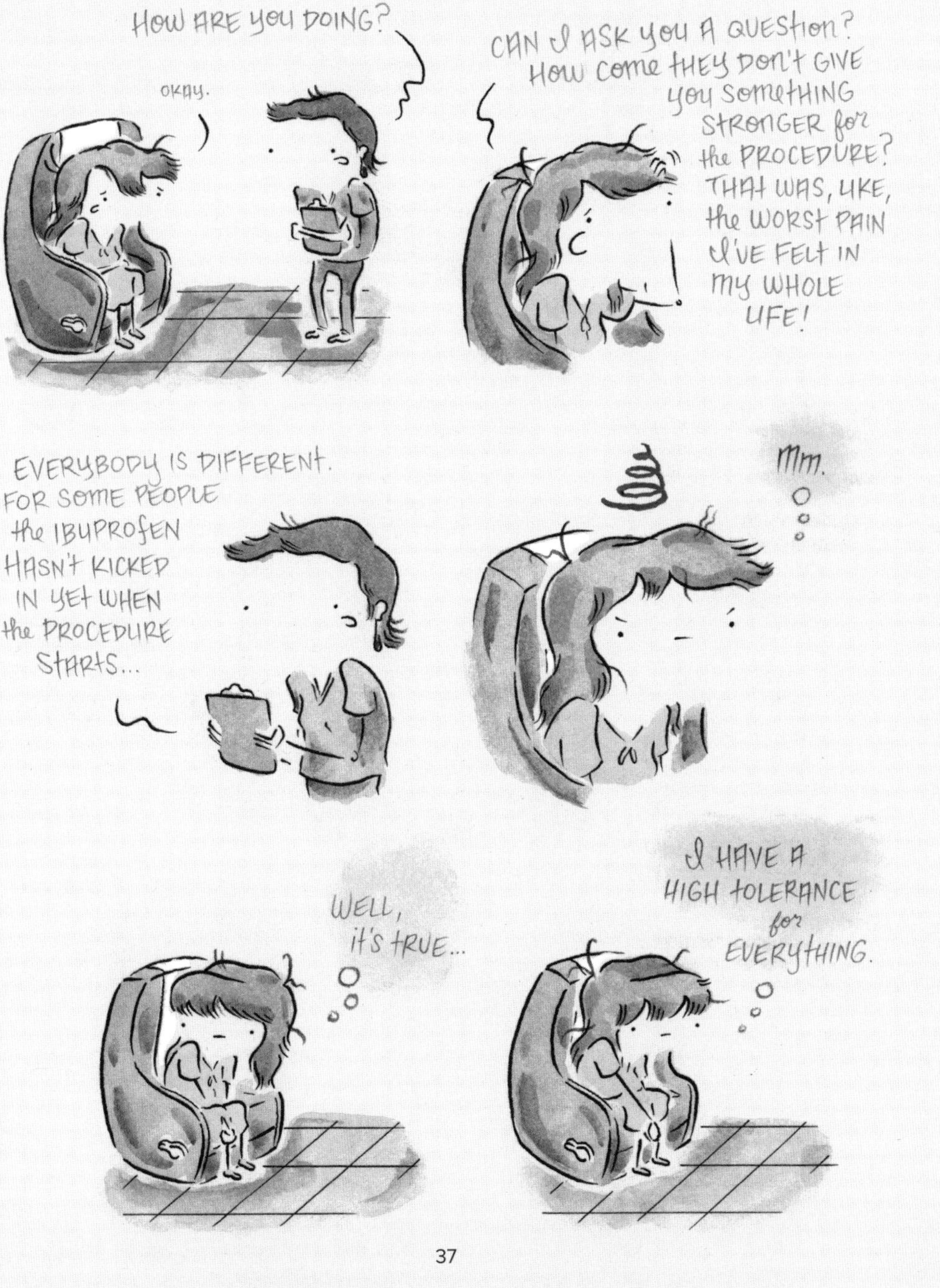
HOW ARE YOU DOING?
OKAY.
CAN I ASK YOU A QUESTION? HOW COME THEY DON'T GIVE YOU SOMETHING STRONGER FOR THE PROCEDURE? THAT WAS, LIKE, THE WORST PAIN I'VE FELT IN MY WHOLE LIFE!
EVERYBODY IS DIFFERENT. FOR SOME PEOPLE THE IBUPROFEN HASN'T KICKED IN YET WHEN THE PROCEDURE STARTS...
Mm.
WELL, IT'S TRUE...
I HAVE A HIGH TOLERANCE FOR EVERYTHING.

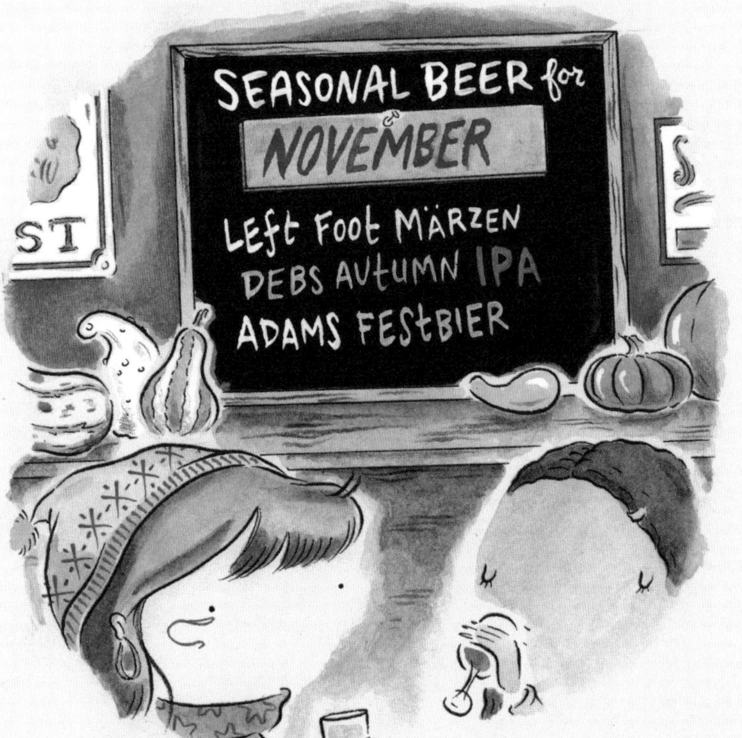
SEASONAL BEER for
NOVEMBER
Left Foot MÄRZEN
DEBS AUTUMN IPA
ADAMS FESTBIER

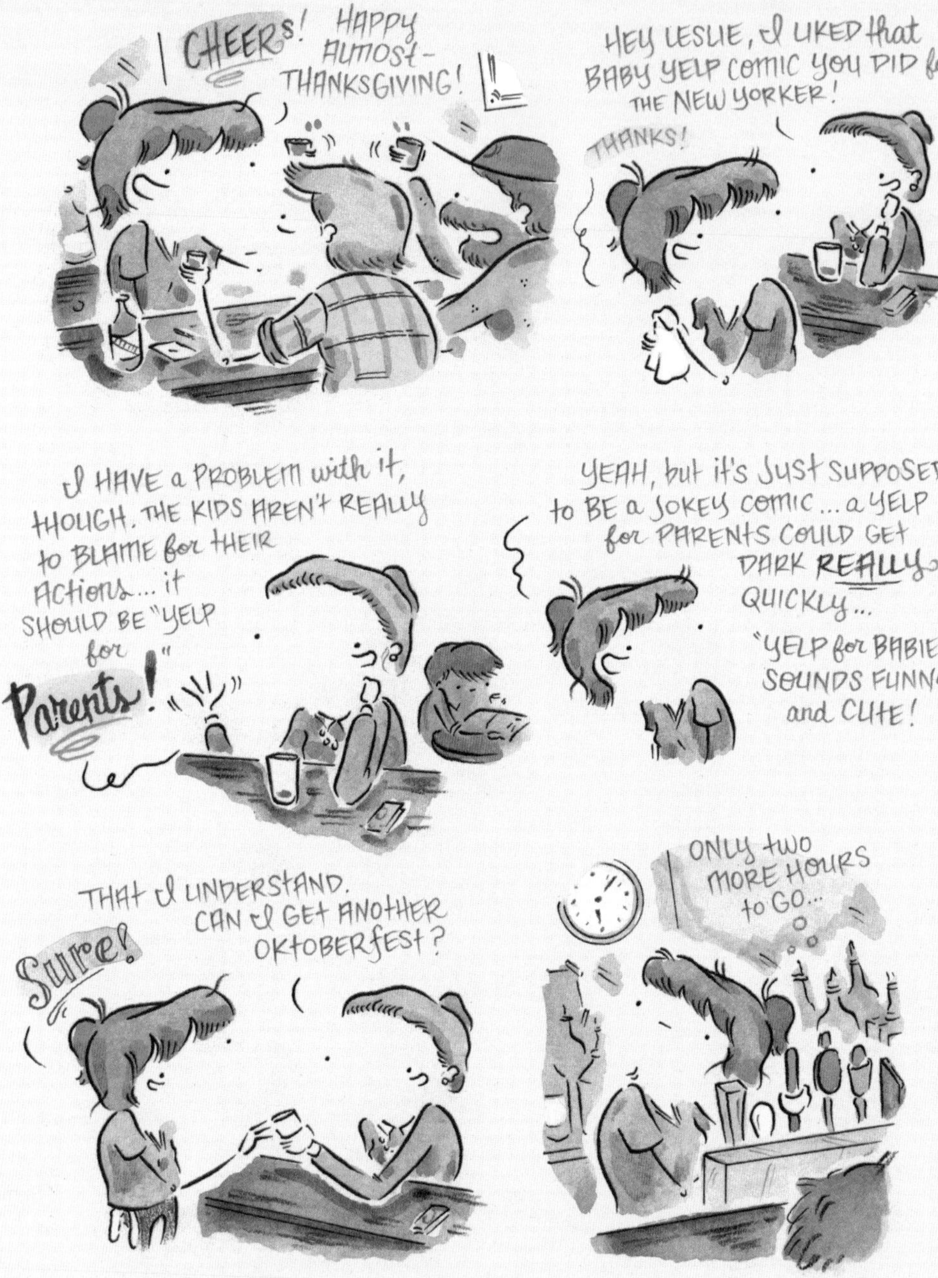

CHEERS! HAPPY ALMOST-THANKSGIVING!
HEY LESLIE, I LIKED that BABY YELP COMIC YOU DID for THE NEW YORKER!
THANKS!
I HAVE a PROBLEM with it, THOUGH. THE KIDS AREN'T REALLY to BLAME for THEIR Actions... it SHOULD BE "YELP for Parents!"
YEAH, but it's JUST SUPPOSED to BE a JOKEY COMIC... a YELP for PARENTS COULD GET DARK REALLY QUICKLY...
"YELP for BABIES" SOUNDS FUNNY and CUTE!
THAT I UNDERSTAND. CAN I GET ANOTHER OKTOBERFEST?
Sure!
ONLY two MORE HOURS to GO...

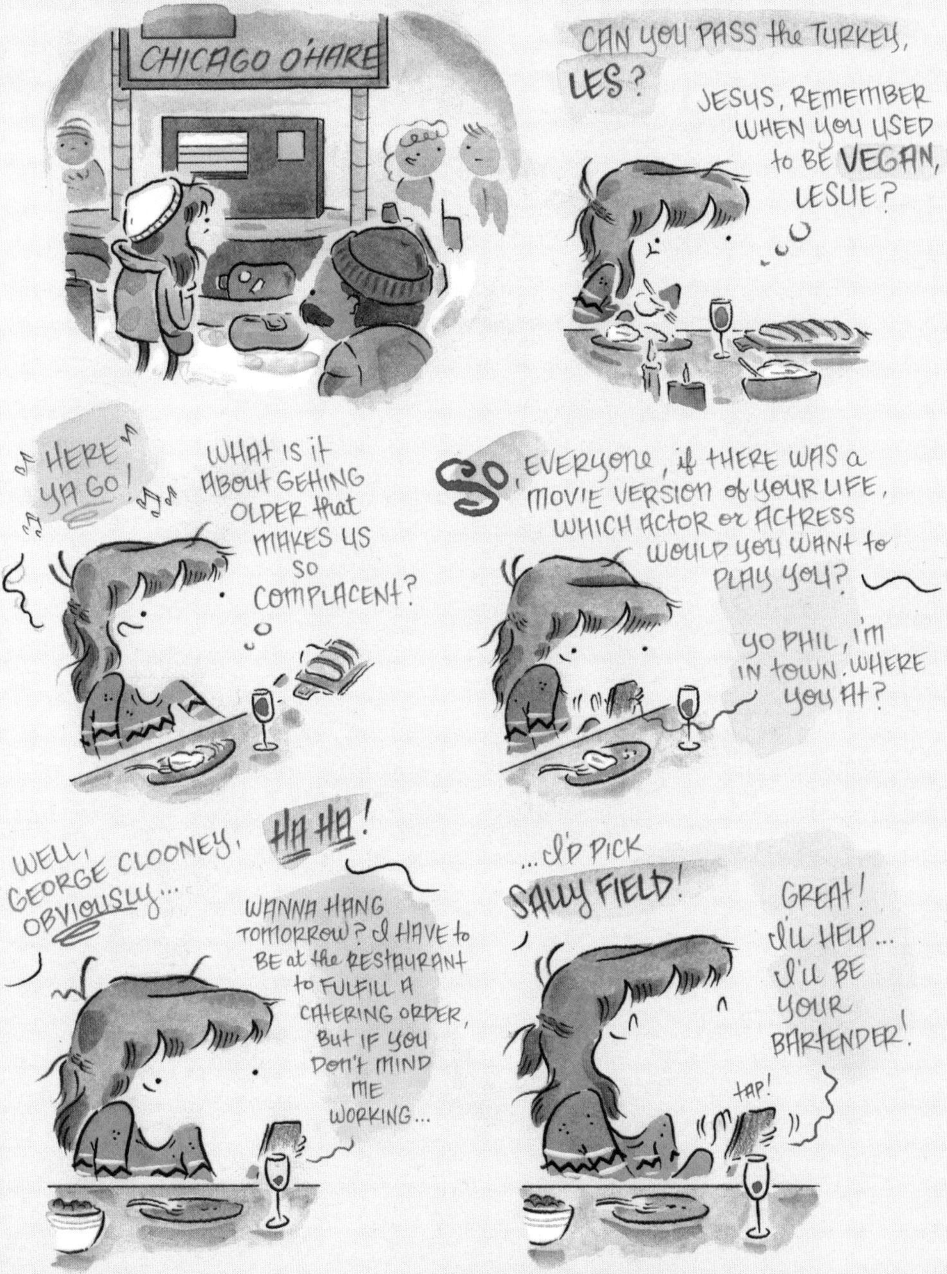
CHICAGO O'HARE
CAN YOU PASS the TURKEY, LES?
JESUS, REMEMBER WHEN YOU USED to BE VEGAN, LESLIE?
HERE YA GO!
WHAT IS IT ABOUT GETTING OLDER that MAKES US SO COMPLACENT?
SO, EVERYONE, if THERE WAS a MOVIE VERSION of YOUR LIFE, WHICH ACTOR or ACTRESS WOULD YOU WANT to PLAY YOU?
YO PHIL, I'M IN TOWN. WHERE YOU AT?
WELL, GEORGE CLOONEY, OBVIOUSLY... HA HA!
WANNA HANG TOMORROW? I HAVE to BE at the RESTAURANT to FULFILL A CATERING ORDER, BUT IF YOU DON'T MIND ME WORKING...
...I'D PICK SALLY FIELD!
GREAT! I'LL HELP... I'LL BE YOUR BARTENDER!
TAP!

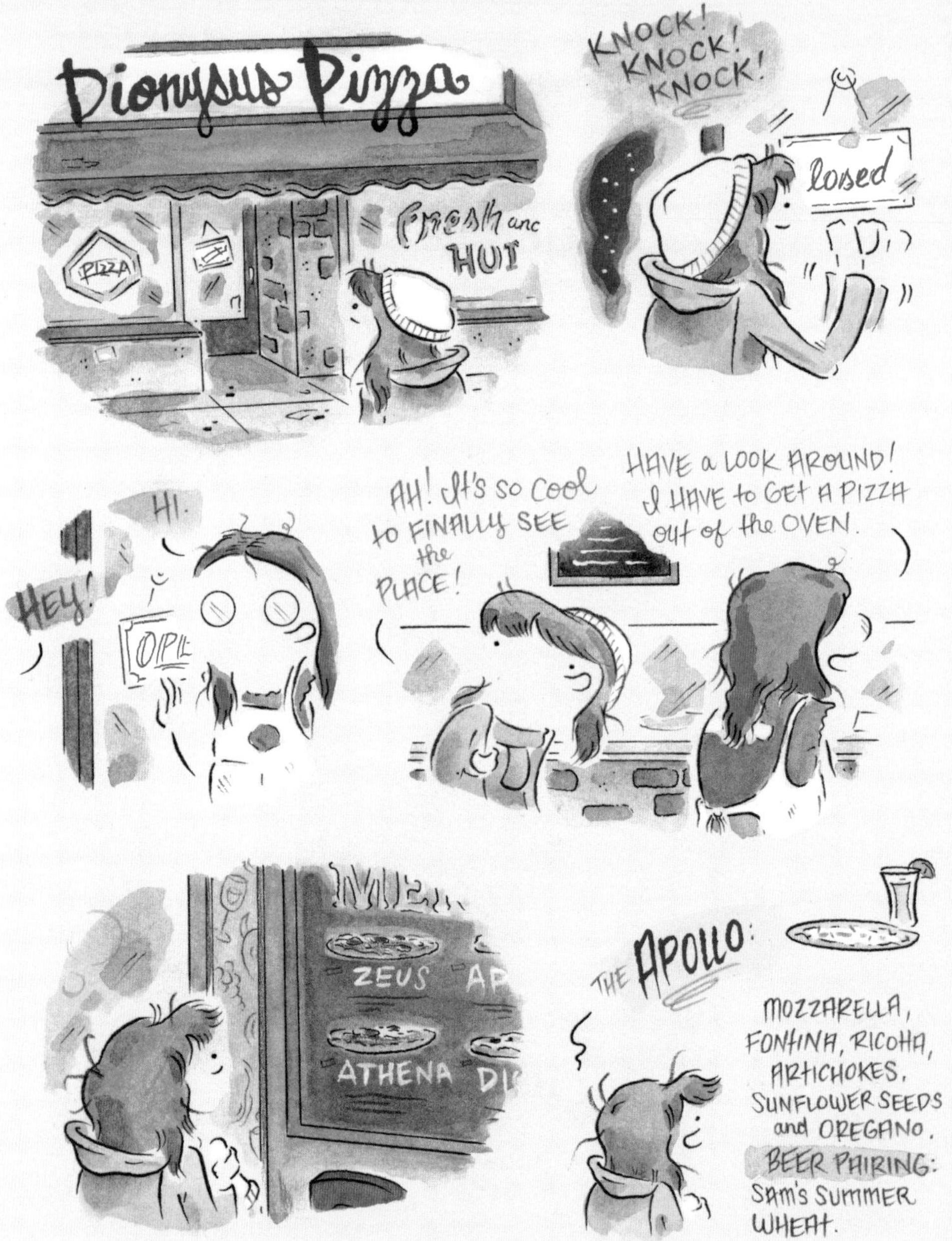
Dionysus Pizza
PIZZA
Fresh and HOT
KNOCK! KNOCK! KNOCK!
losed
HEY!
HI.
OPE
AH! It's so cool to FINALLY SEE the PLACE!
HAVE a LOOK AROUND! I HAVE to GET A PIZZA out of the OVEN.
ZEUS
ATHENA
THE APOLLO:
MOZZARELLA, FONTINA, RICOTTA, ARTICHOKES, SUNFLOWER SEEDS and OREGANO.
BEER PAIRING: SAM'S SUMMER WHEAT.

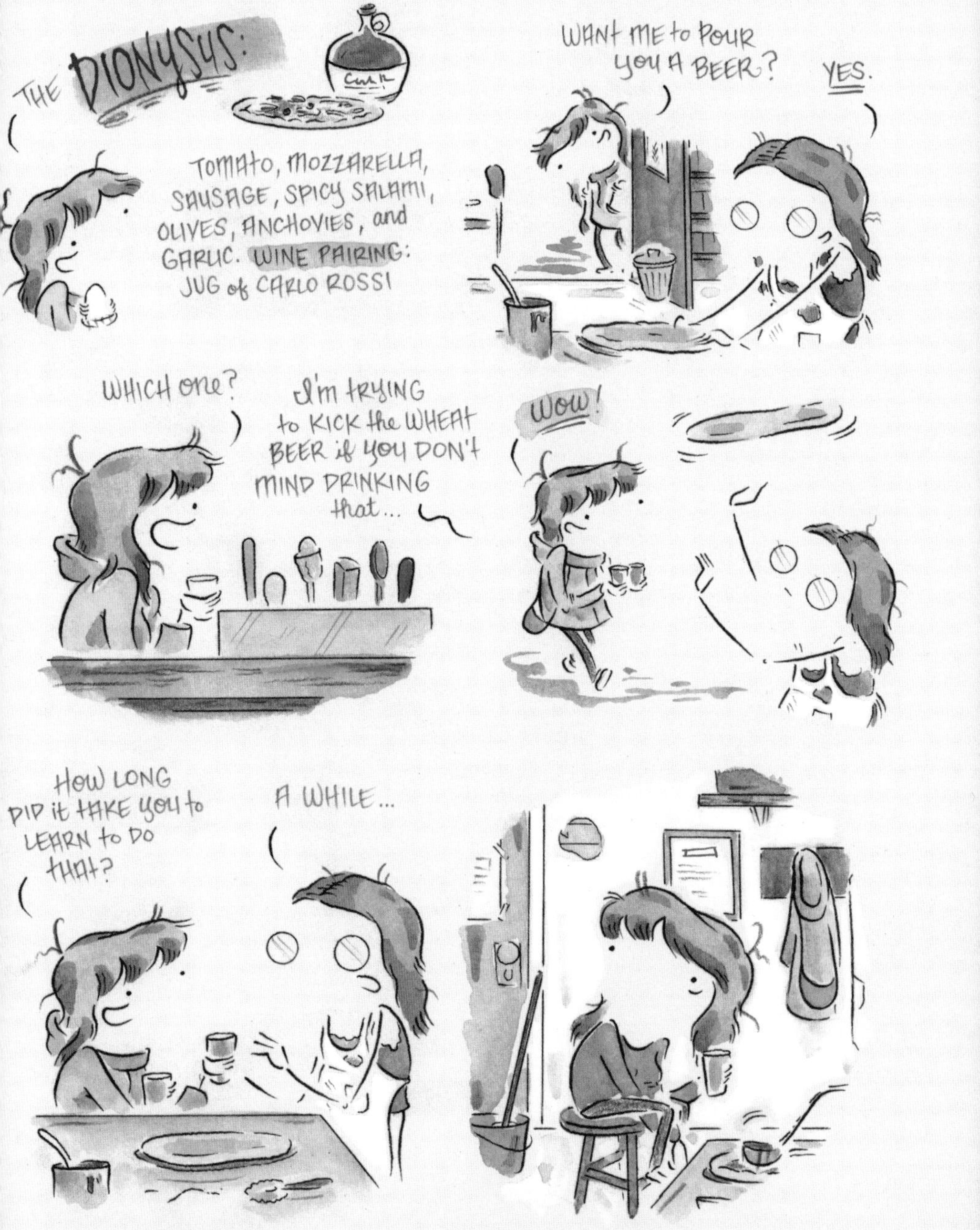
THE DIONYSUS:
CARLO
TOMATO, MOZZARELLA, SAUSAGE, SPICY SALAMI, OLIVES, ANCHOVIES, and GARLIC. WINE PAIRING: JUG of CARLO ROSSI
WANT ME to POUR YOU A BEER?
YES.
WHICH one?
I'm TRYING to KICK the WHEAT BEER if YOU DON'T MIND DRINKING that...
WOW!
HOW LONG DID it TAKE YOU to LEARN to DO THAT?
A WHILE...

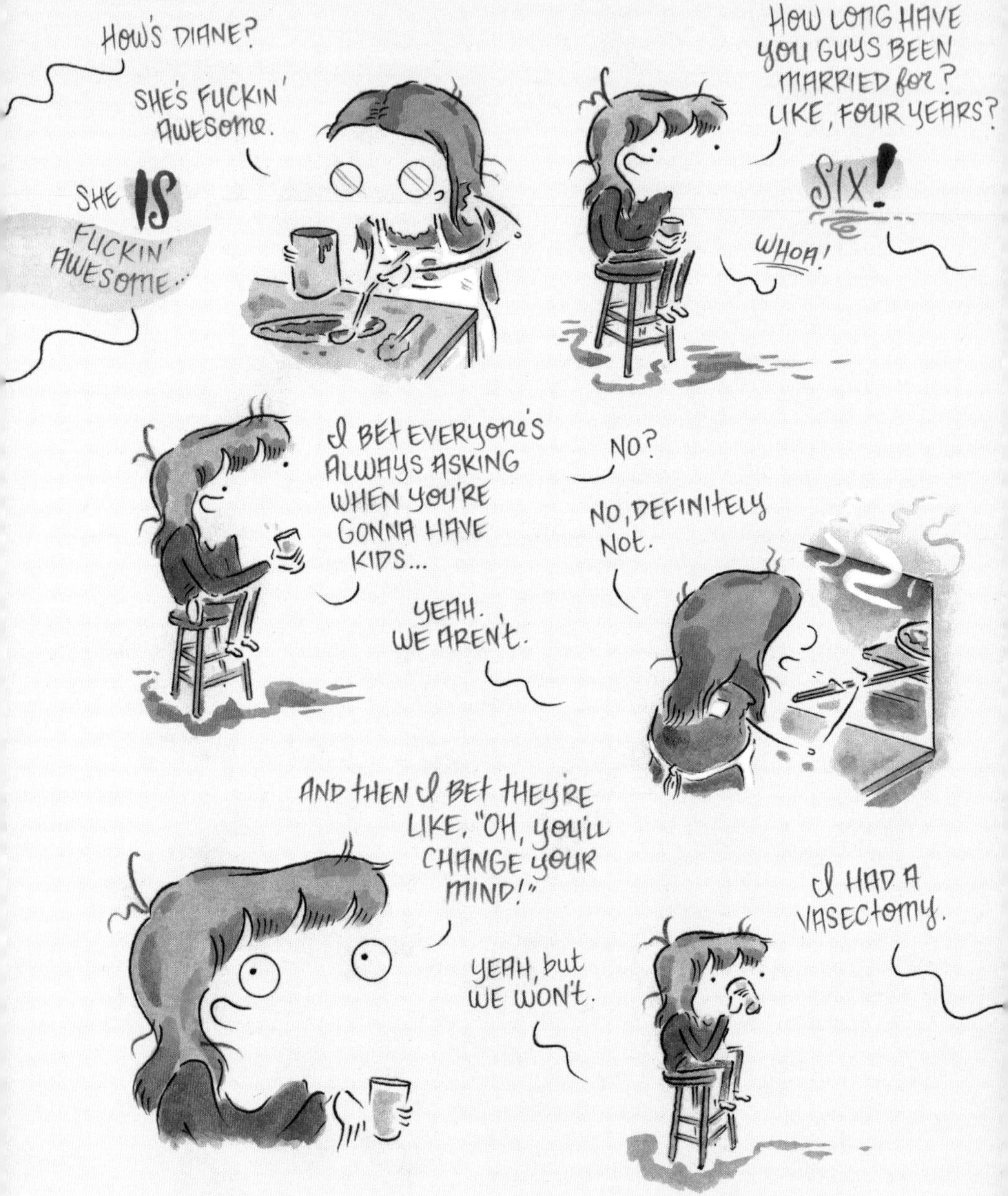
HOW'S DIANE?
SHE'S FUCKIN' AWESOME.
SHE IS FUCKIN' AWESOME...
HOW LONG HAVE YOU GUYS BEEN MARRIED FOR? LIKE, FOUR YEARS?
SIX!
WHOA!
I BET EVERYONE'S ALWAYS ASKING WHEN YOU'RE GONNA HAVE KIDS...
YEAH. WE AREN'T.
NO?
NO, DEFINITELY NOT.
AND THEN I BET THEY'RE LIKE, "OH, YOU'LL CHANGE YOUR MIND!"
YEAH, BUT WE WON'T.
I HAD A VASECTOMY.

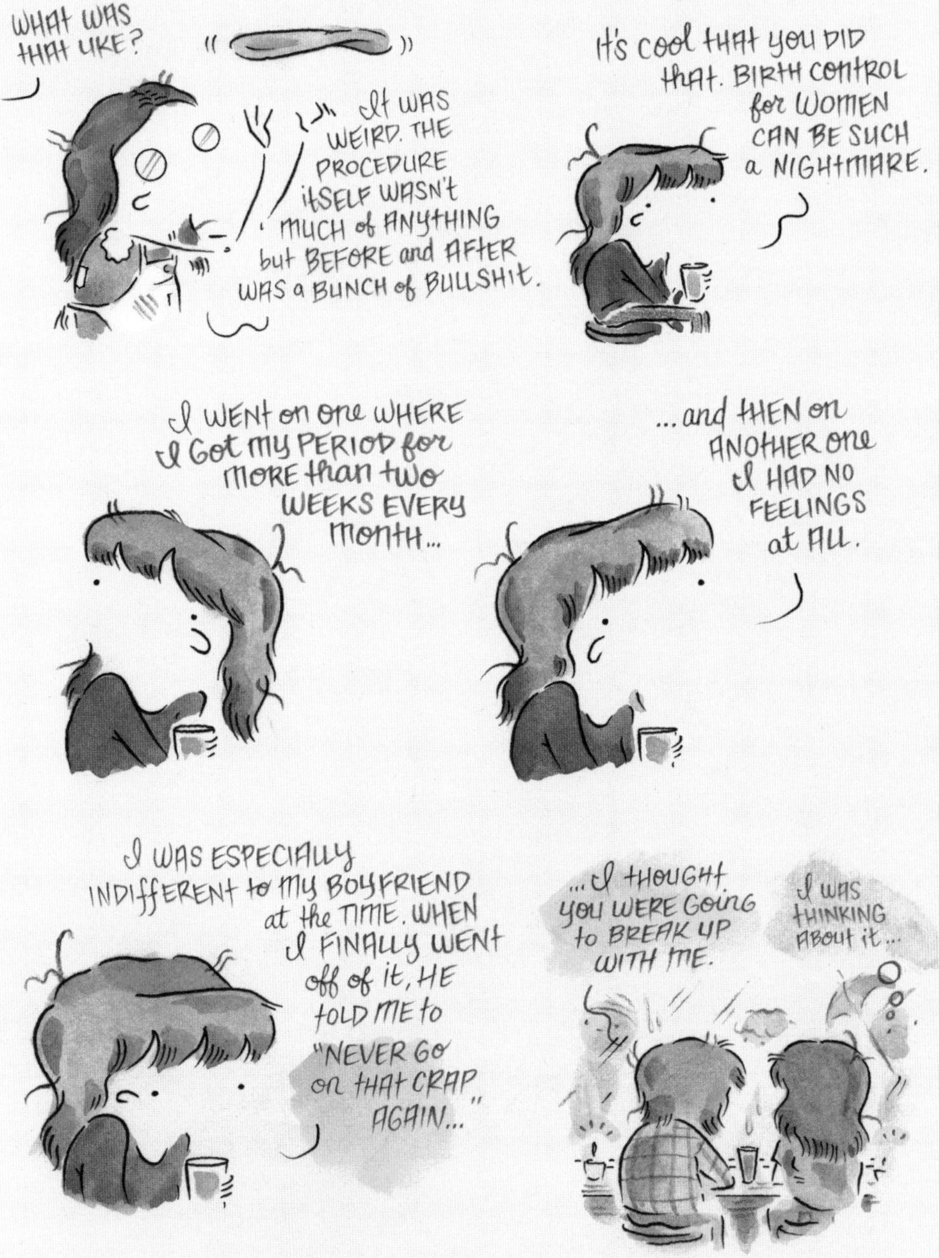
WHAT WAS THAT LIKE?
" "
IT WAS WEIRD. THE PROCEDURE ITSELF WASN'T MUCH OF ANYTHING BUT BEFORE AND AFTER WAS A BUNCH OF BULLSHIT.
IT'S COOL THAT YOU DID THAT. BIRTH CONTROL FOR WOMEN CAN BE SUCH A NIGHTMARE.
I WENT ON ONE WHERE I GOT MY PERIOD FOR MORE THAN TWO WEEKS EVERY MONTH...
...AND THEN ON ANOTHER ONE I HAD NO FEELINGS AT ALL.
I WAS ESPECIALLY INDIFFERENT TO MY BOYFRIEND AT THE TIME. WHEN I FINALLY WENT OFF OF IT, HE TOLD ME TO "NEVER GO ON THAT CRAP AGAIN..."
...I THOUGHT YOU WERE GOING TO BREAK UP WITH ME.
I WAS THINKING ABOUT IT...

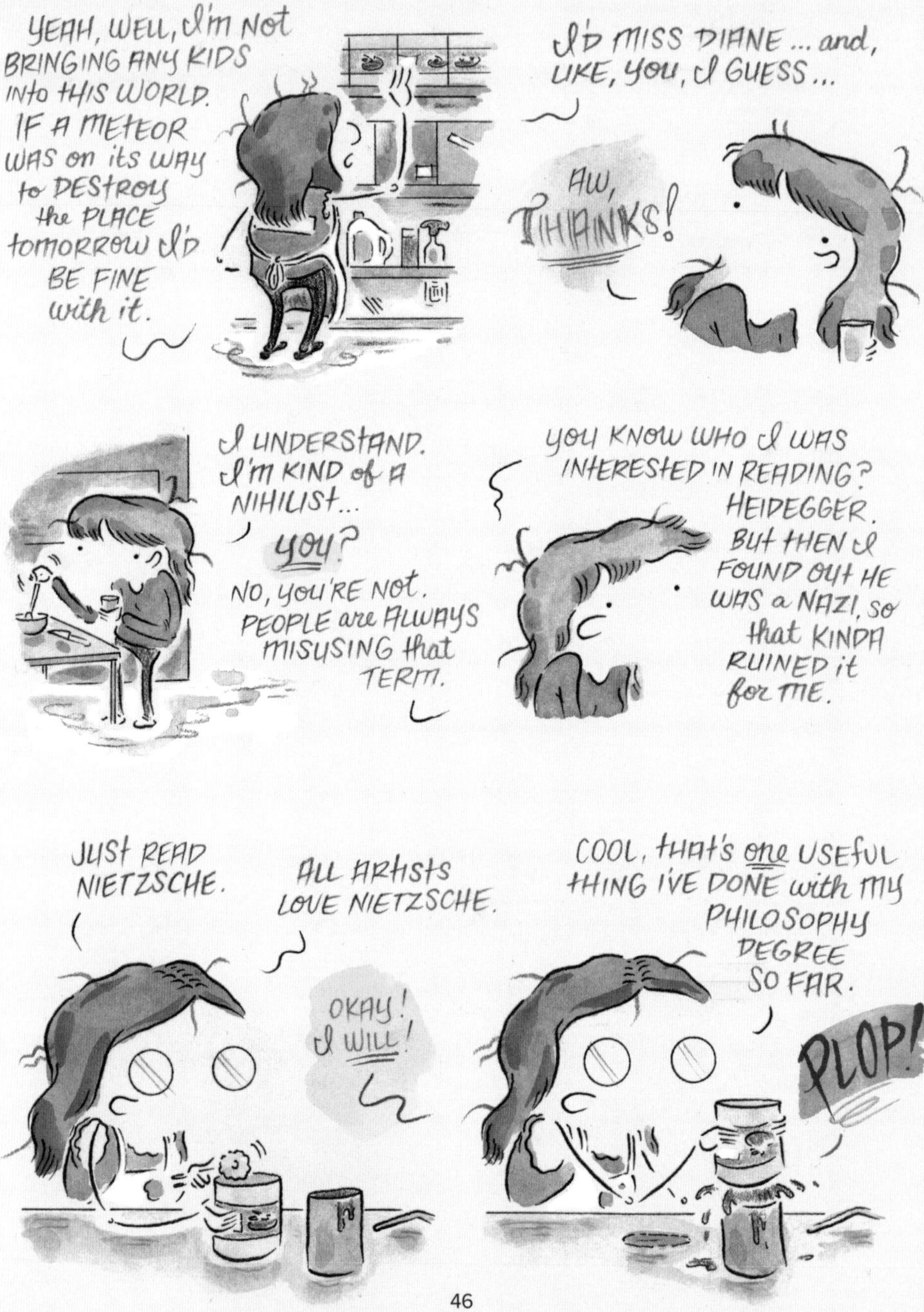
YEAH, WELL, I'M NOT BRINGING ANY KIDS INTO THIS WORLD. IF A METEOR WAS ON ITS WAY TO DESTROY THE PLACE TOMORROW I'D BE FINE WITH IT.
I'D MISS DIANE ... and, LIKE, YOU, I GUESS ...
AW, THANKS!
I UNDERSTAND. I'M KIND of A NIHILIST...
YOU?
NO, YOU'RE NOT. PEOPLE are ALWAYS MISUSING that TERM.
YOU KNOW WHO I WAS INTERESTED IN READING? HEIDEGGER. BUT THEN I FOUND OUT HE WAS a NAZI, so that KINDA RUINED it for ME.
JUST READ NIETZSCHE.
ALL ARTISTS LOVE NIETZSCHE.
OKAY! I WILL!
COOL, that's one USEFUL THING I'VE DONE with my PHILOSOPHY DEGREE SO FAR.
PLOP!

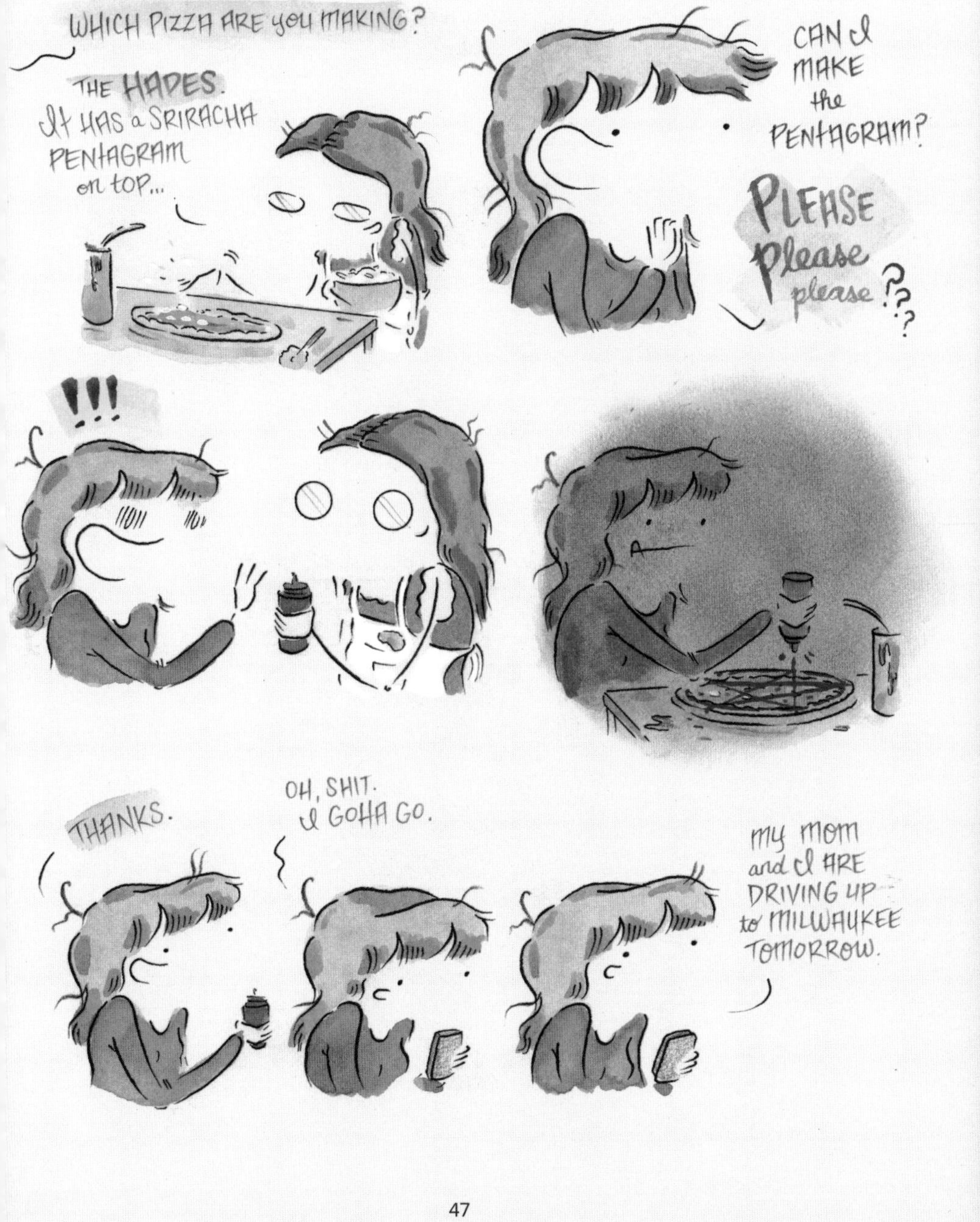
WHICH PIZZA ARE YOU MAKING?
THE HADES. It HAS a SRIRACHA PENTAGRAM on top...
CAN I MAKE the PENTAGRAM?
PLEASE please please ???
!!!
THANKS.
OH, SHIT. I GOTTA GO.
my mom and I ARE DRIVING UP to MILWAUKEE TOMORROW.

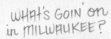
WHAT'S GOIN' ON in MILWAUKEE?

MY BEST FRIEND from CHILDHOOD JUST HAD tWINS, SO WE'RE GOING UP to MEET them.

SOUNDS LIKE a BLAST.

MY MOM WILL BE in HEAVEN.

THANKS for KEEPING ME COMPANY WHILE I WORKED. NEXT time WE'LL DO SOMETHING FUN.

THAT WAS FUN!

YOU'RE the BEST.

LOVE YA, MAN! THANKS for the BEER!

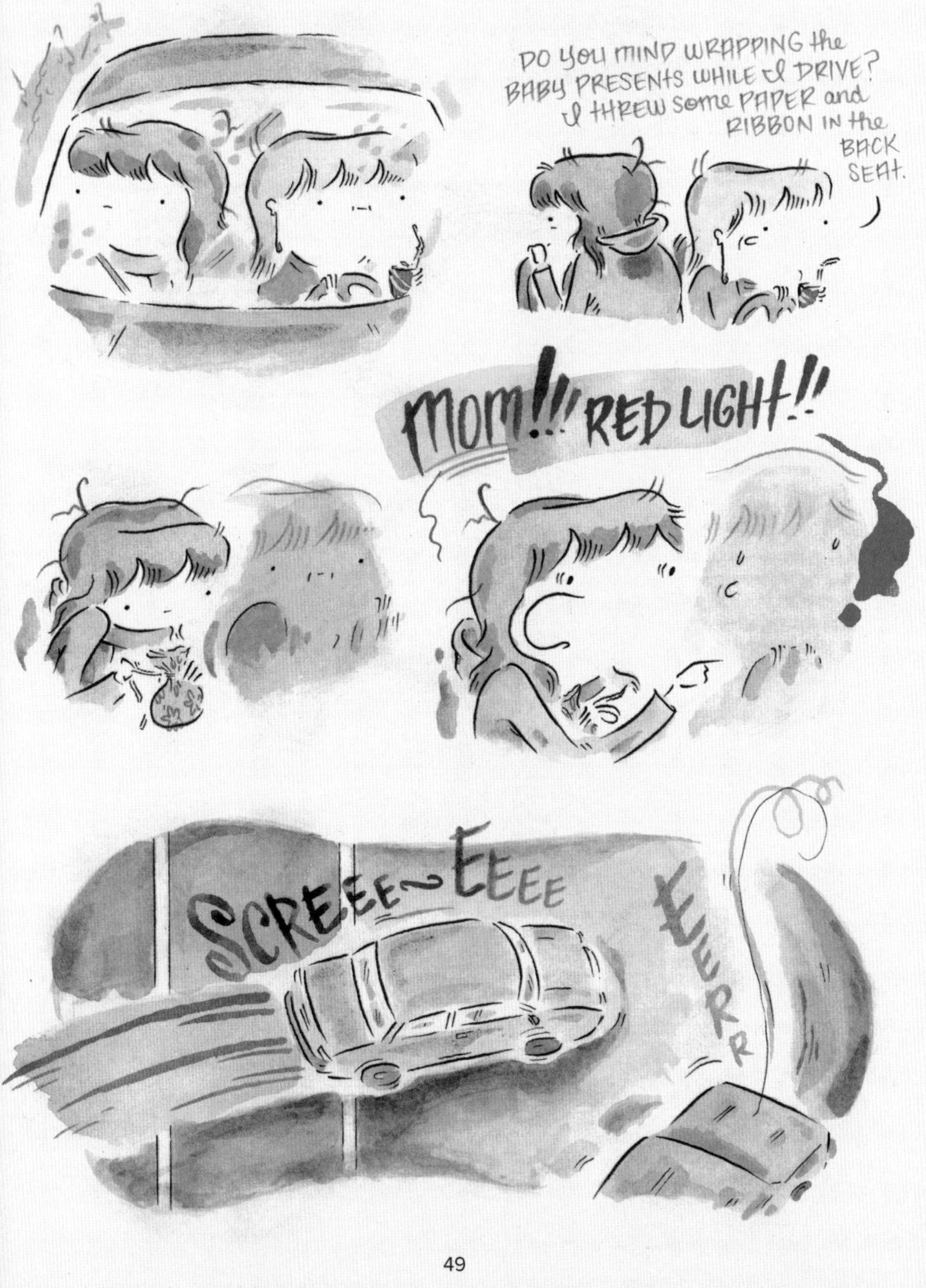
DO YOU MIND WRAPPING the BABY PRESENTS WHILE I DRIVE? I THREW Some PAPER and RIBBON IN the BACK SEAT.
MOM!!! RED LIGHT!!
SCREEE~EEEE
EEERR

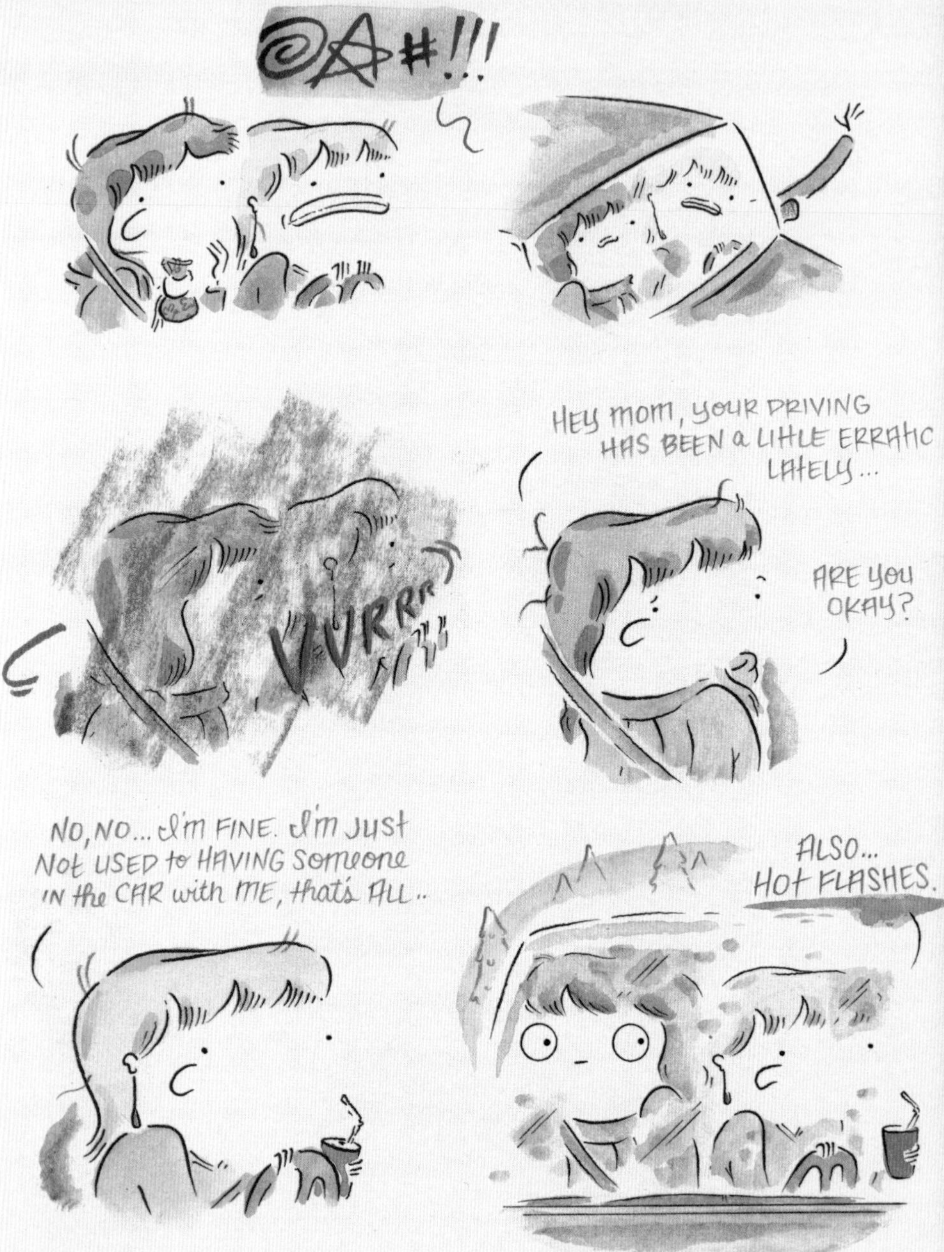
@A#!!!
VVURRR
HEY MOM, YOUR DRIVING HAS BEEN A LITTLE ERRATIC LATELY...
ARE YOU OKAY?
NO, NO... I'M FINE. I'M JUST NOT USED TO HAVING SOMEONE IN THE CAR WITH ME, THAT'S ALL..
ALSO... HOT FLASHES.

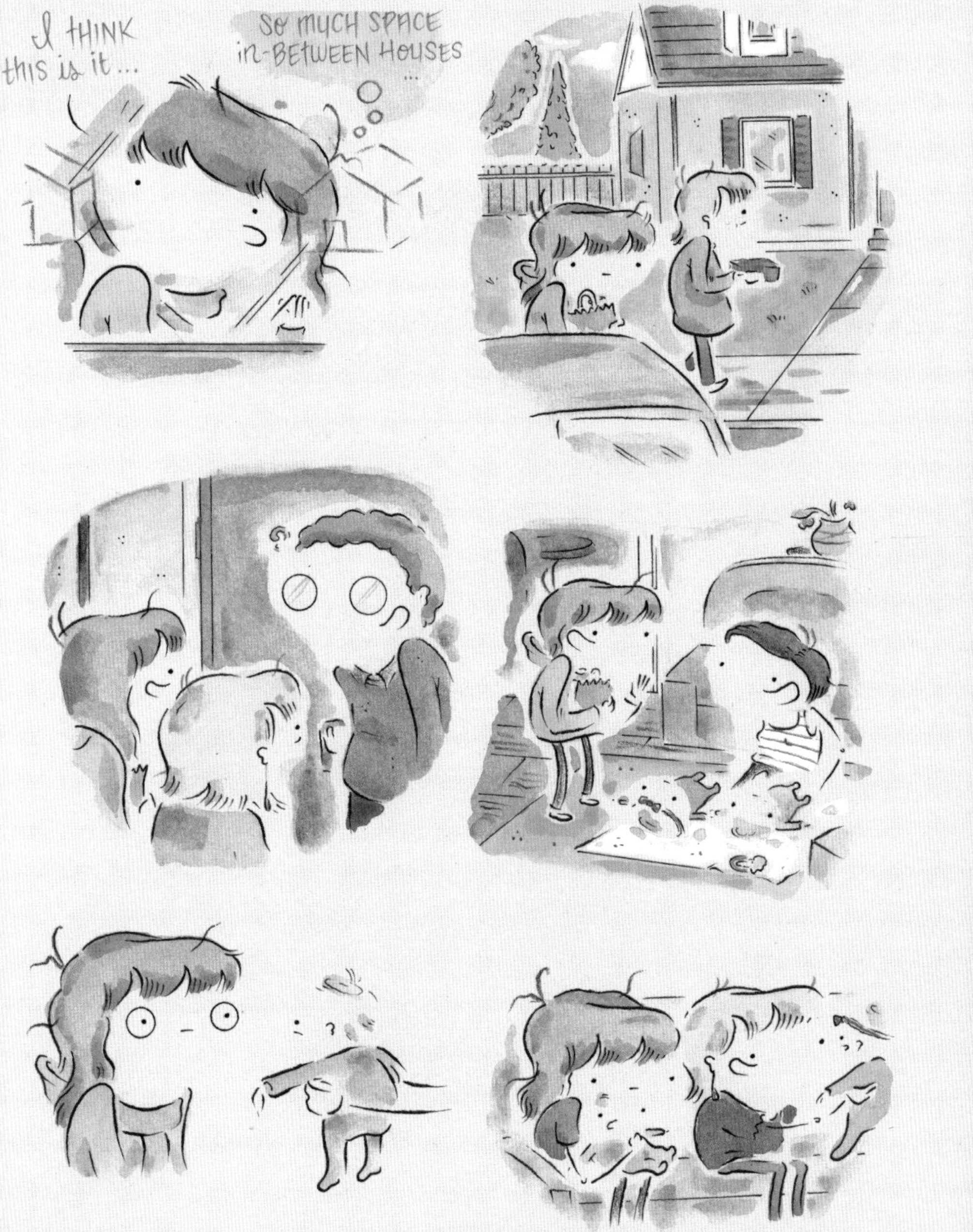
I THINK this is it...
SO MUCH SPACE in-BETWEEN HOUSES ...

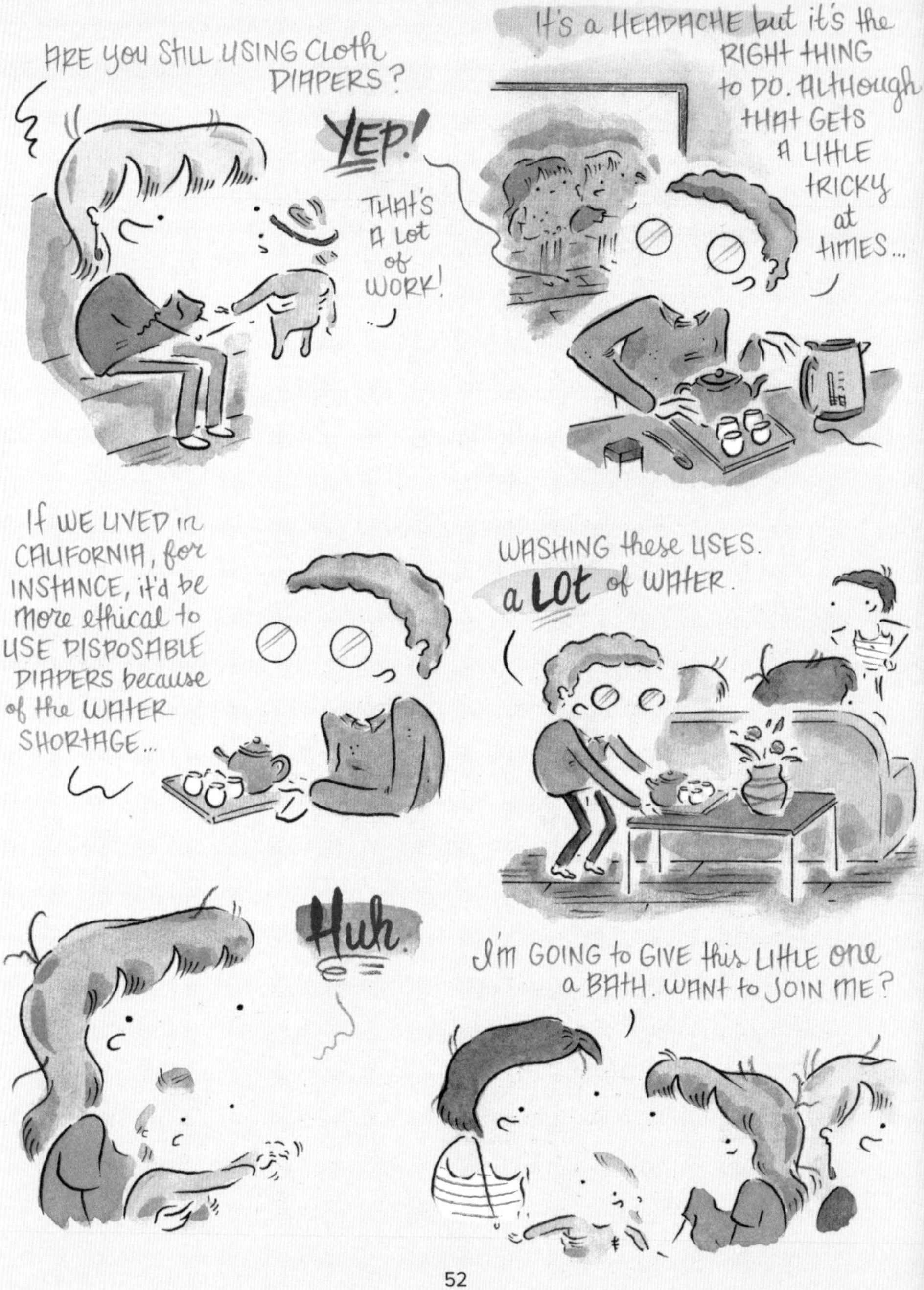
ARE YOU STILL USING CLOTH DIAPERS?
YEP!
THAT'S A LOT OF WORK!
It's a HEADACHE but it's the RIGHT THING to DO. ALTHOUGH THAT GETS A LITTLE TRICKY at TIMES...
If WE LIVED in CALIFORNIA, for INSTANCE, it'd be more ethical to USE DISPOSABLE DIAPERS because of the WATER SHORTAGE...
WASHING these USES a LOT of WATER.
Huh.
I'M GOING to GIVE this LITTLE ONE a BATH. WANT to JOIN ME?

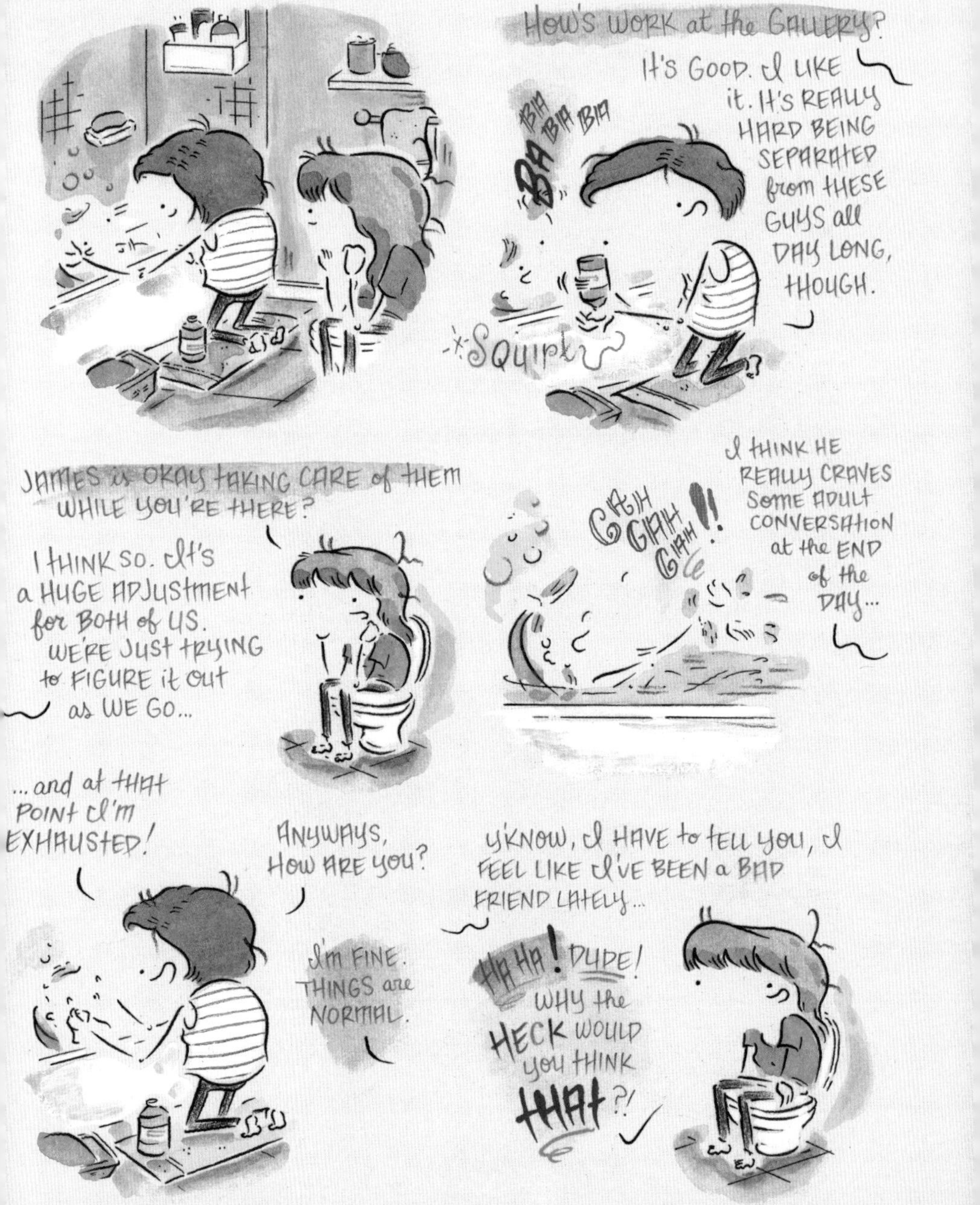
HOW'S WORK at the GALLERY?
IT'S GOOD. I LIKE it. IT'S REALLY HARD BEING SEPARATED from THESE GUYS all DAY LONG, THOUGH.
BLA BLA BLA BA
SQUIRK
JAMES is OKAY TAKING CARE of THEM WHILE YOU'RE THERE?
I THINK SO. IT'S a HUGE ADJUSTMENT for BOTH of US. WE'RE JUST TRYING to FIGURE it OUT as WE GO...
I THINK HE REALLY CRAVES SOME ADULT CONVERSATION at the END of the DAY...
GAH GAH GAH!!
...and at THAT POINT I'M EXHAUSTED!
ANYWAYS, HOW ARE YOU?
I'M FINE. THINGS are NORMAL.
Y'KNOW, I HAVE to TELL YOU, I FEEL LIKE I'VE BEEN a BAD FRIEND LATELY...
HA HA! DUDE! WHY the HECK WOULD YOU THINK THAT?!

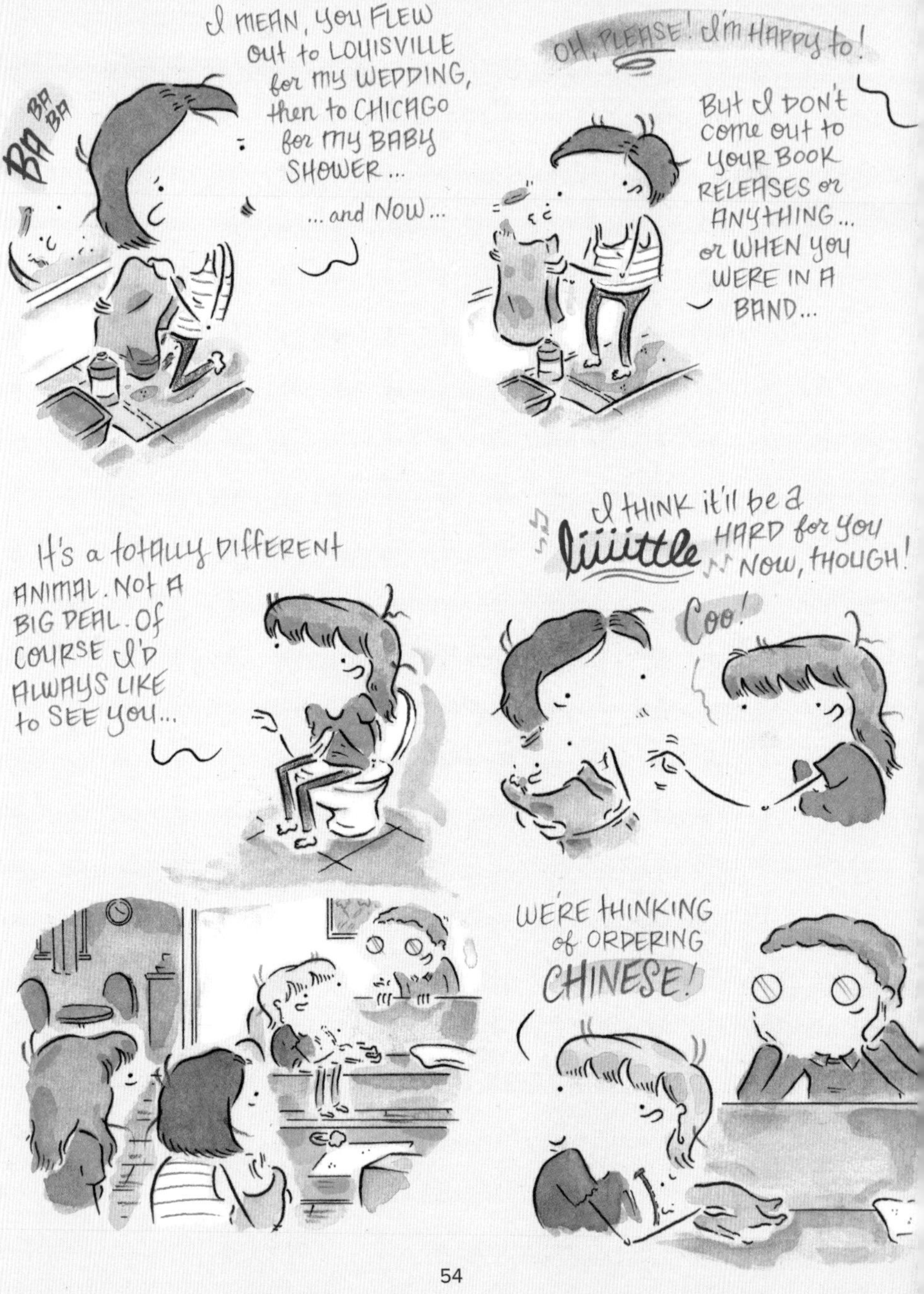

I MEAN, YOU FLEW OUT TO LOUISVILLE FOR MY WEDDING, THEN TO CHICAGO FOR MY BABY SHOWER...
...AND NOW...
BA BA BA
OH, PLEASE! I'M HAPPY TO!
BUT I DON'T COME OUT TO YOUR BOOK RELEASES OR ANYTHING... OR WHEN YOU WERE IN A BAND...
IT'S A TOTALLY DIFFERENT ANIMAL. NOT A BIG DEAL. OF COURSE I'D ALWAYS LIKE TO SEE YOU...
I THINK IT'LL BE A LIIIITTLE HARD FOR YOU NOW, THOUGH!
COO!
WE'RE THINKING OF ORDERING CHINESE!

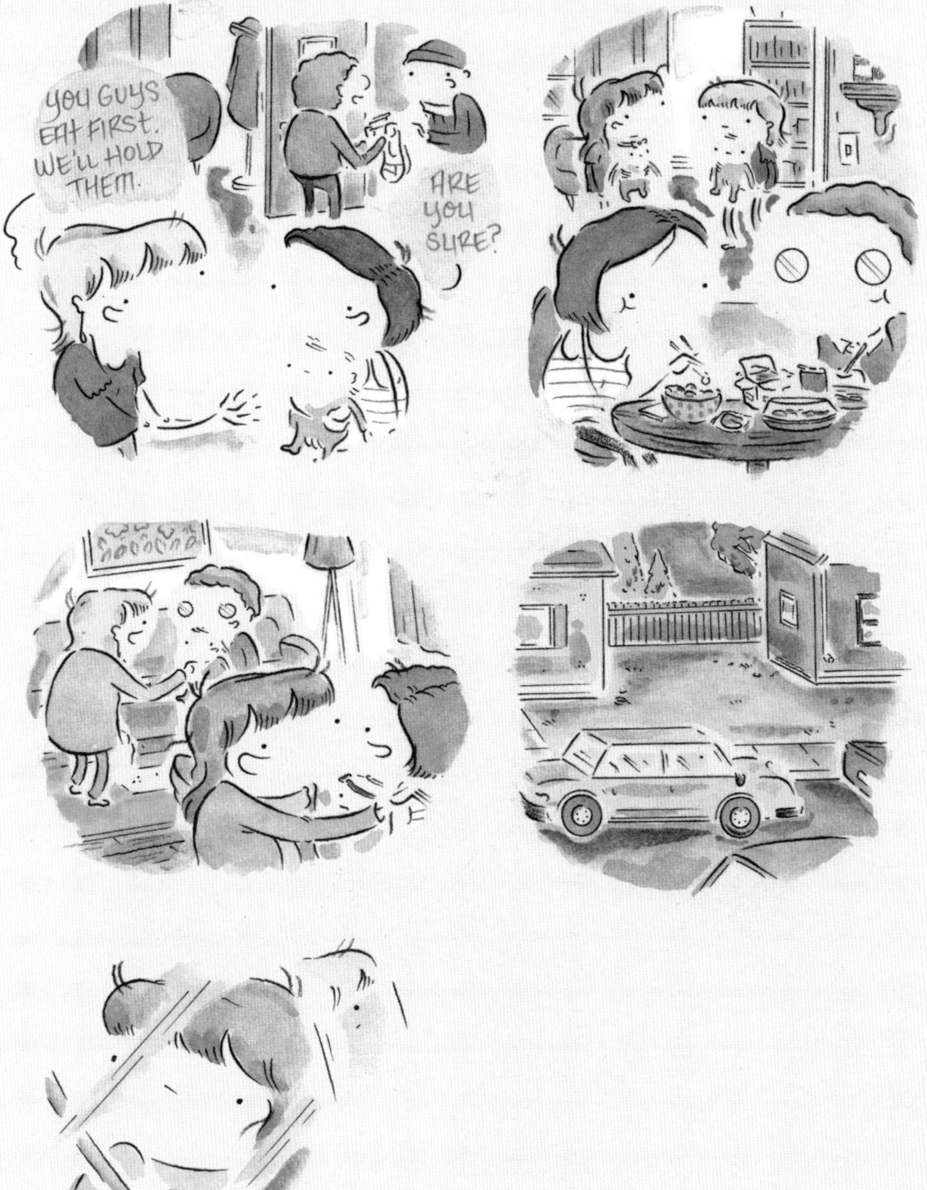
YOU GUYS EAT FIRST. WE'LL HOLD THEM.
ARE YOU SURE?

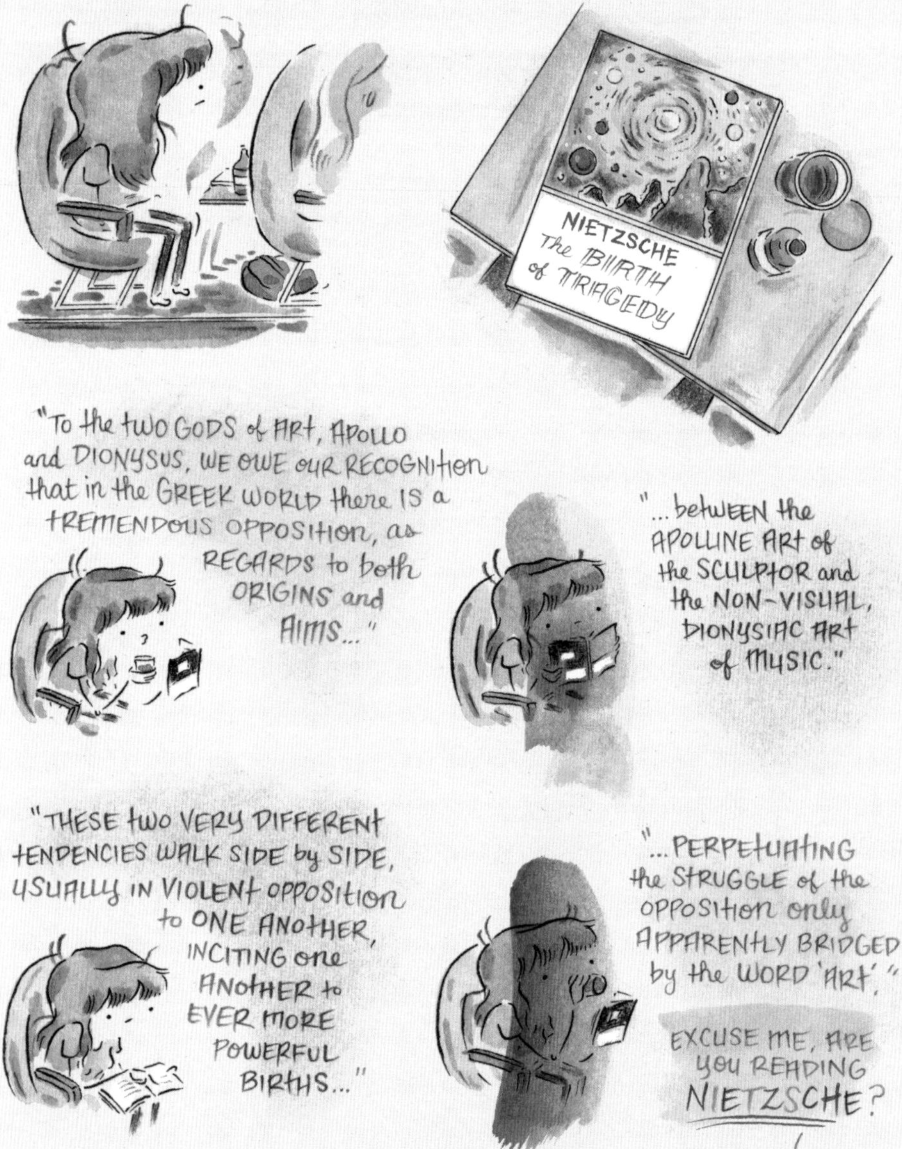
NIETZSCHE
The BIRTH of TRAGEDY
"To the two GODS of ART, APOLLO and DIONYSUS, WE OWE OUR RECOGNITION that in the GREEK WORLD there IS a TREMENDOUS OPPOSITION, as REGARDS to both ORIGINS and AIMS..."
"...between the APOLLINE ART of the SCULPTOR and the NON-VISUAL, DIONYSIAC ART of MUSIC."
"THESE two VERY DIFFERENT TENDENCIES WALK SIDE by SIDE, USUALLY IN VIOLENT OPPOSITION to ONE ANOTHER, INCITING one ANOTHER to EVER MORE POWERFUL BIRTHS..."
"...PERPETUATING the STRUGGLE of the OPPOSITION only APPARENTLY BRIDGED by the WORD 'ART'."
EXCUSE ME, ARE YOU READING NIETZSCHE?

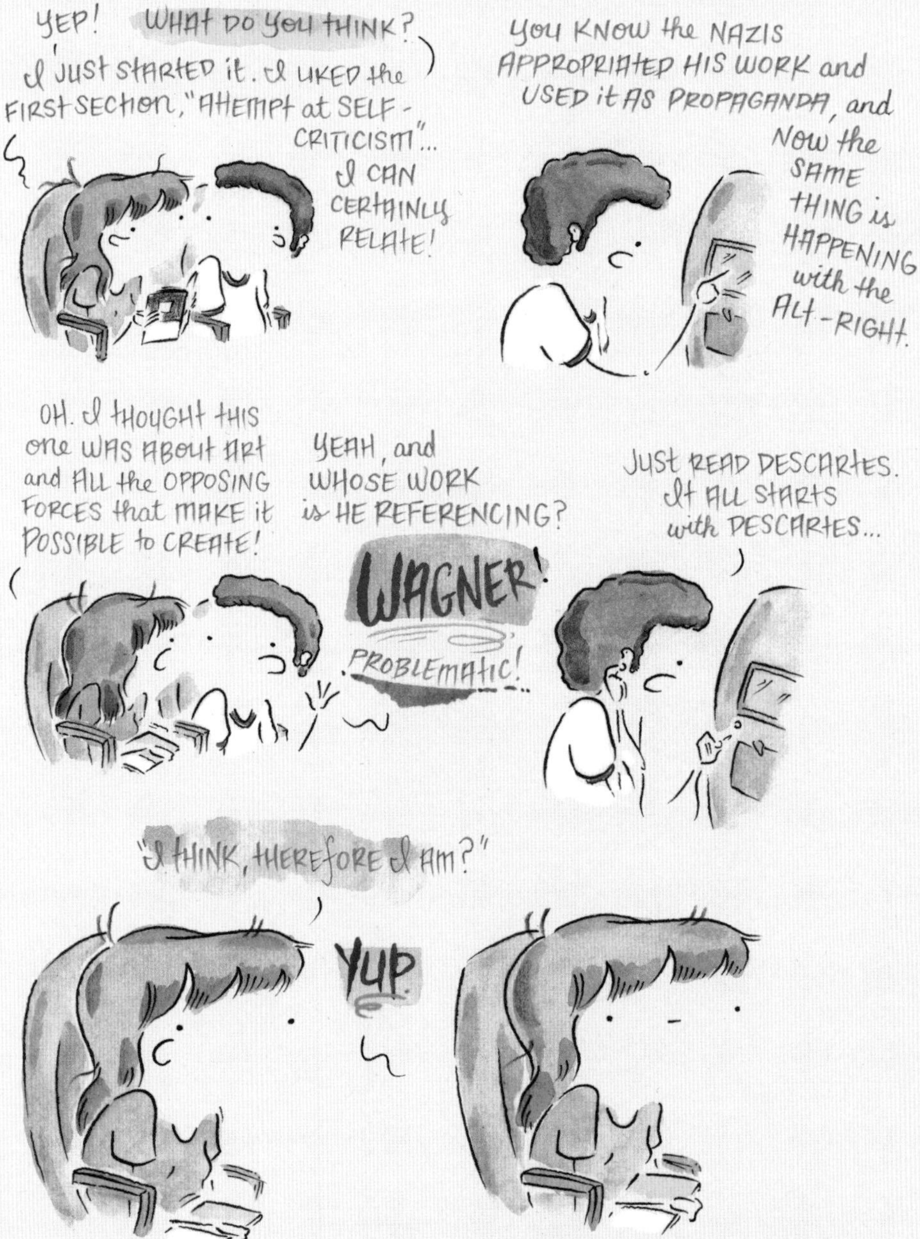
YEP!
WHAT DO YOU THINK?
I JUST STARTED IT. I LIKED THE FIRST SECTION, "ATTEMPT AT SELF-CRITICISM"... I CAN CERTAINLY RELATE!
YOU KNOW THE NAZIS APPROPRIATED HIS WORK AND USED IT AS PROPAGANDA, AND NOW THE SAME THING IS HAPPENING WITH THE ALT-RIGHT.
OH. I THOUGHT THIS ONE WAS ABOUT ART AND ALL THE OPPOSING FORCES THAT MAKE IT POSSIBLE TO CREATE!
YEAH, AND WHOSE WORK IS HE REFERENCING?
WAGNER!
PROBLEMATIC!
JUST READ DESCARTES. IT ALL STARTS WITH DESCARTES...
"I THINK, THEREFORE I AM?"
YUP.

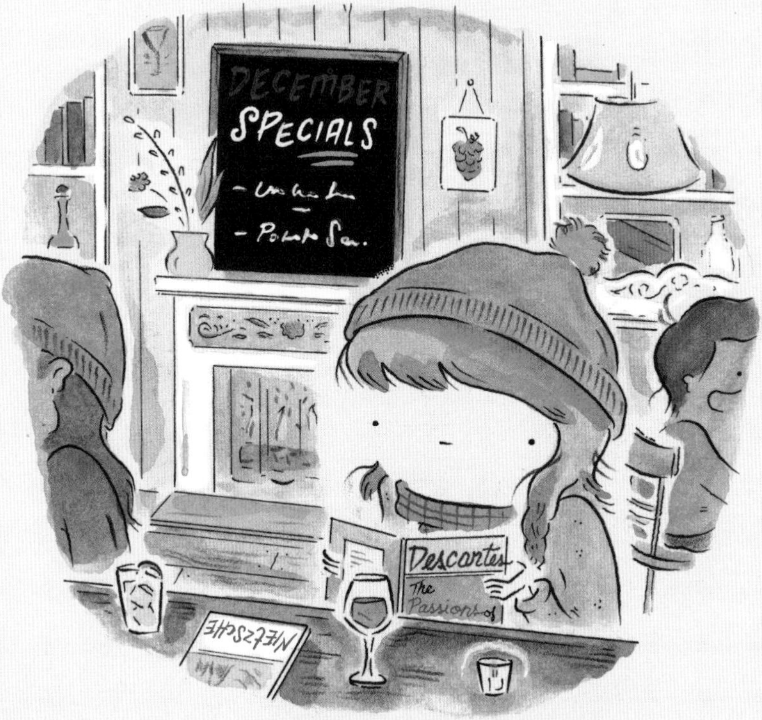
DECEMBER
SPECIALS
Descartes
The Passions of
NIETZSCHE

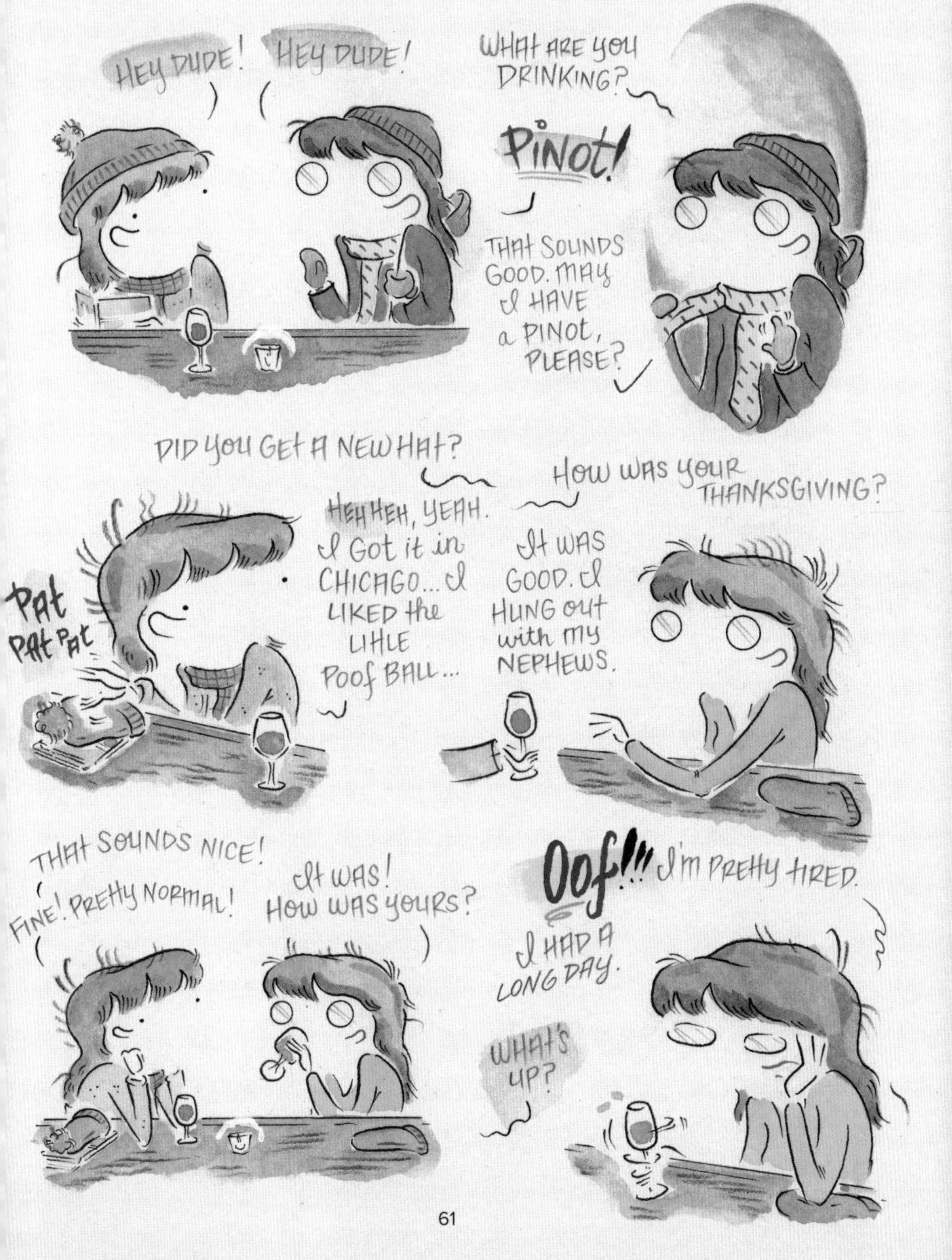

HEY DUDE!
HEY DUDE!
WHAT ARE YOU DRINKING?
PINOT!
THAT SOUNDS GOOD. MAY I HAVE A PINOT, PLEASE?
DID YOU GET A NEW HAT?
HEH HEH, YEAH. I GOT IT IN CHICAGO... I LIKED THE LITTLE POOF BALL...
PAT PAT PAT
HOW WAS YOUR THANKSGIVING?
IT WAS GOOD. I HUNG OUT WITH MY NEPHEWS.
THAT SOUNDS NICE!
IT WAS! HOW WAS YOURS?
FINE! PRETTY NORMAL!
OOF!!! I'M PRETTY TIRED.
I HAD A LONG DAY.
WHAT'S UP?

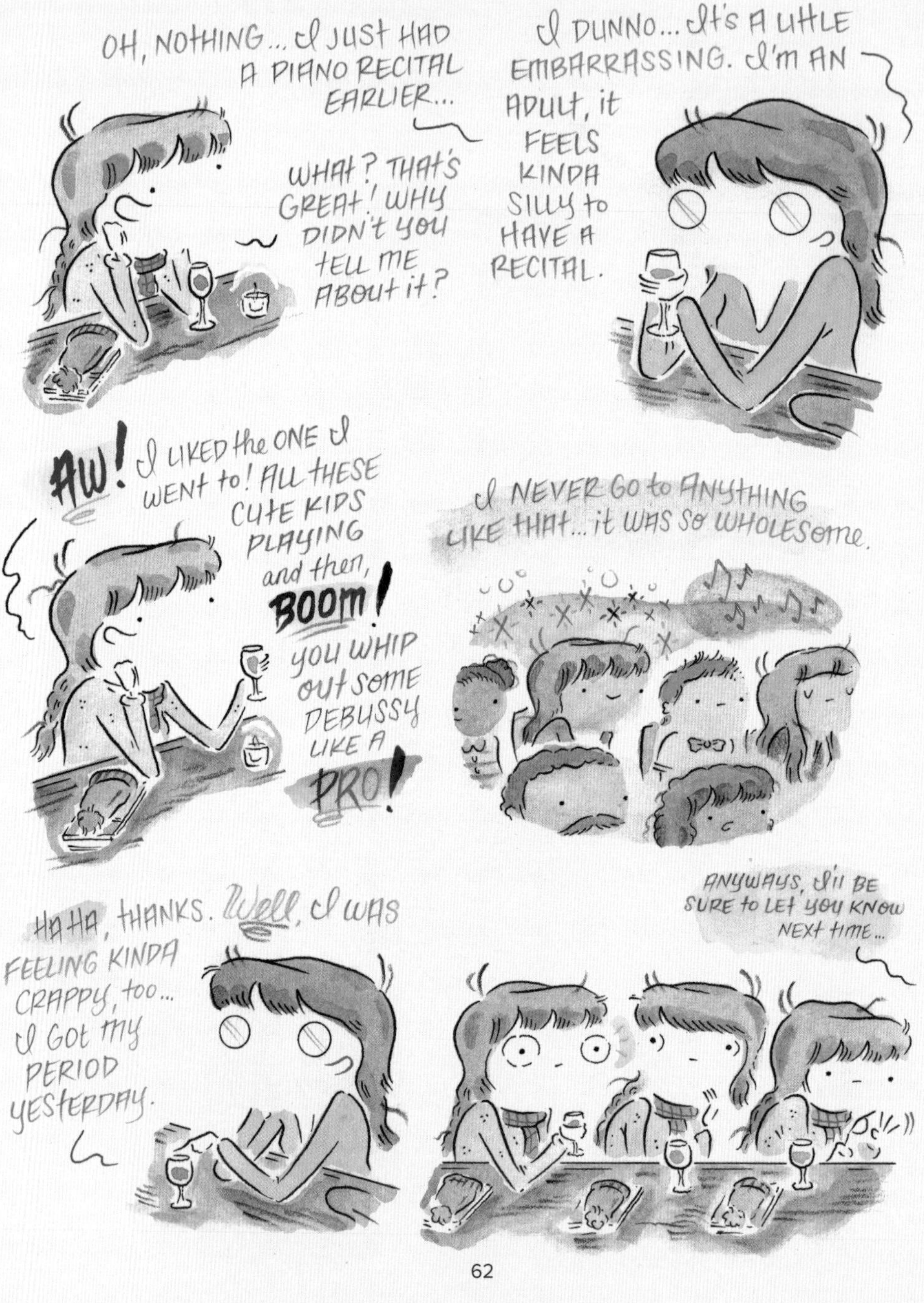
OH, NOTHING... I JUST HAD A PIANO RECITAL EARLIER...
WHAT? THAT'S GREAT! WHY DIDN'T YOU TELL ME ABOUT IT?
I DUNNO... IT'S A LITTLE EMBARRASSING. I'M AN ADULT, IT FEELS KINDA SILLY TO HAVE A RECITAL.
AW! I LIKED THE ONE I WENT TO! ALL THESE CUTE KIDS PLAYING AND THEN, BOOM! YOU WHIP OUT SOME DEBUSSY LIKE A PRO!
I NEVER GO TO ANYTHING LIKE THAT... IT WAS SO WHOLESOME.
HA HA, THANKS. WELL, I WAS FEELING KINDA CRAPPY, TOO... I GOT MY PERIOD YESTERDAY.
ANYWAYS, I'LL BE SURE TO LET YOU KNOW NEXT TIME...

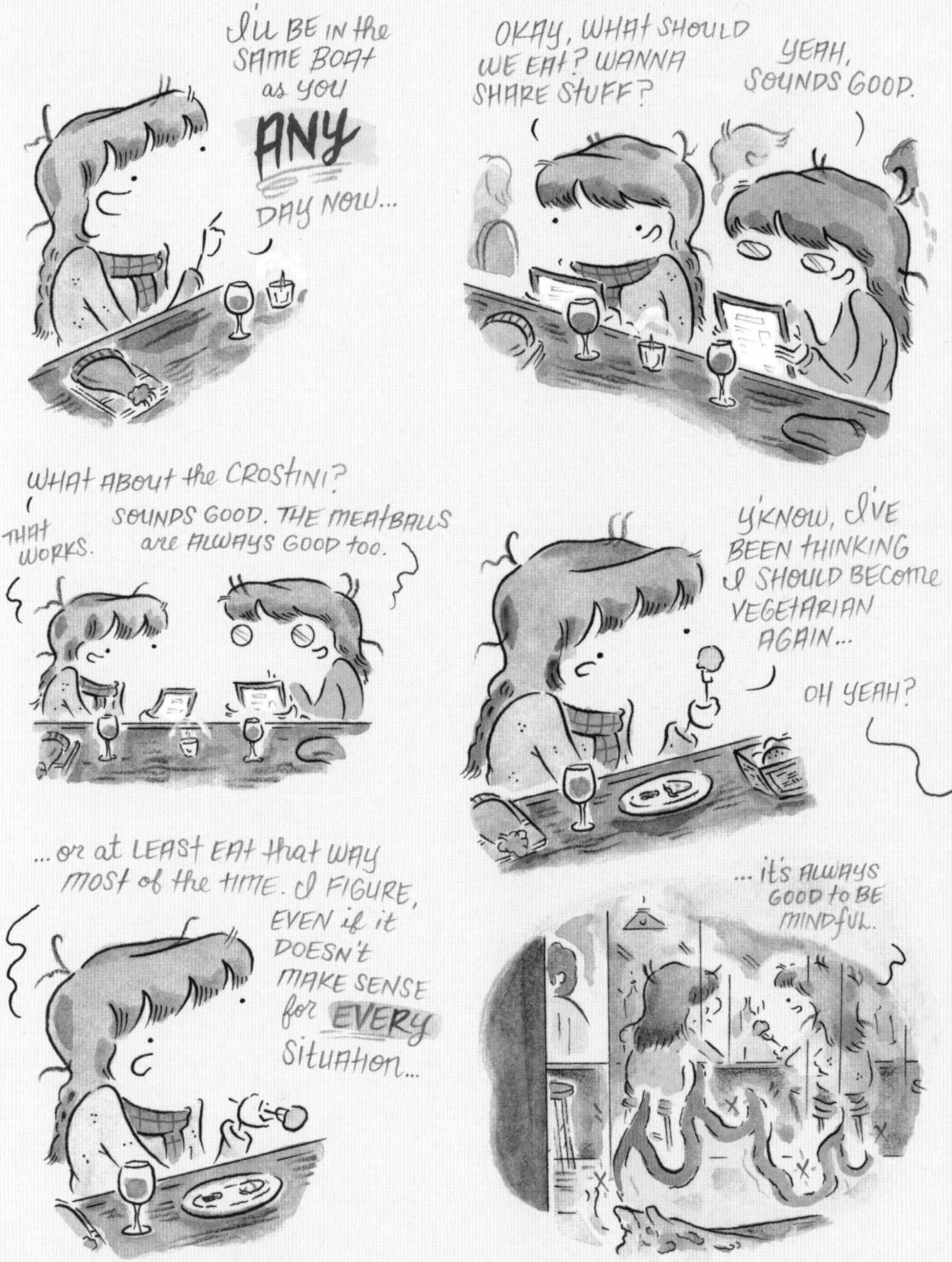
I'LL BE IN THE SAME BOAT AS YOU ANY DAY NOW...
OKAY, WHAT SHOULD WE EAT? WANNA SHARE STUFF?
YEAH, SOUNDS GOOD.
WHAT ABOUT THE CROSTINI?
THAT WORKS.
SOUNDS GOOD. THE MEATBALLS ARE ALWAYS GOOD TOO.
Y'KNOW, I'VE BEEN THINKING I SHOULD BECOME VEGETARIAN AGAIN...
OH YEAH?
...OR AT LEAST EAT THAT WAY MOST OF THE TIME. I FIGURE, EVEN IF IT DOESN'T MAKE SENSE FOR EVERY SITUATION...
...IT'S ALWAYS GOOD TO BE MINDFUL.

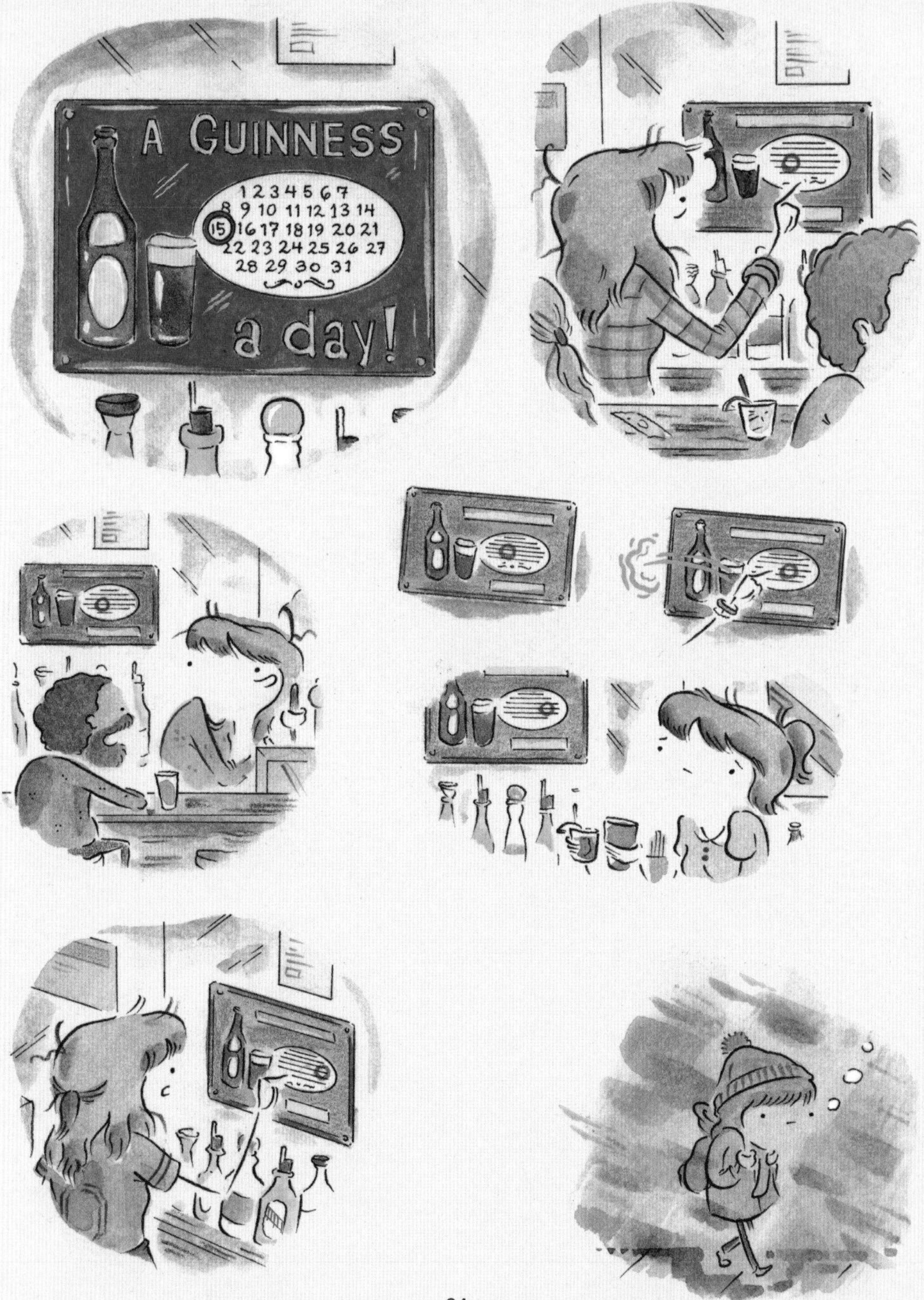
A GUINNESS
1 2 3 4 5 6 7
8 9 10 11 12 13 14
15 16 17 18 19 20 21
22 23 24 25 26 27
28 29 30 31
a day!

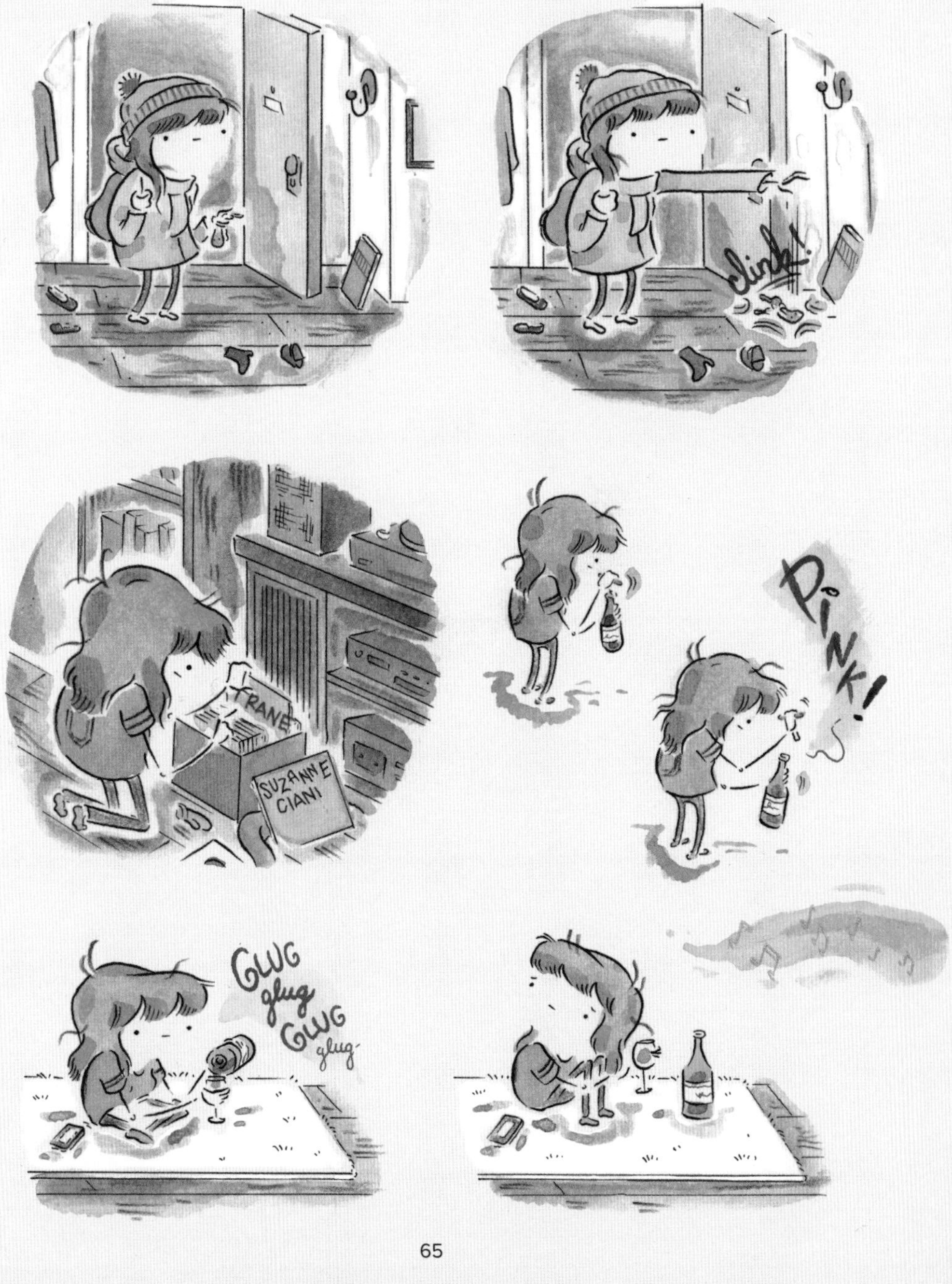
clink!
TRANE
SUZANNE CIANI
PINK!
GLUG
glug
GLUG
glug

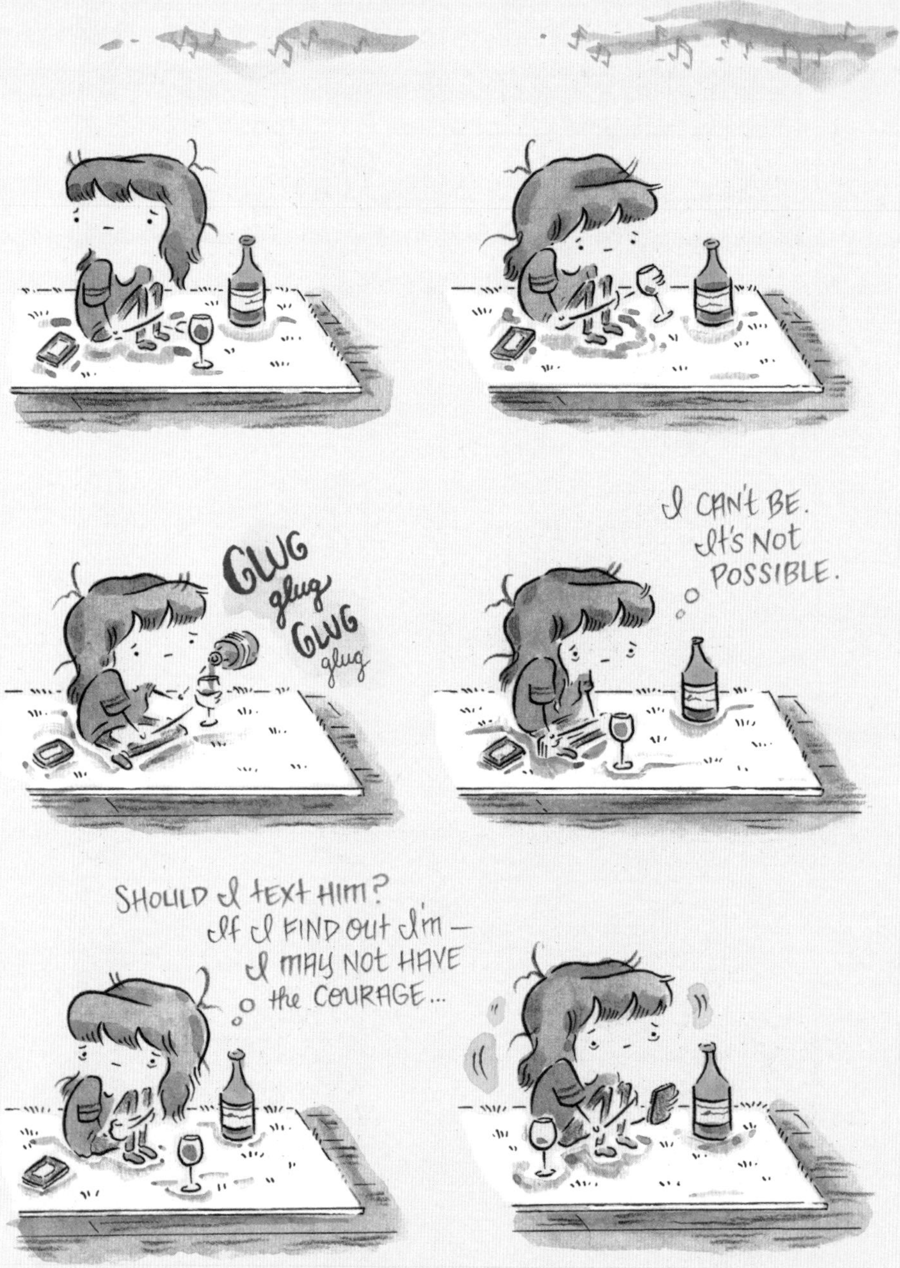
GLUG
glug
GLUG
glug
I CAN'T BE. It's NOT POSSIBLE.
SHOULD I TEXT HIM?
IF I FIND OUT I'M —
I MAY NOT HAVE
THE COURAGE...

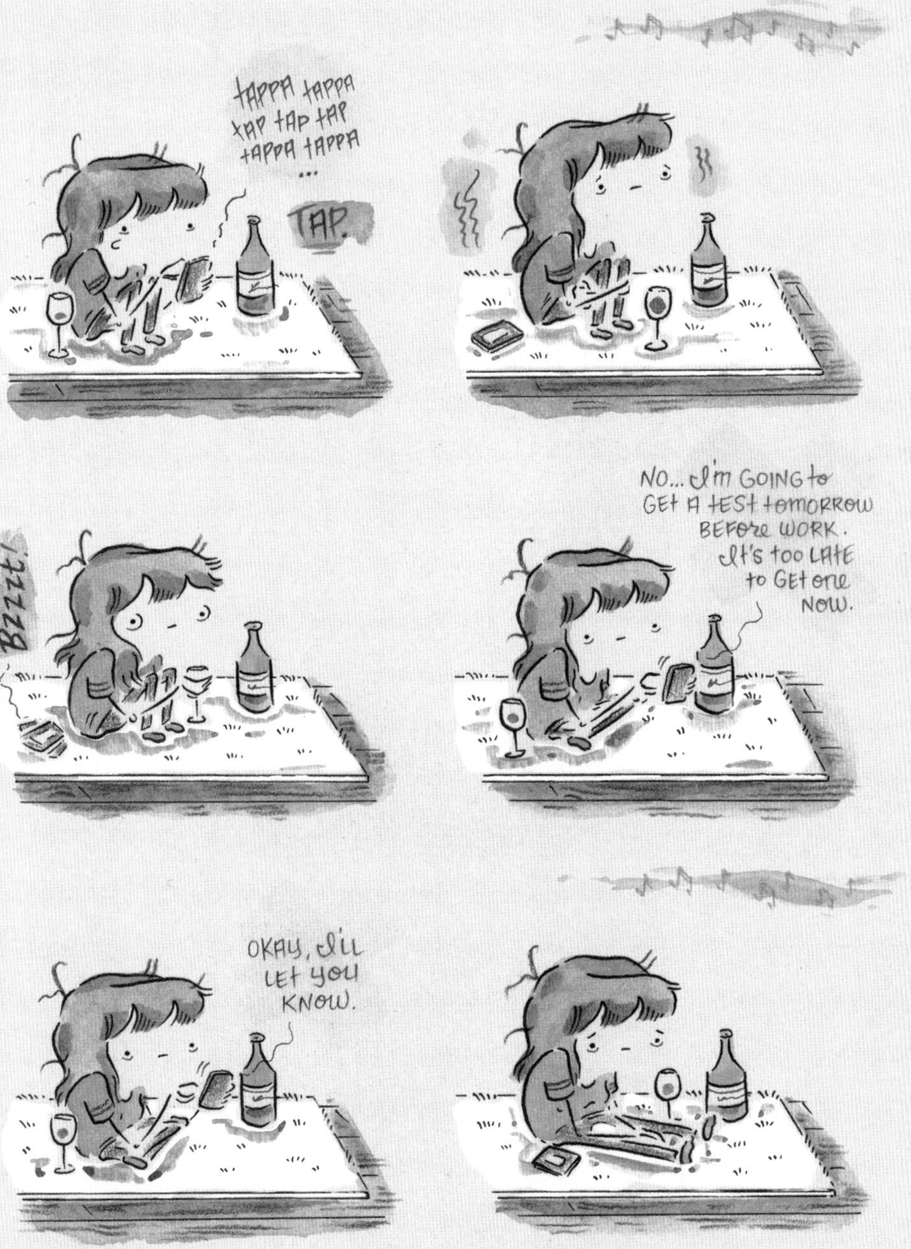
TAPPA TAPPA
TAP TAP TAP
TAPPA TAPPA
...
TAP.
Bzzzt!
NO... I'M GOING TO GET A TEST TOMORROW BEFORE WORK. IT'S TOO LATE TO GET ONE NOW.
OKAY, I'LL LET YOU KNOW.

Bzzzt!
I HOPE YOU'RE OKAY.

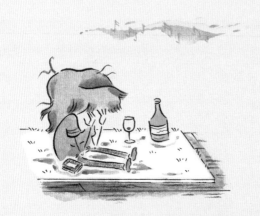

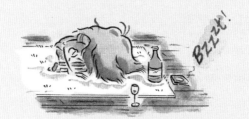

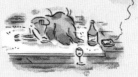

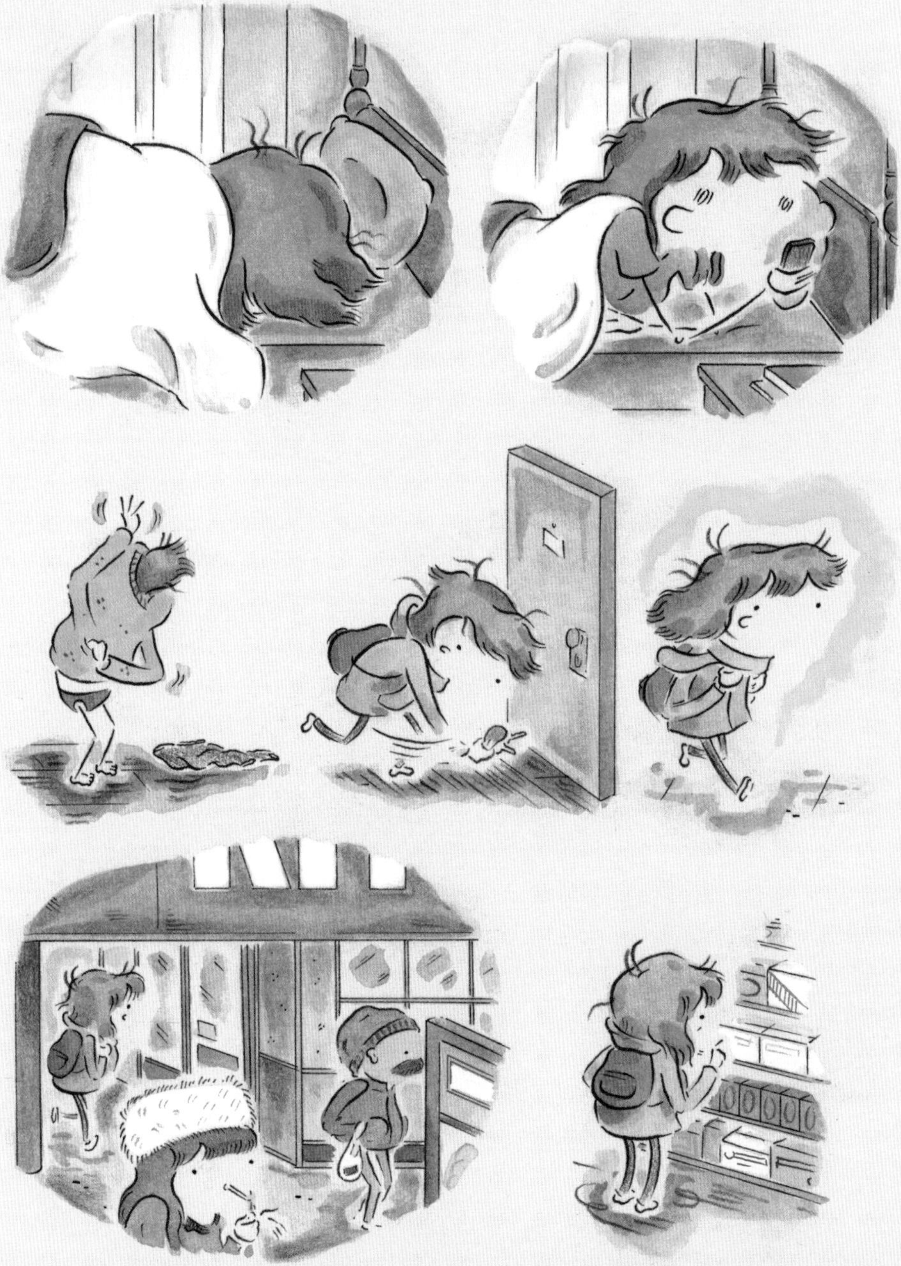

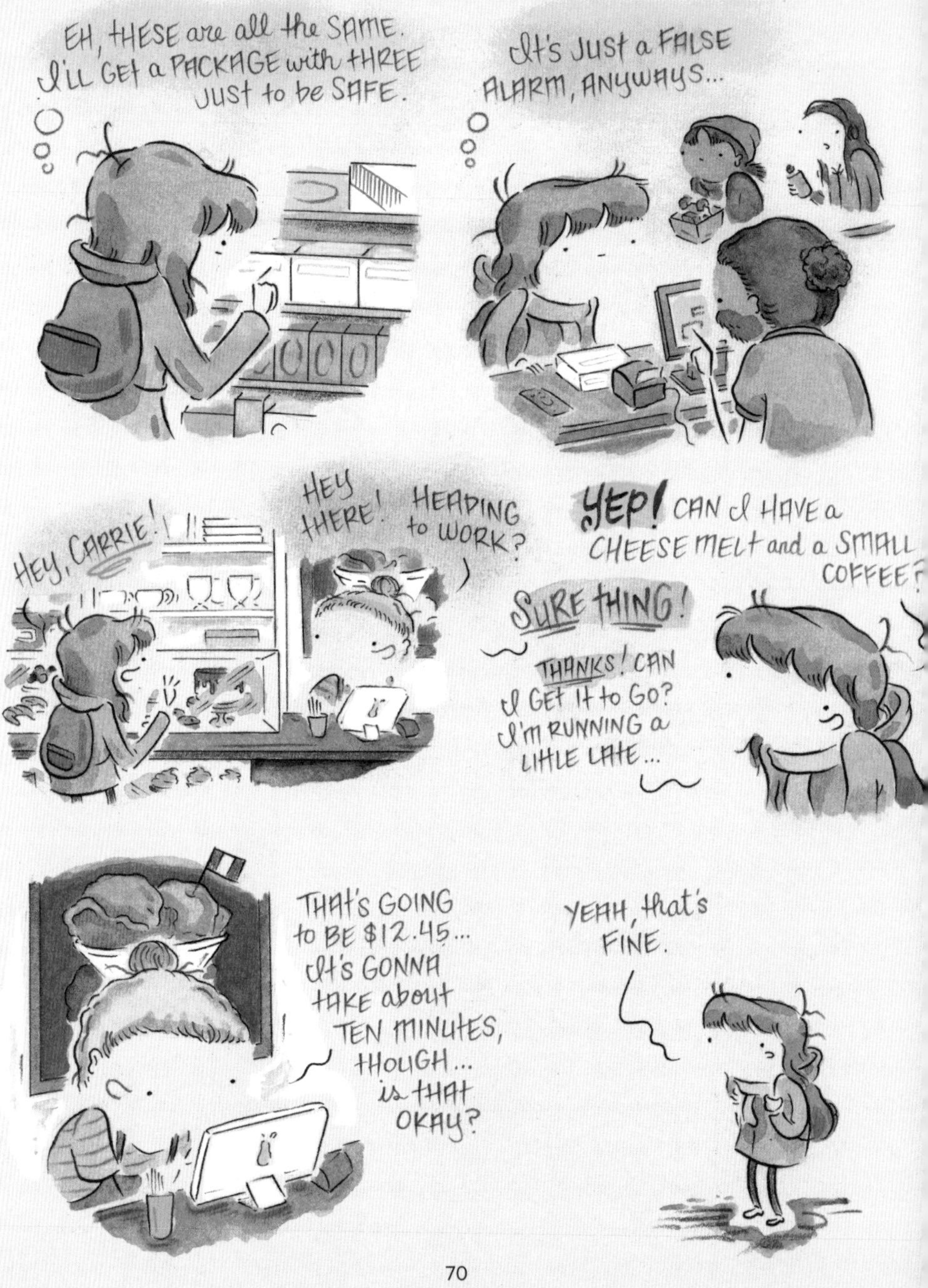
EH, THESE are all the SAME. I'LL GET a PACKAGE with THREE JUST to be SAFE.
It's JUST a FALSE ALARM, ANYWAYS...
HEY, CARRIE!
HEY THERE! HEADING to WORK?
YEP! CAN I HAVE a CHEESE MELT and a SMALL COFFEE?
SURE THING!
THANKS! CAN I GET IT to GO? I'M RUNNING a LITTLE LATE...
THAT's GOING to BE $12.45... It's GONNA TAKE about TEN MINUTES, THOUGH... is THAT OKAY?
YEAH, that's FINE.

HAHA! I'm JUST GOING to USE YOUR BATHROOM REALLY QUICK ...
YEAH, THEY'RE all the SAME.

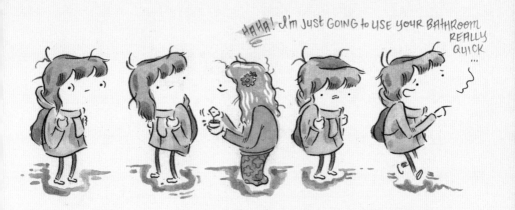

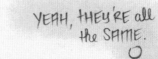

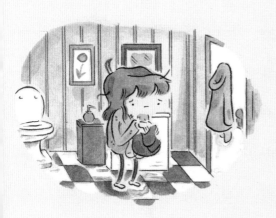

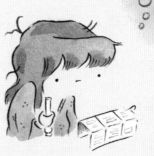

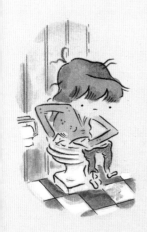

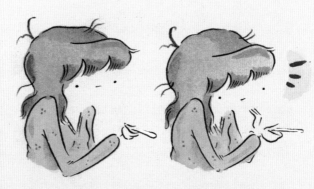

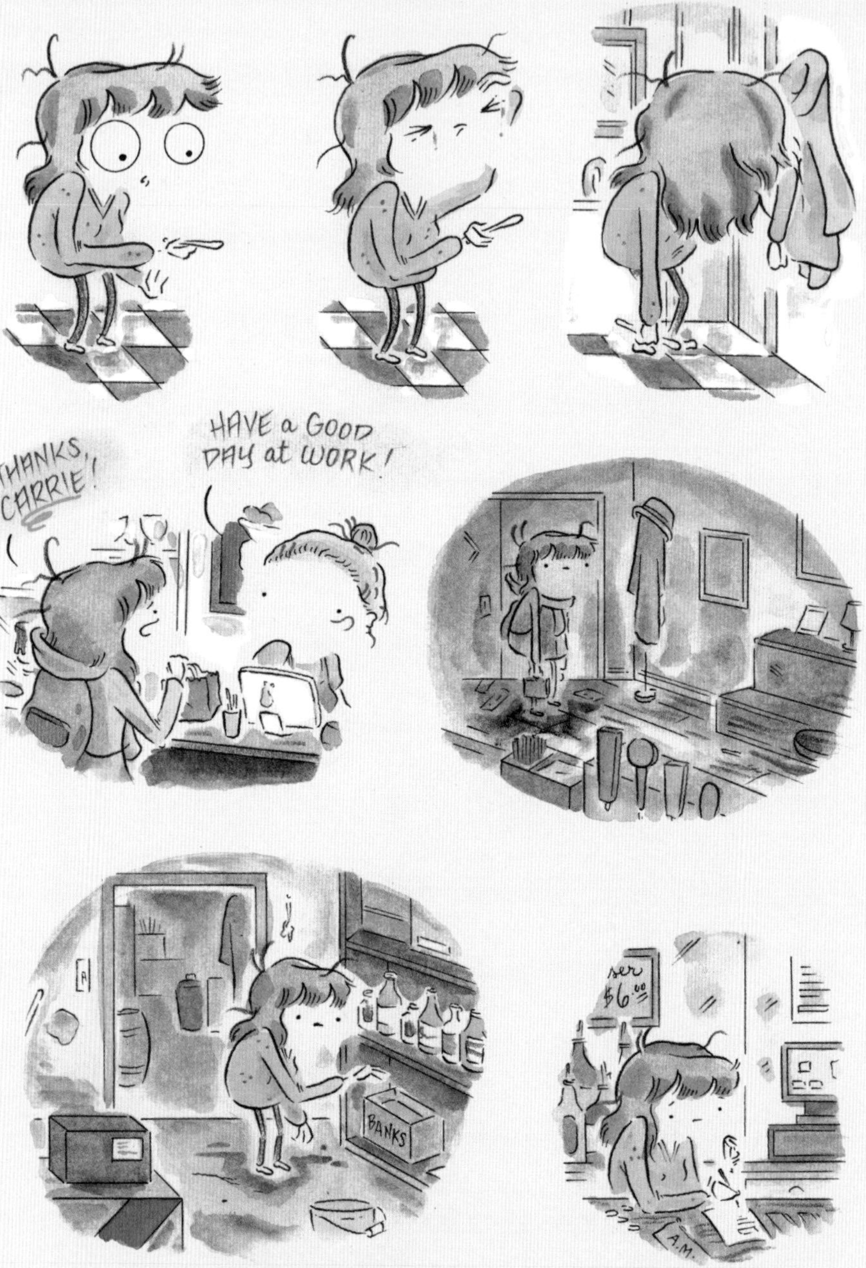
THANKS, CARRIE!
HAVE a GOOD DAY at WORK!
BANKS
ser
$6.00
A.M.

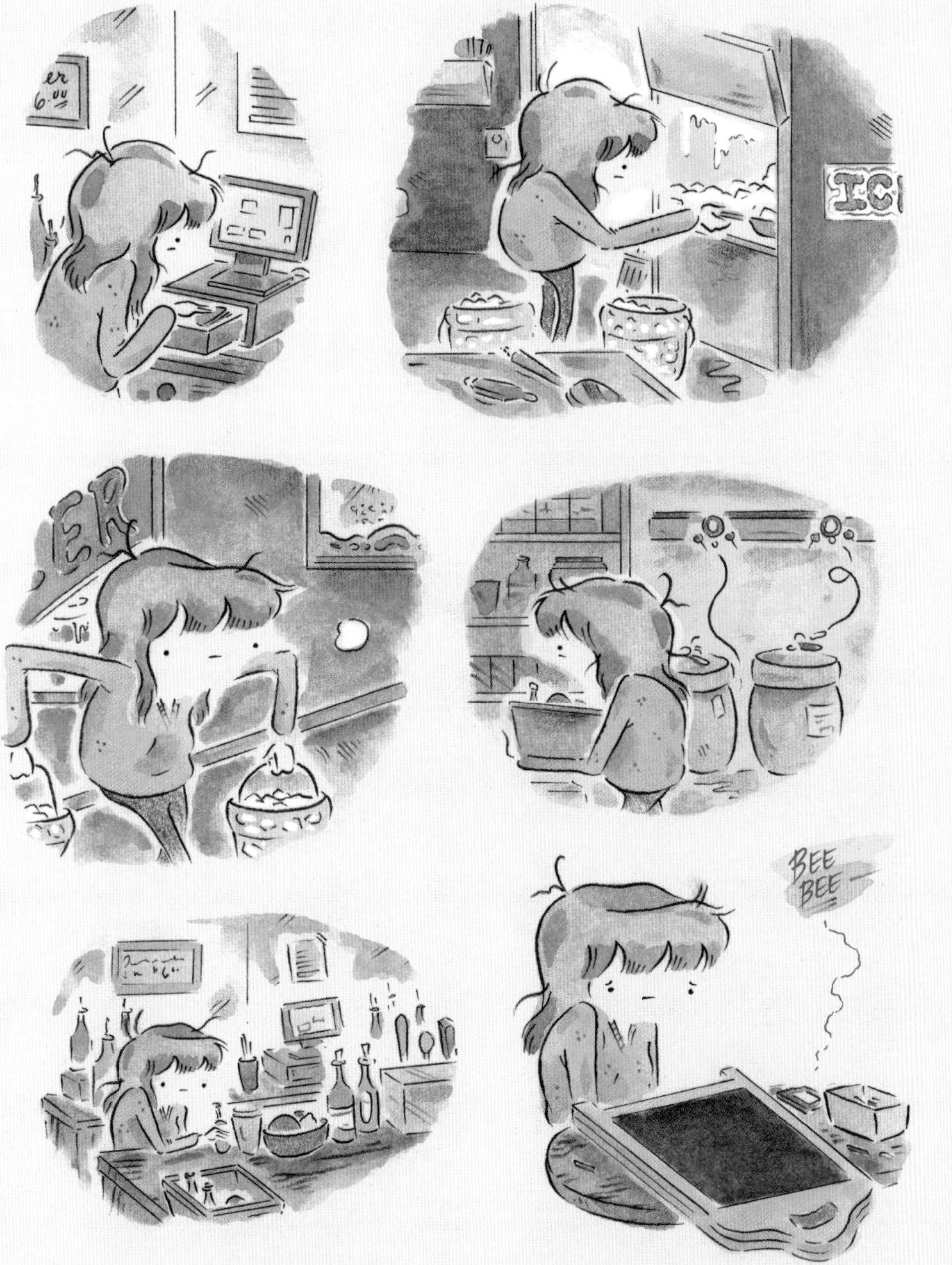
BEE
BEE

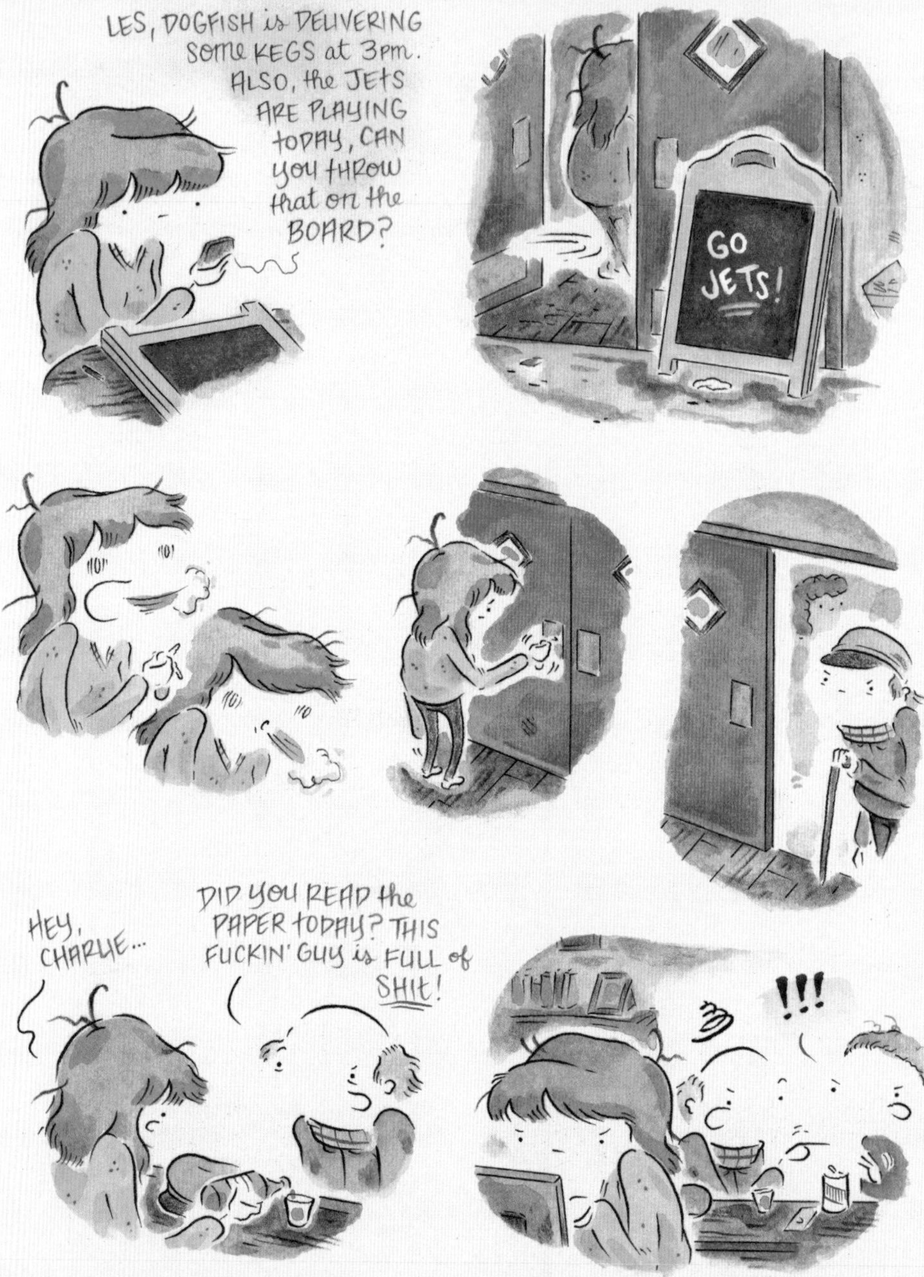
LES, DOGFISH is DELIVERING SOME KEGS at 3pm. ALSO, the JETS ARE PLAYING TODAY, CAN YOU THROW THAT ON THE BOARD?
GO JETS!
HEY, CHARLIE...
DID YOU READ the PAPER TODAY? THIS FUCKIN' GUY is FULL of SHIT!
!!!

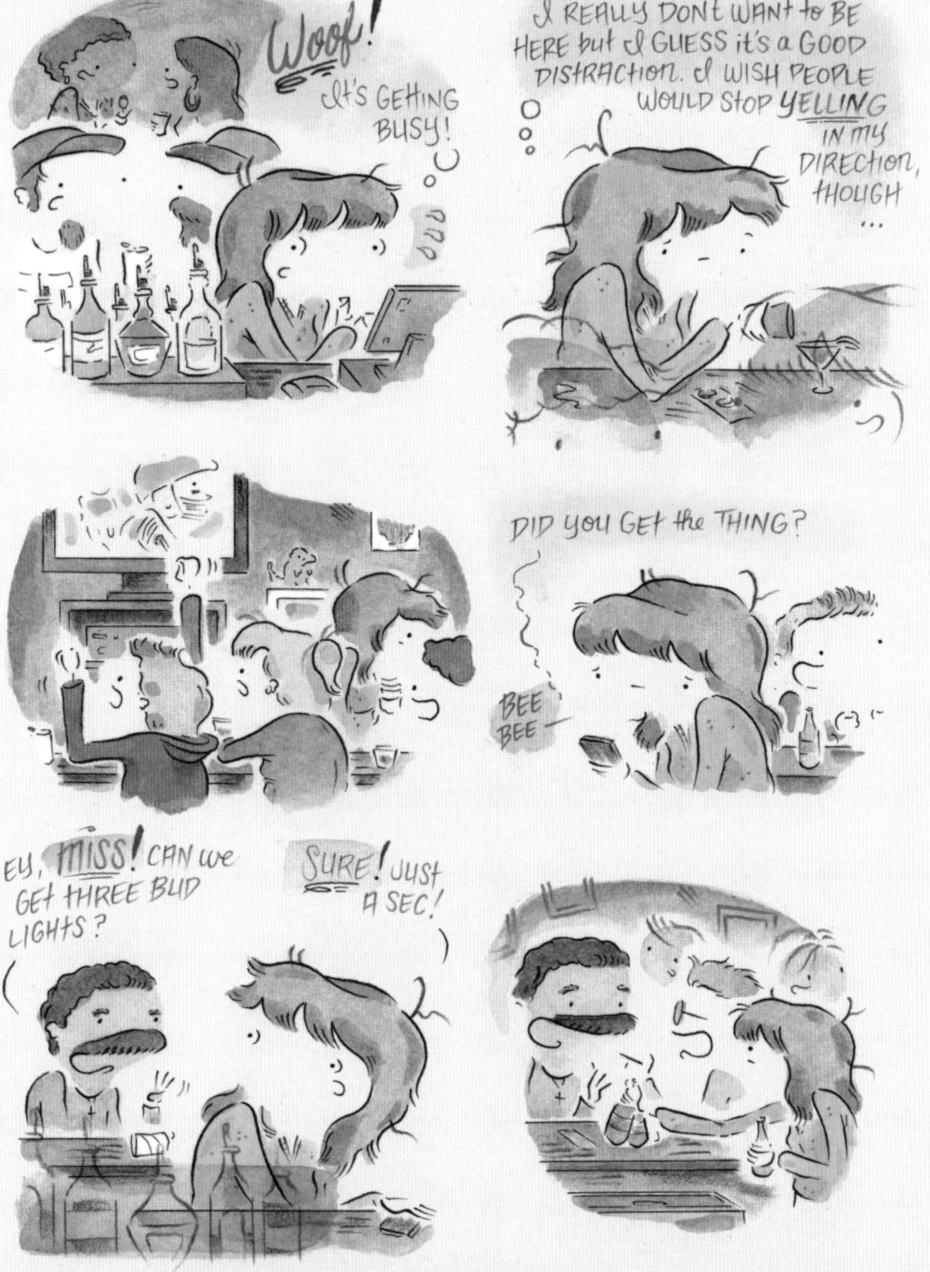
Woof!
It's GETTING BUSY!
I REALLY DON'T WANT to BE HERE but I GUESS it's a GOOD DISTRACTION. I WISH PEOPLE WOULD STOP YELLING IN MY DIRECTION, THOUGH ...
DID YOU GET the THING?
BEE BEE
EY, MISS! CAN WE GET THREE BUD LIGHTS?
SURE! JUST A SEC!

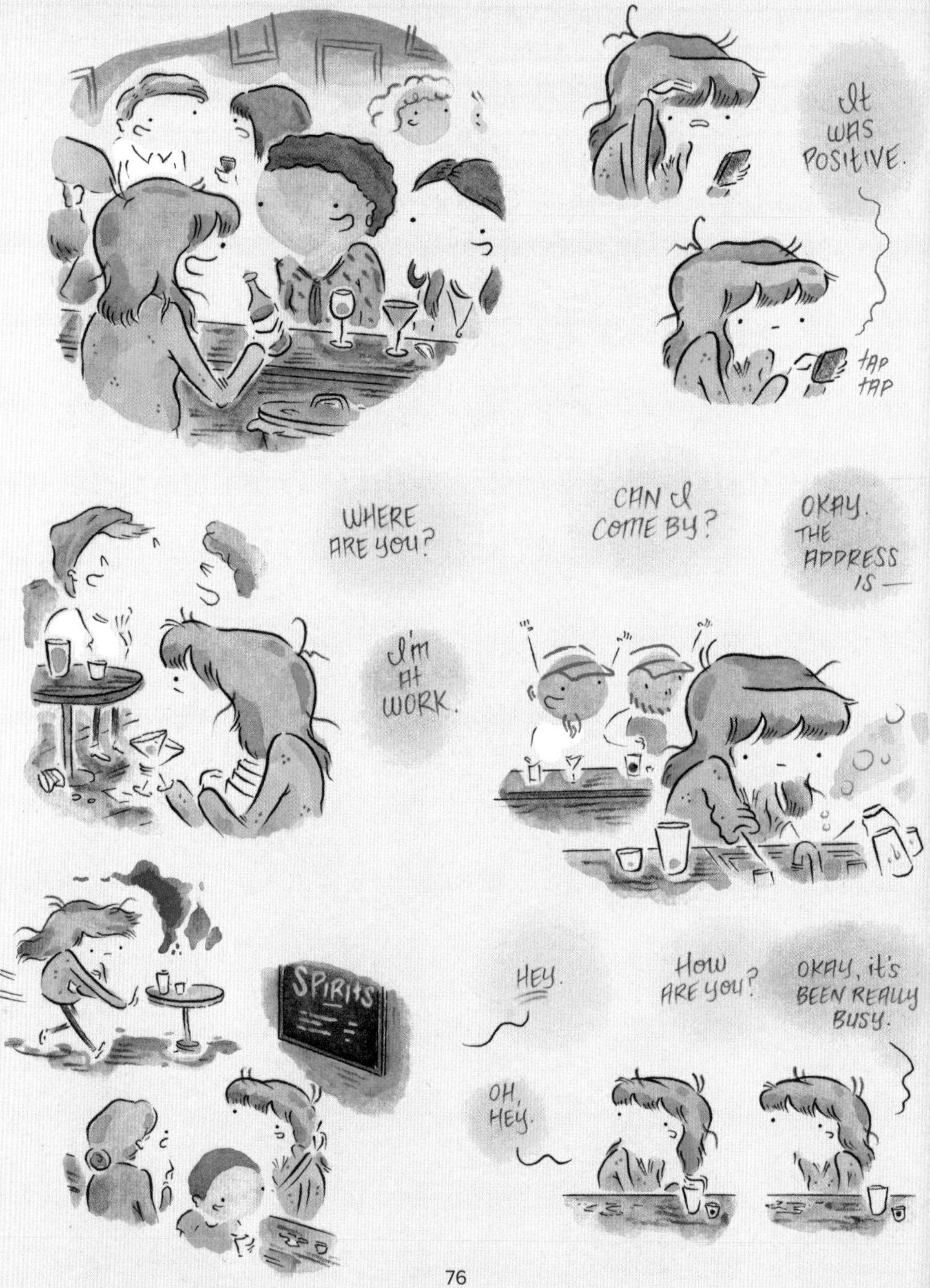

It WAS POSITIVE.
TAP TAP
WHERE ARE YOU?
I'm AT WORK.
CAN I COME BY?
OKAY. THE ADDRESS IS—
HEY.
OH, HEY.
How ARE you?
OKAY, it's BEEN REALLY BUSY.

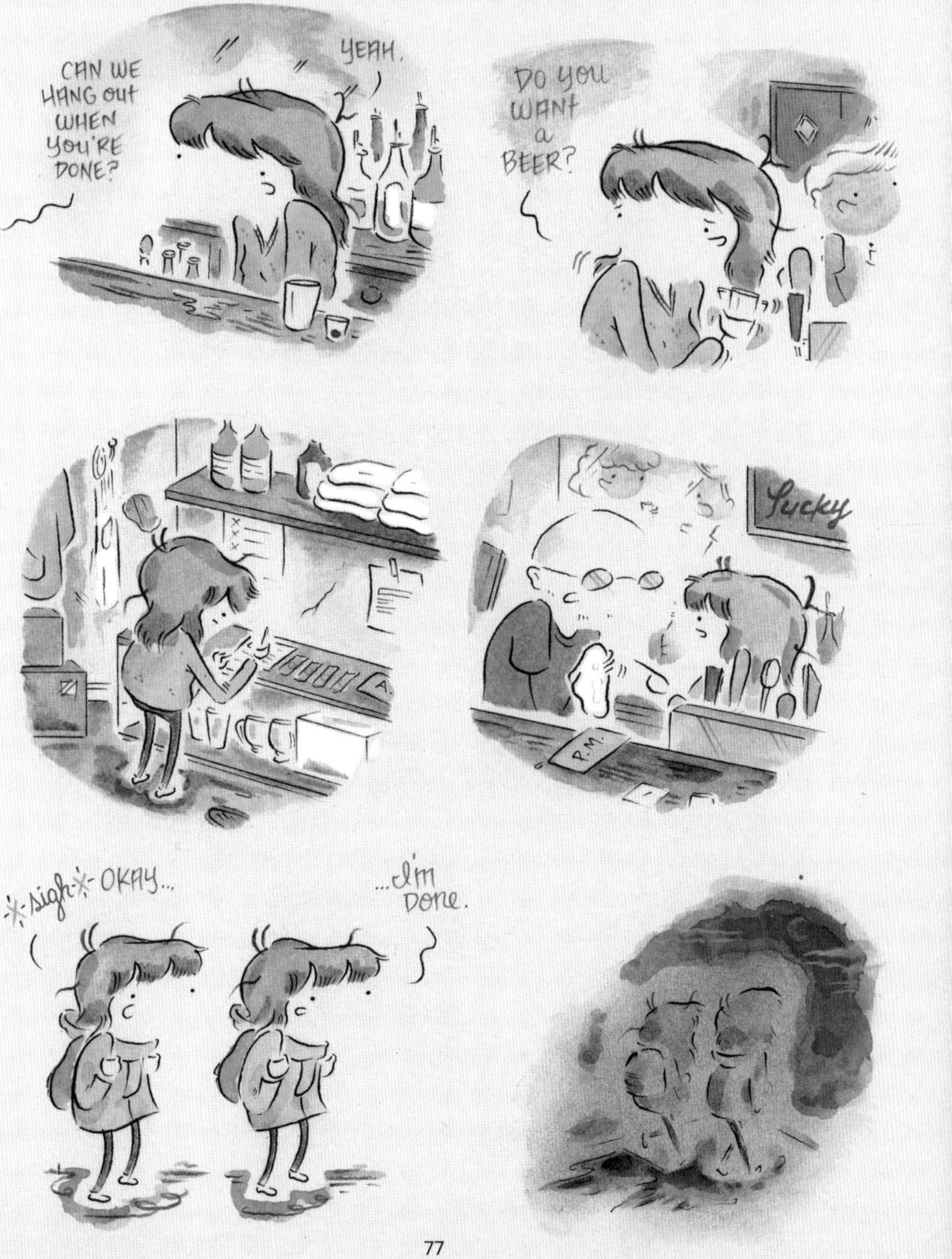
CAN WE HANG OUT WHEN YOU'RE DONE?
YEAH.
DO YOU WANT a BEER?
Lucky
A.
P.M.
sigh OKAY...
...I'm DONE.

SORRY. I DON'T HAVE A COUCH.
WHY DON'T YOU HAVE A COUCH?
ERM...
...because I WANT all of my ENERGY to be focused over there.

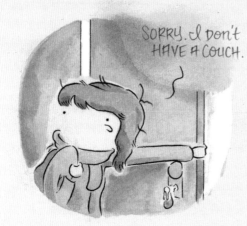

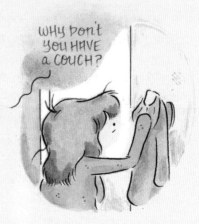

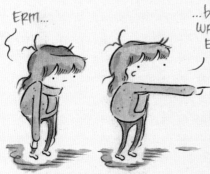

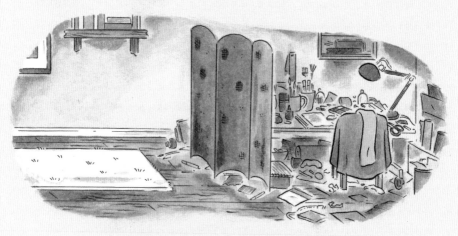

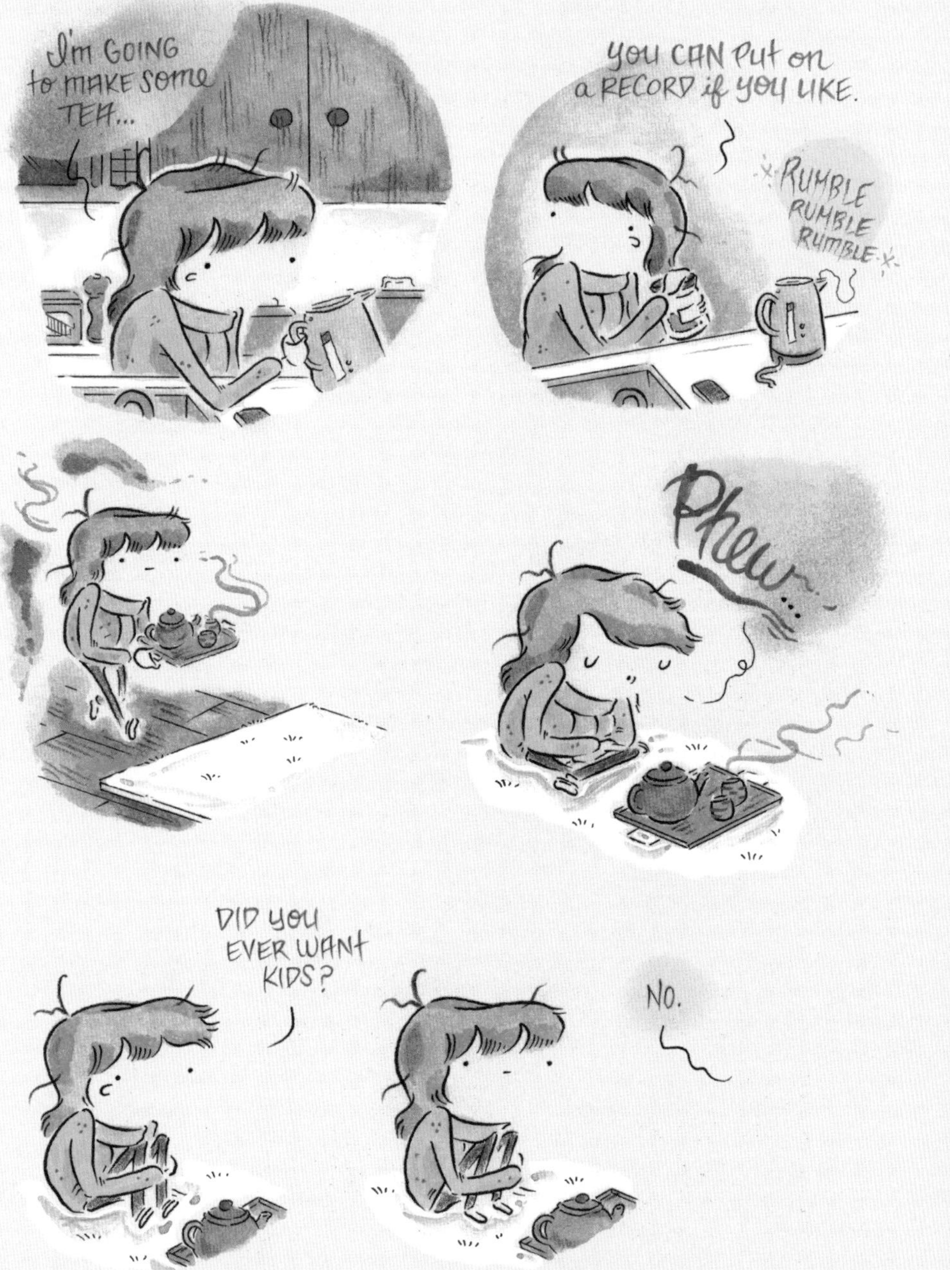
I'm GOING to MAKE SOME TEA...
YOU CAN PUT ON A RECORD IF YOU LIKE.
RUMBLE RUMBLE RUMBLE RUMBLE
Phew...
DID YOU EVER WANT KIDS?
NO.

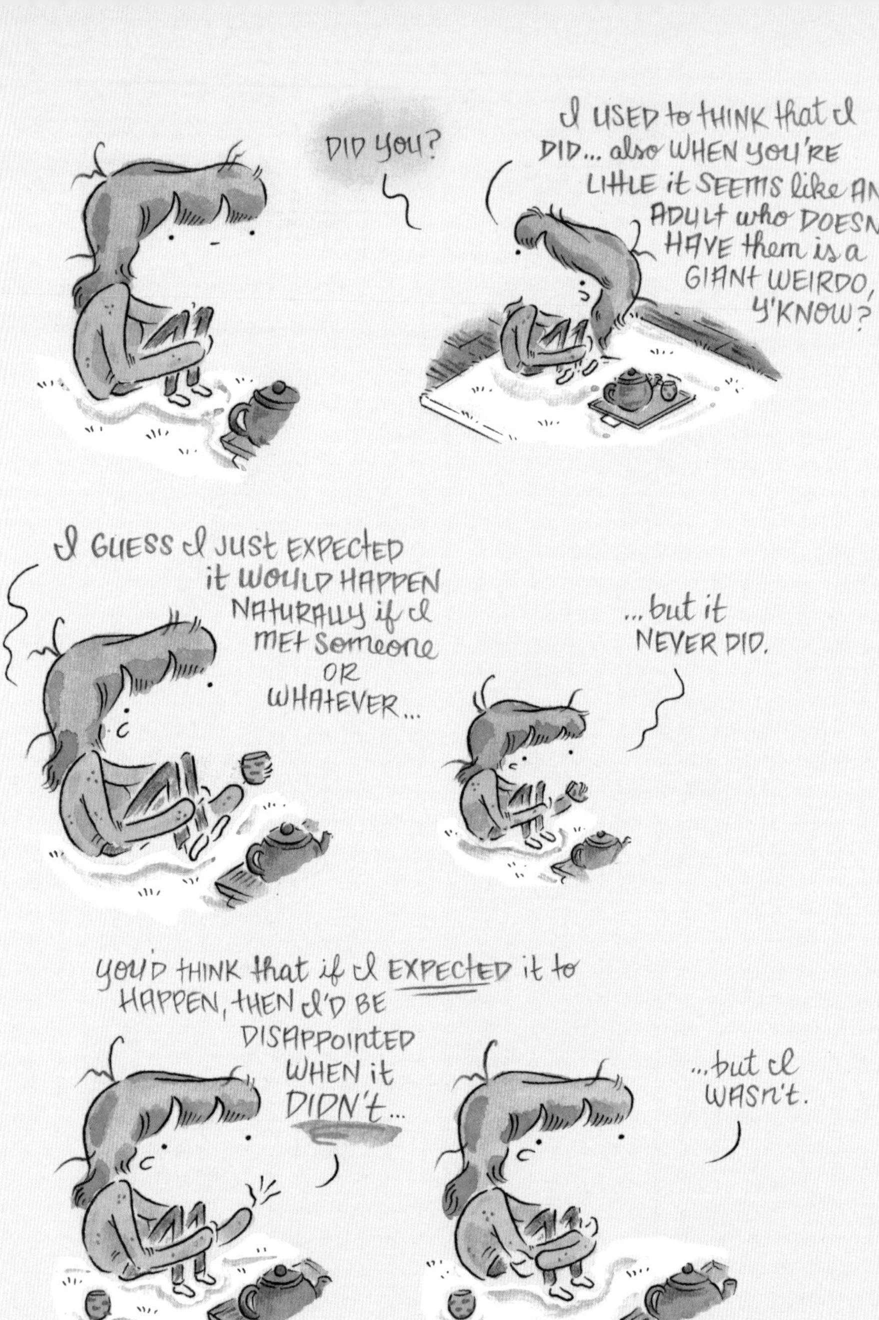
DID YOU?
I USED to THINK that I DID... also WHEN YOU'RE LITTLE it SEEMS like ANY ADULT who DOESN'T HAVE them is a GIANT WEIRDO, Y'KNOW?
I GUESS I JUST EXPECTED it WOULD HAPPEN NATURALLY if I MET Someone OR WHATEVER...
...but it NEVER DID.
YOU'D THINK that if I EXPECTED it to HAPPEN, THEN I'D BE DISAPPOINTED WHEN it DIDN'T...
...but I WASN'T.

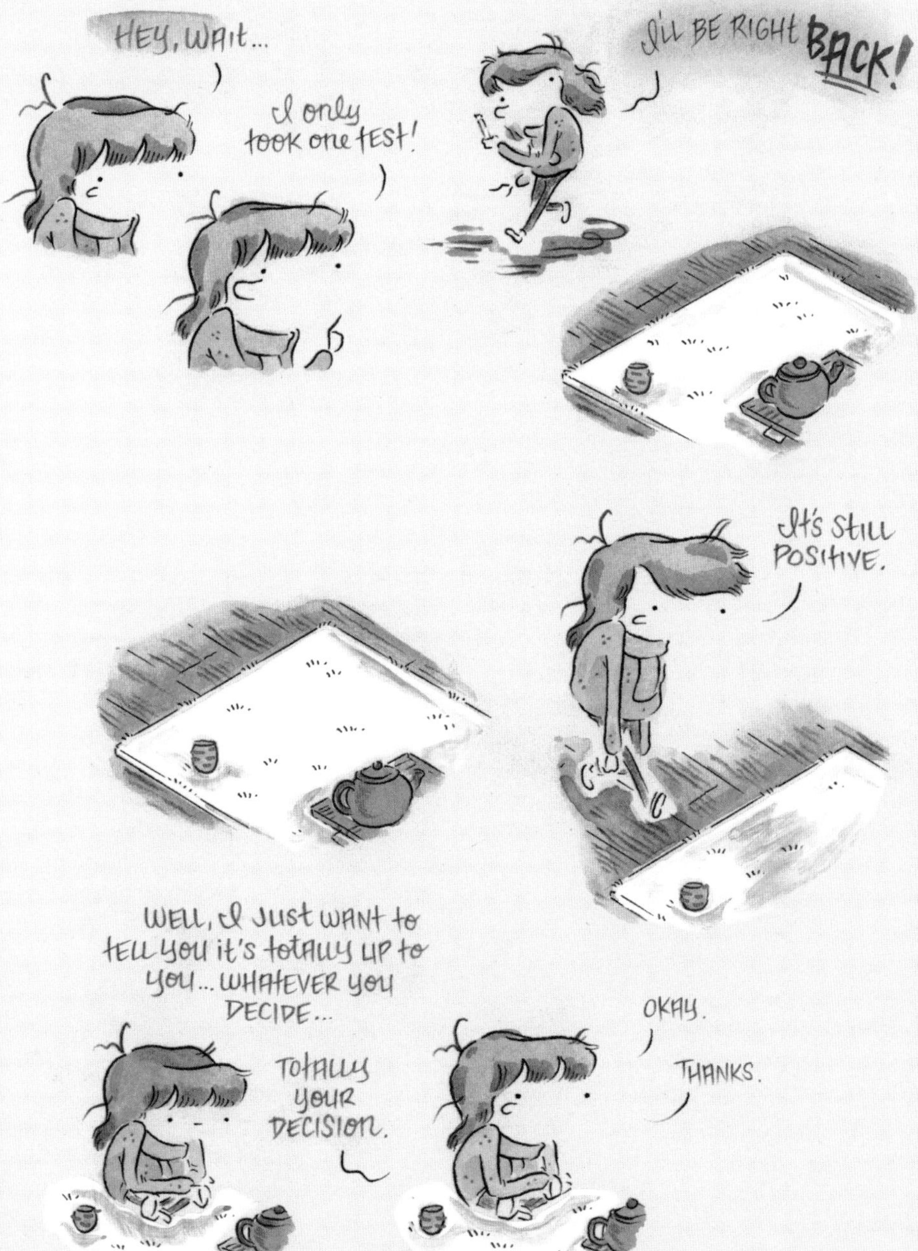

HEY, WAIT...
I only took one test!
I'LL BE RIGHT BACK!
It's still POSITIVE.
WELL, I JUST WANT TO TELL YOU IT'S TOTALLY UP TO YOU... WHATEVER YOU DECIDE...
TOTALLY YOUR DECISION.
OKAY.
THANKS.

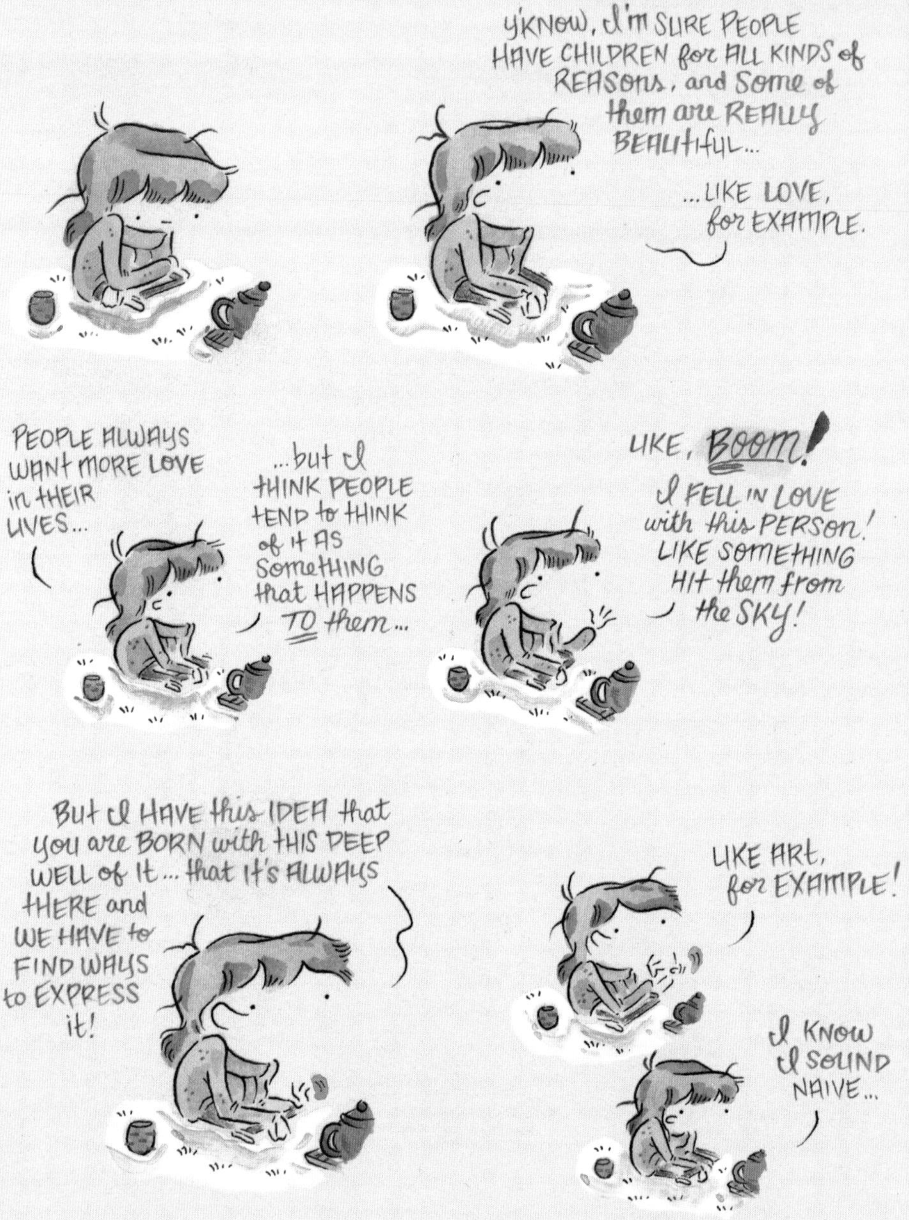

Y'KNOW, I'M SURE PEOPLE HAVE CHILDREN for ALL KINDS of REASONS, and Some of them are REALLY BEAUTIFUL...
...LIKE LOVE, for EXAMPLE.
PEOPLE ALWAYS WANT MORE LOVE in THEIR LIVES...
...but I THINK PEOPLE TEND to THINK of it AS Something that HAPPENS TO them...
LIKE, BOOM!
I FELL IN LOVE with this PERSON! LIKE SOMETHING HIT them from the SKY!
But I HAVE this IDEA that you are BORN with THIS DEEP WELL of It... that it's ALWAYS THERE and WE HAVE to FIND WAYS to EXPRESS it!
LIKE ART, for EXAMPLE!
I KNOW I SOUND NAIVE...

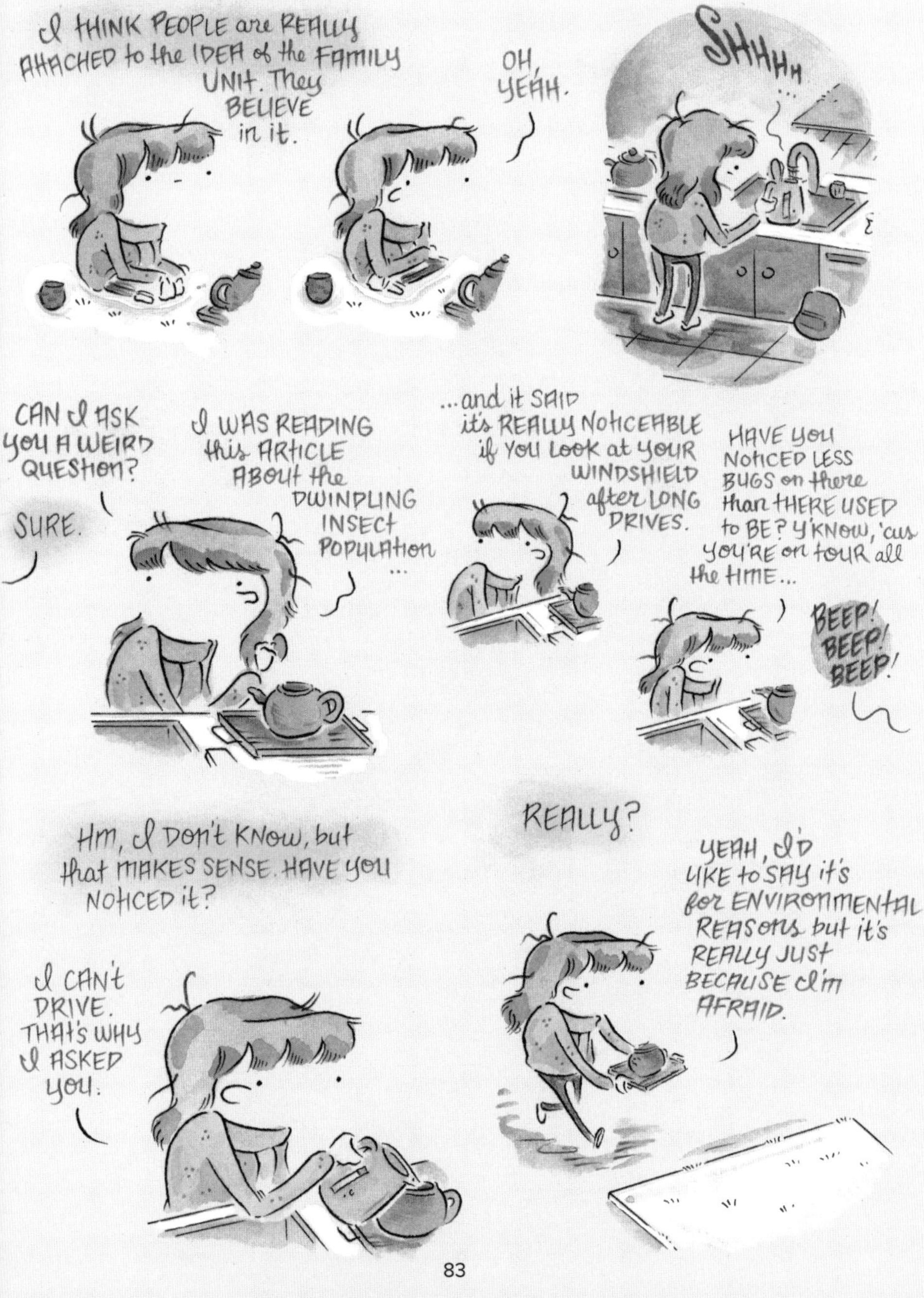
I THINK PEOPLE are REALLY AttACHED to the IDEA of the FAMILY UNIT. They BELIEVE in it.
OH, YEAH.
SHHHH
CAN I ASK YOU A WEIRD QUESTION?
SURE.
I WAS READING this ARTICLE ABOUT the DWINDLING INSECT POPULATION...
...and it SAID it's REALLY NOTICEABLE if YOU LOOK at YOUR WINDSHIELD after LONG DRIVES.
HAVE YOU NOTICED LESS BUGS on there than THERE USED to BE? Y'KNOW, 'cus YOU'RE on TOUR all the TIME...
BEEP! BEEP! BEEP!
Hm, I DON'T KNOW, but that MAKES SENSE. HAVE YOU NOTICED it?
REALLY?
I CAN'T DRIVE. THAT'S WHY I ASKED YOU.
YEAH, I'D LIKE to SAY it's for ENVIRONMENTAL REASONS but it's REALLY JUST BECAUSE I'M AFRAID.

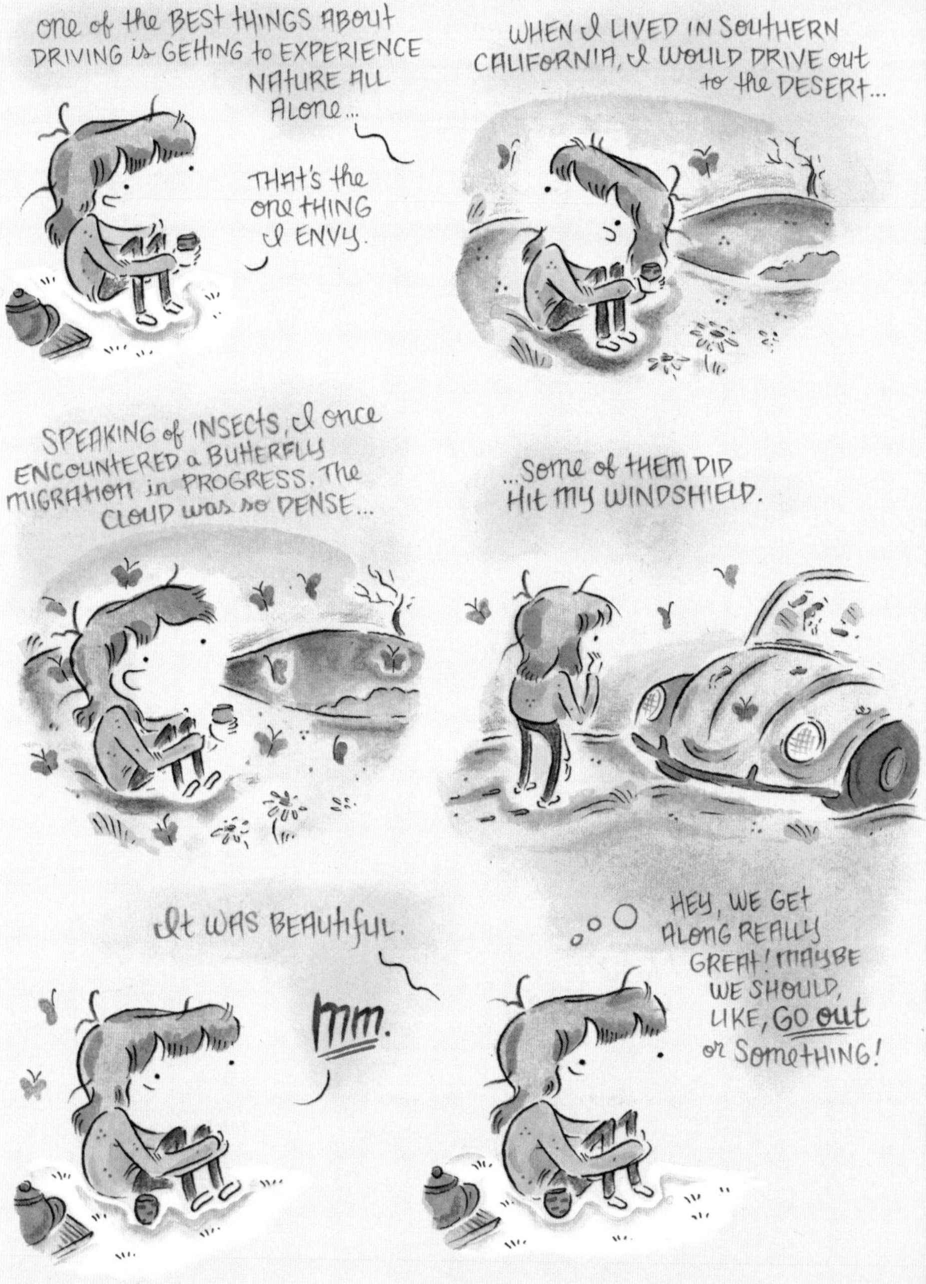
one of the BEST THINGS ABOUT DRIVING is GETTING to EXPERIENCE NATURE ALL ALONE...
THAT'S the one THING I ENVY.
WHEN I LIVED IN SOUTHERN CALIFORNIA, I WOULD DRIVE out to the DESERT...
SPEAKING of INSECTS, I once ENCOUNTERED a BUTTERFLY MIGRATION in PROGRESS. The CLOUD was so DENSE...
...Some of THEM DID Hit my WINDSHIELD.
It WAS BEAUTIFUL.
Mm.
HEY, WE GET ALONG REALLY GREAT! MAYBE WE SHOULD, LIKE, GO out or SOMETHING!

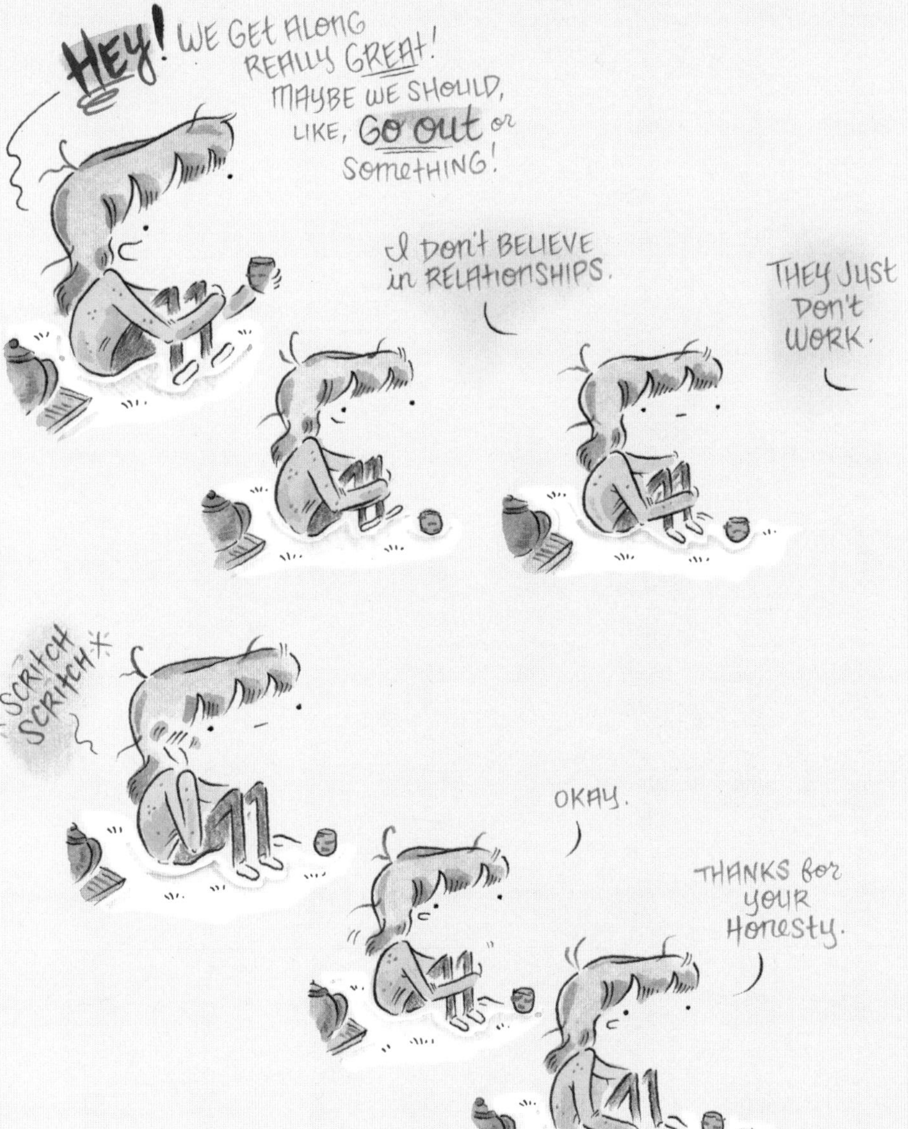
HEY! WE GET ALONG REALLY GREAT! MAYBE WE SHOULD, LIKE, GO OUT or SOMETHING!
I DON'T BELIEVE in RELATIONSHIPS.
THEY JUST DON'T WORK.
SCRITCH SCRITCH
OKAY.
THANKS for YOUR HONESTY.

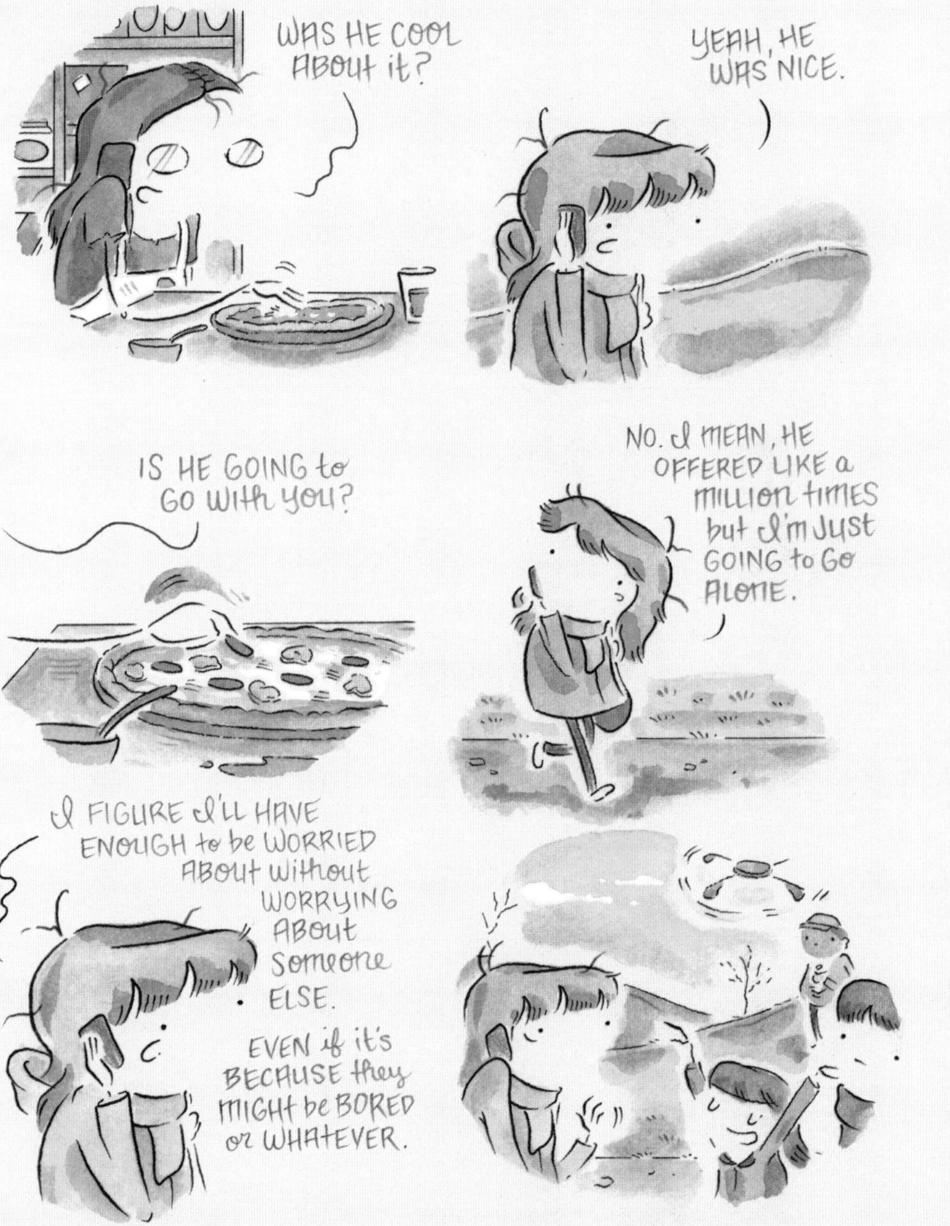
WAS HE COOL ABOUT it?
YEAH, HE WAS NICE.
IS HE GOING to GO WITH YOU?
NO. I MEAN, HE OFFERED LIKE a MILLION TIMES but I'm JUST GOING to GO ALONE.
I FIGURE I'LL HAVE ENOUGH to be WORRIED ABOUT without WORRYING ABOUT SOMEONE ELSE.
EVEN if it's BECAUSE they MIGHT be BORED or WHATEVER.

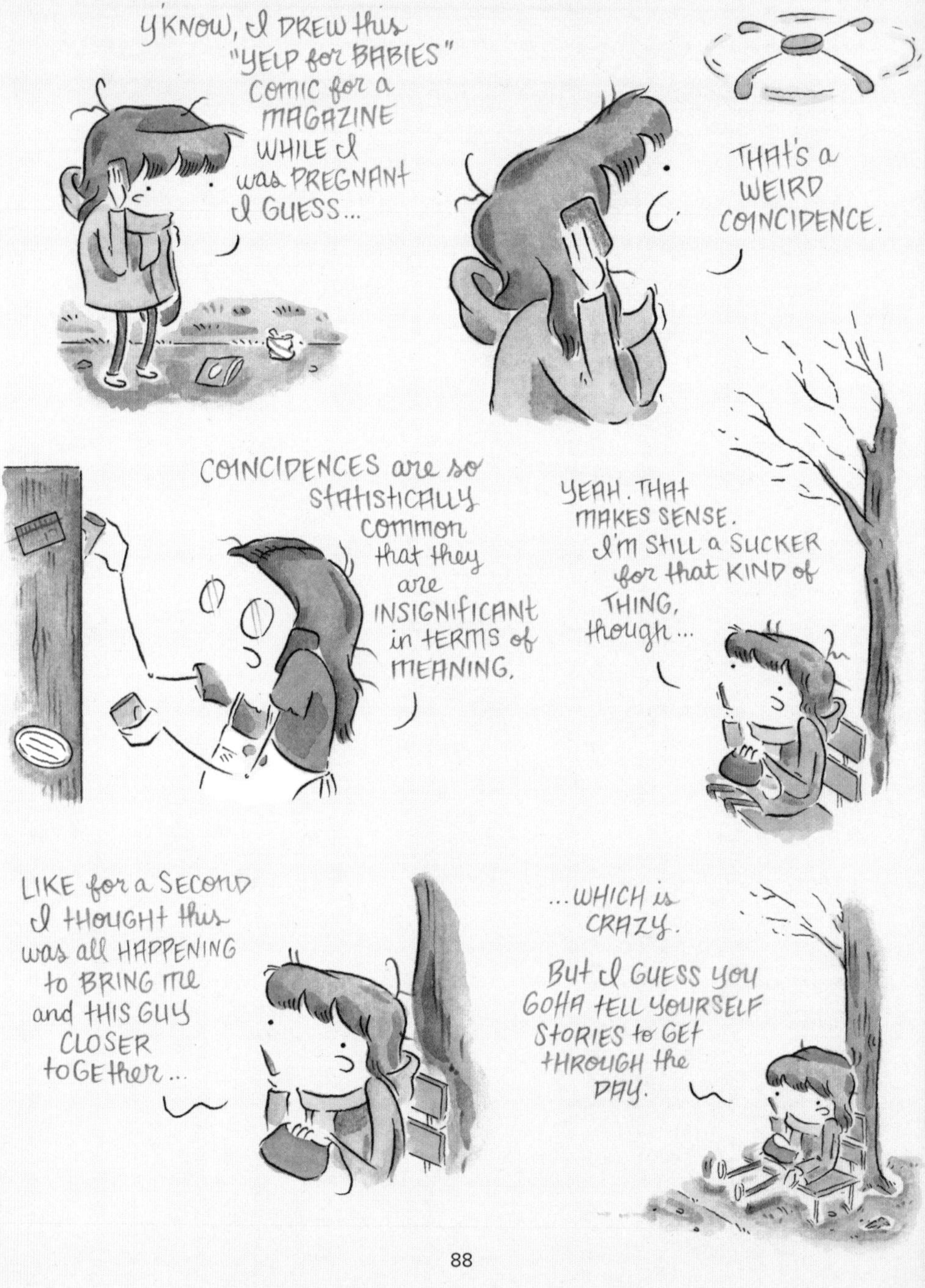
Y'KNOW, I DREW this "YELP for BABIES" comic for a MAGAZINE WHILE I was PREGNANT I GUESS...
THAT's a WEIRD COINCIDENCE.
COINCIDENCES are so statistically common that they are INSIGNIFICANT in TERMS of MEANING.
YEAH. THAT MAKES SENSE. I'm STILL a SUCKER for that KIND of THING, though...
LIKE for a SECOND I THOUGHT this was all HAPPENING to BRING me and THIS GUY CLOSER toGEther...
...WHICH is CRAZY.
But I GUESS you GOTTA tell YOURSELF STORIES to GET THROUGH the DAY.

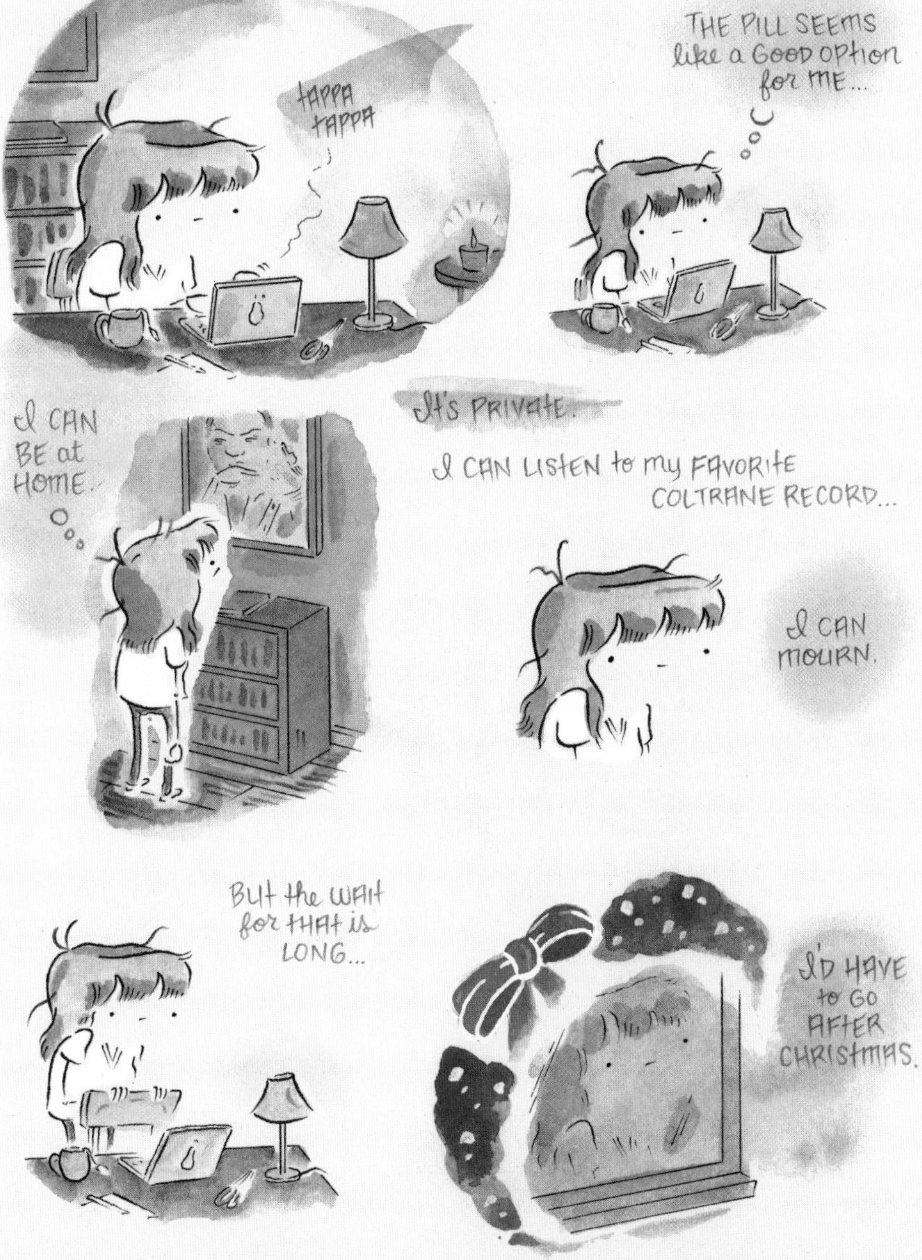
tappa tappa
THE PILL SEEMS like a GOOD option for ME...
It's PRIVATE.
I CAN BE at HOME.
I CAN LISTEN to my FAVORITE COLTRANE RECORD...
I CAN MOURN.
But the WAIT for THAT is LONG...
I'D HAVE to GO AFTER CHRISTMAS.

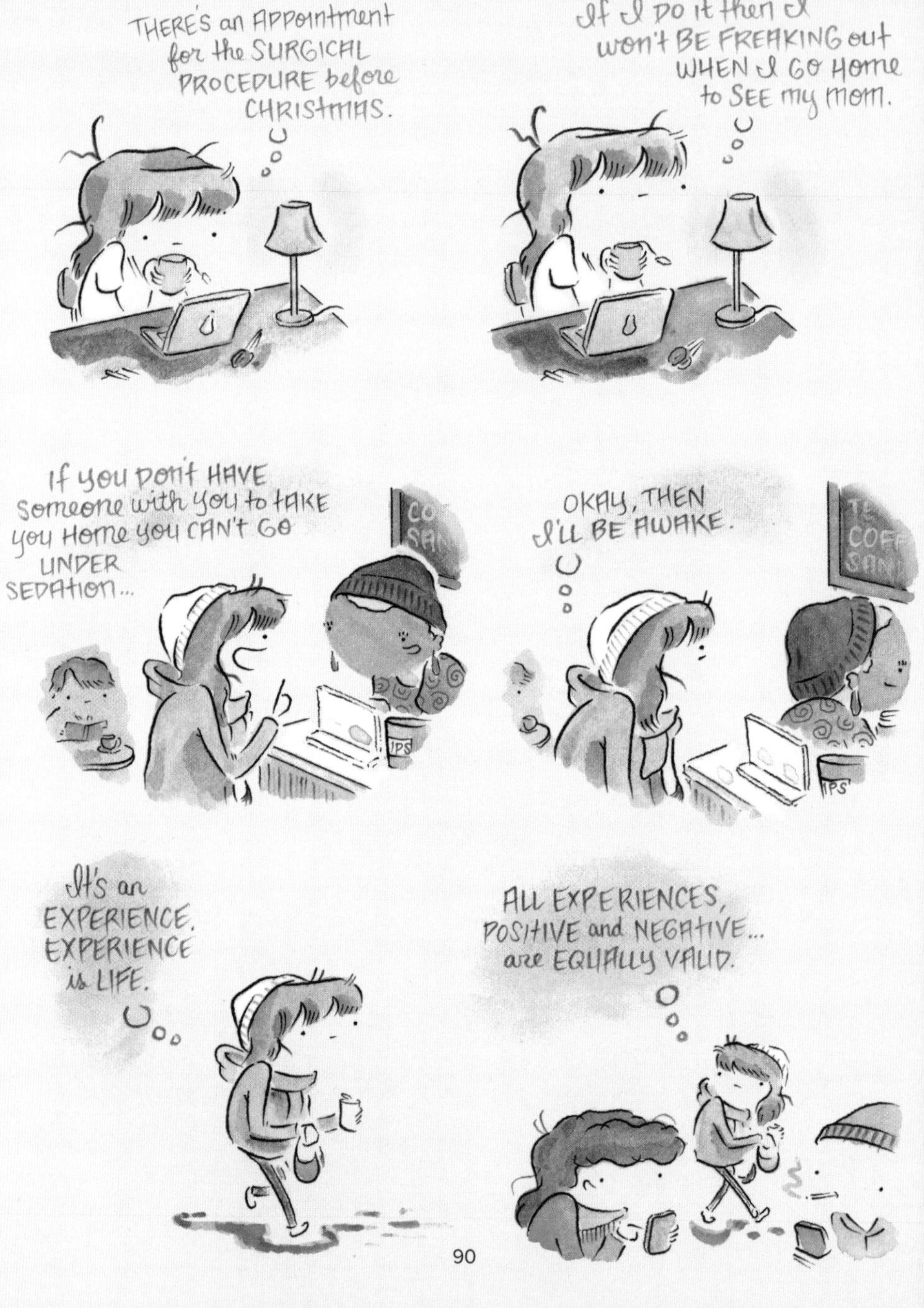
THERE'S an Appointment for the SURGICAL PROCEDURE before CHRISTMAS.
If I Do it then I won't BE FREAKING out WHEN I GO Home to SEE my mom.
If you Don't HAVE someone with you to tAKE you Home you CAN'T GO UNDER SEDAtion...
OKAY, THEN I'LL BE AWAKE.
It's an EXPERIENCE. EXPERIENCE is LIFE.
ALL EXPERIENCES, POSITIVE and NEGATIVE... are EQUALLY VALID.

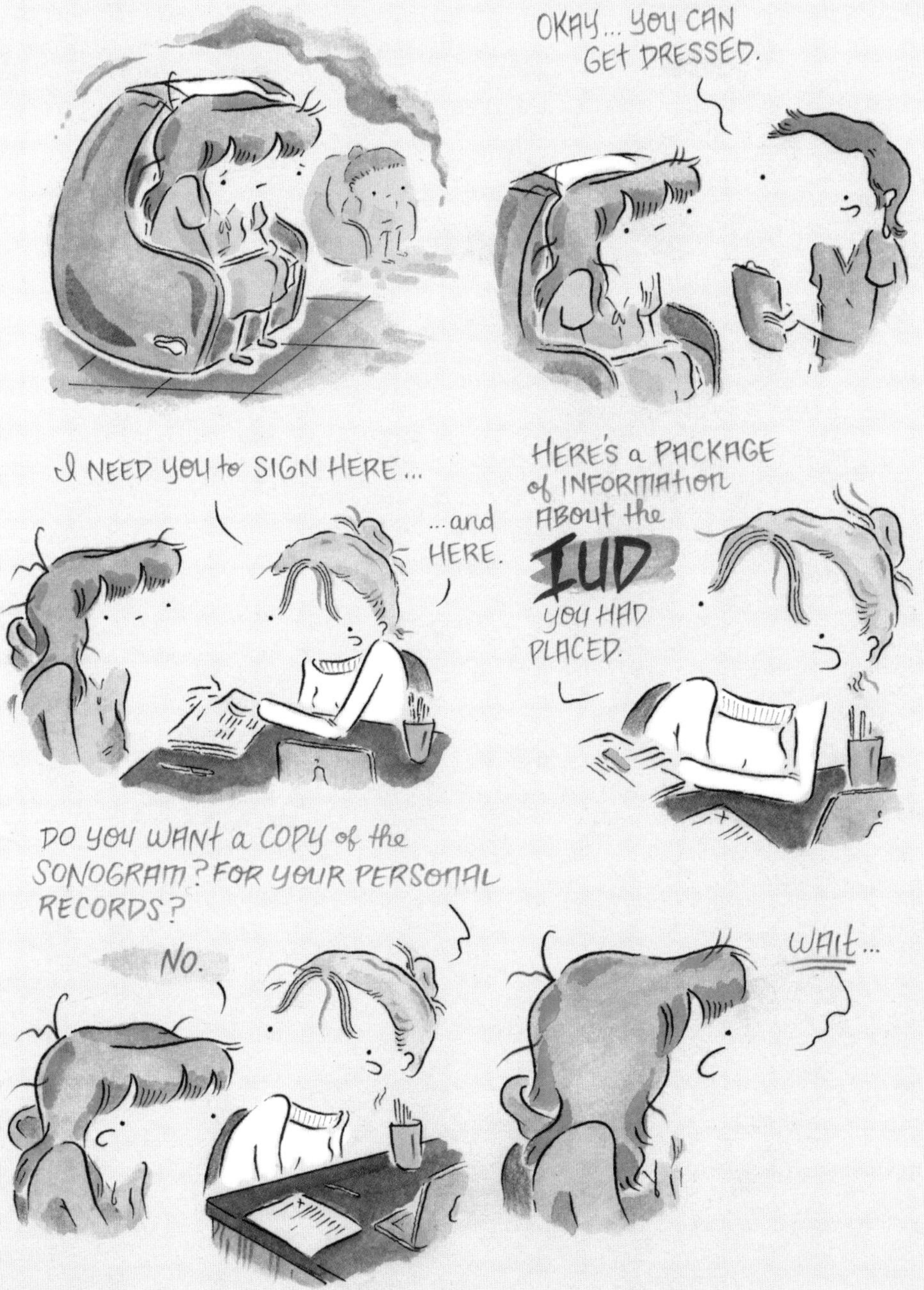
OKAY... YOU CAN GET DRESSED.
I NEED YOU to SIGN HERE...
...and HERE.
HERE'S a PACKAGE of INFORMATION ABOUT the IUD YOU HAD PLACED.
DO YOU WANT a COPY of the SONOGRAM? FOR YOUR PERSONAL RECORDS?
NO.
WAIT...

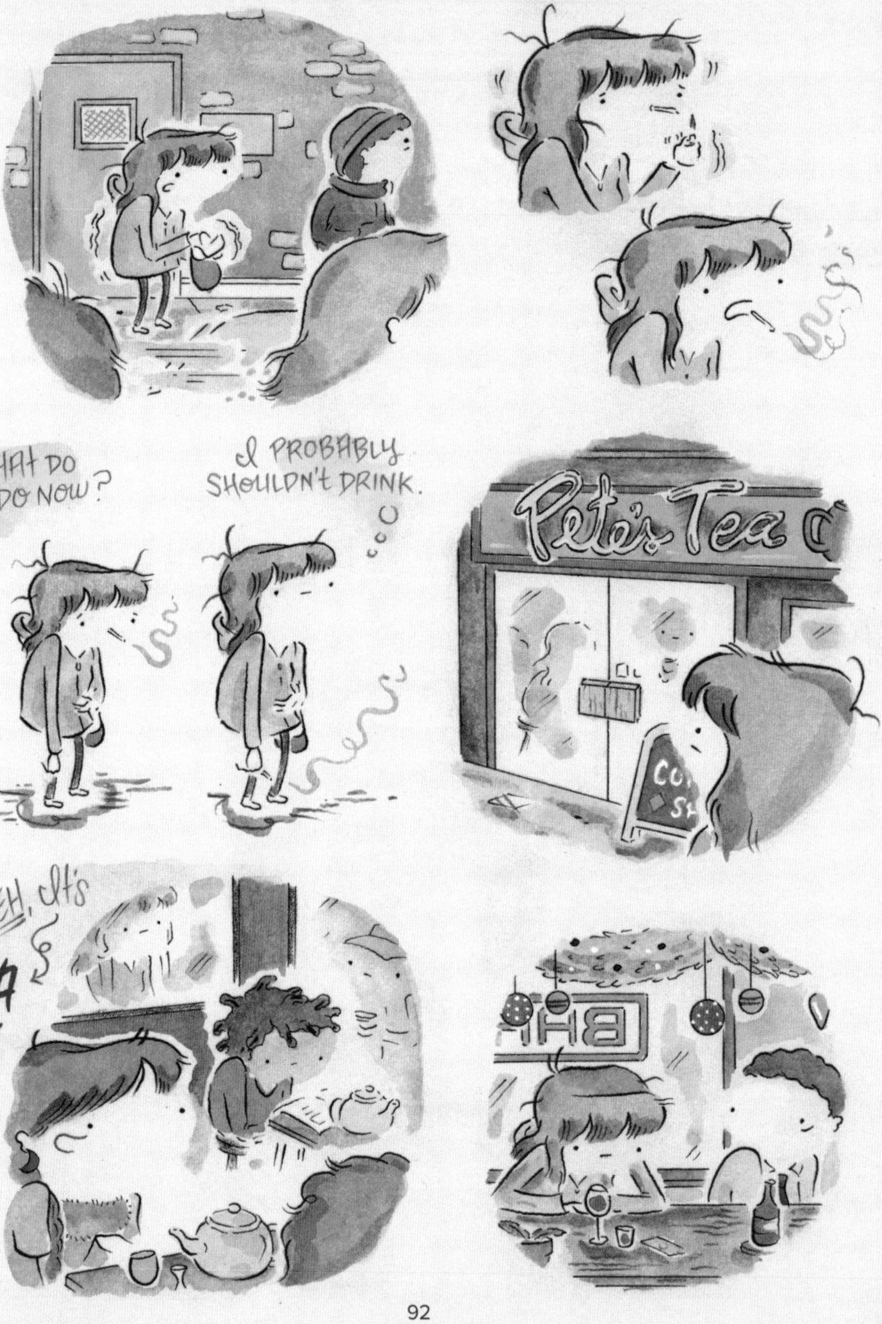
WHAT DO I DO NOW?
I PROBABLY SHOULDN'T DRINK.
Pete's Tea
EH, IT'S
PACKED…

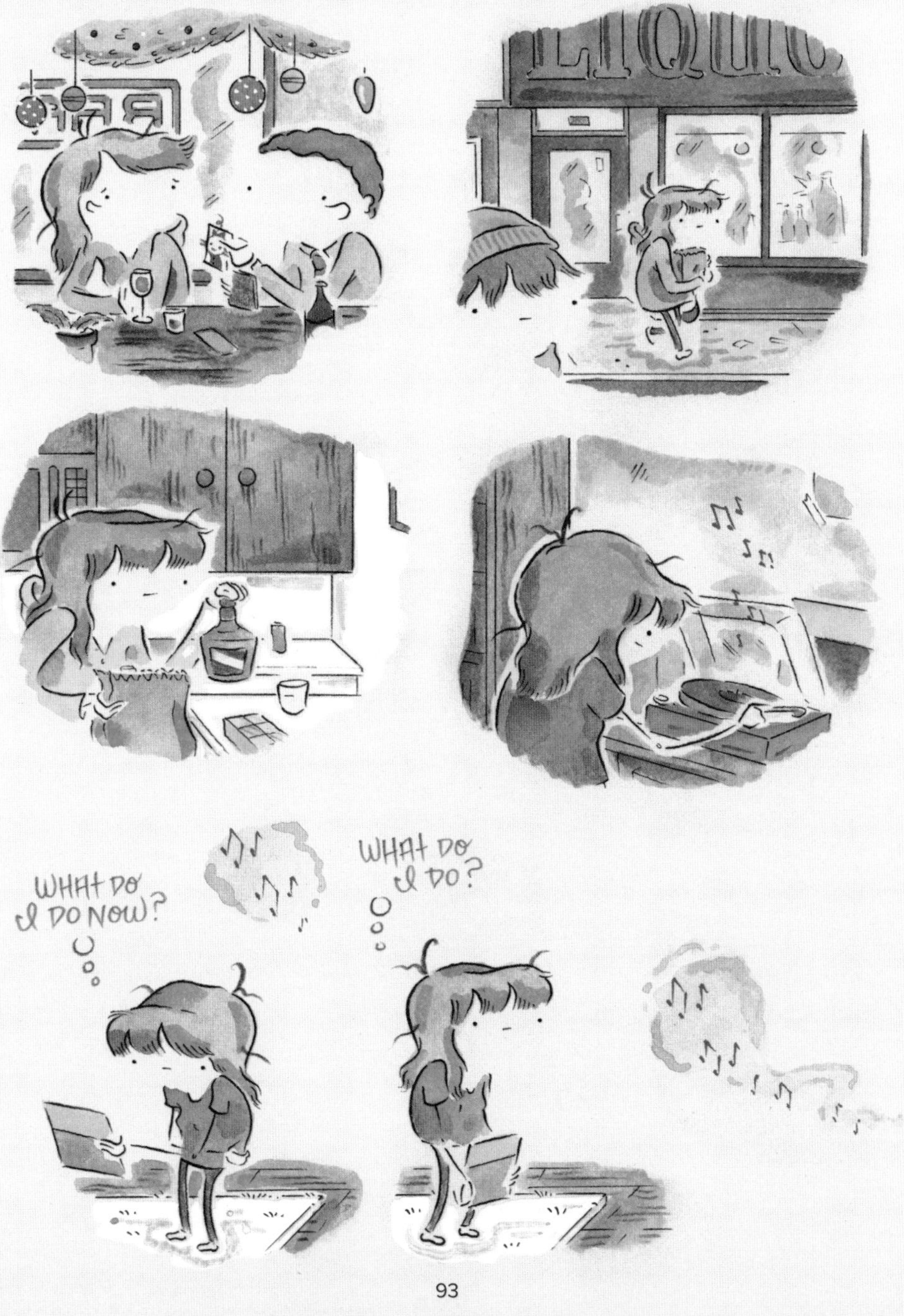
LIQUO
WHAT DO I DO NOW?
WHAT DO I DO?

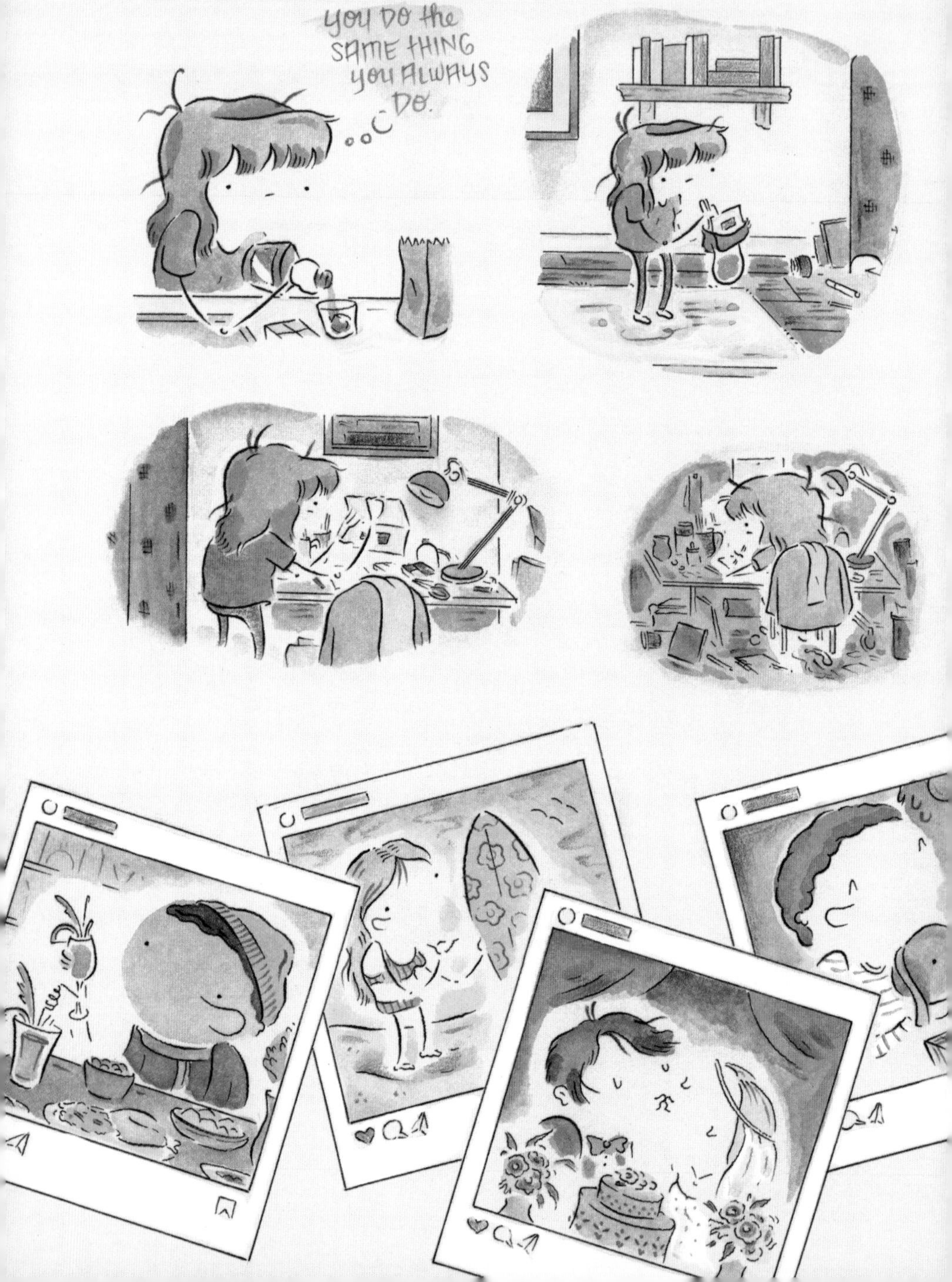
you DO the SAME THING you ALWAYS DO.

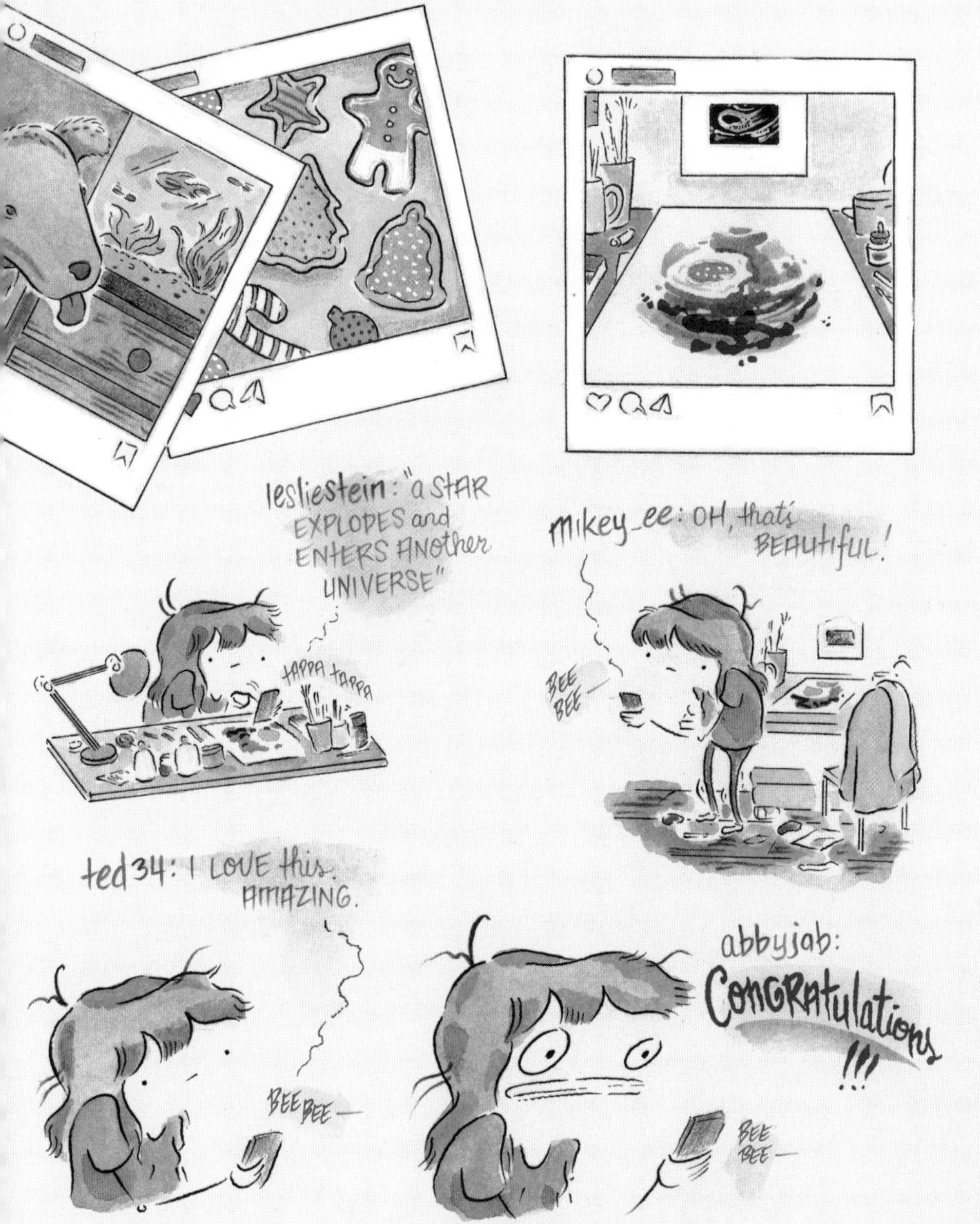

lesliestein: "a STAR EXPLODES and ENTERS ANother UNIVERSE"
TAPPA TAPPA
mikey_ee: OH, that's BEAUTIFUL!
BEE BEE—
ted34: I LOVE this. AMAZING.
BEE BEE—
abbyjab: CONGRATulations!!!
BEE BEE—

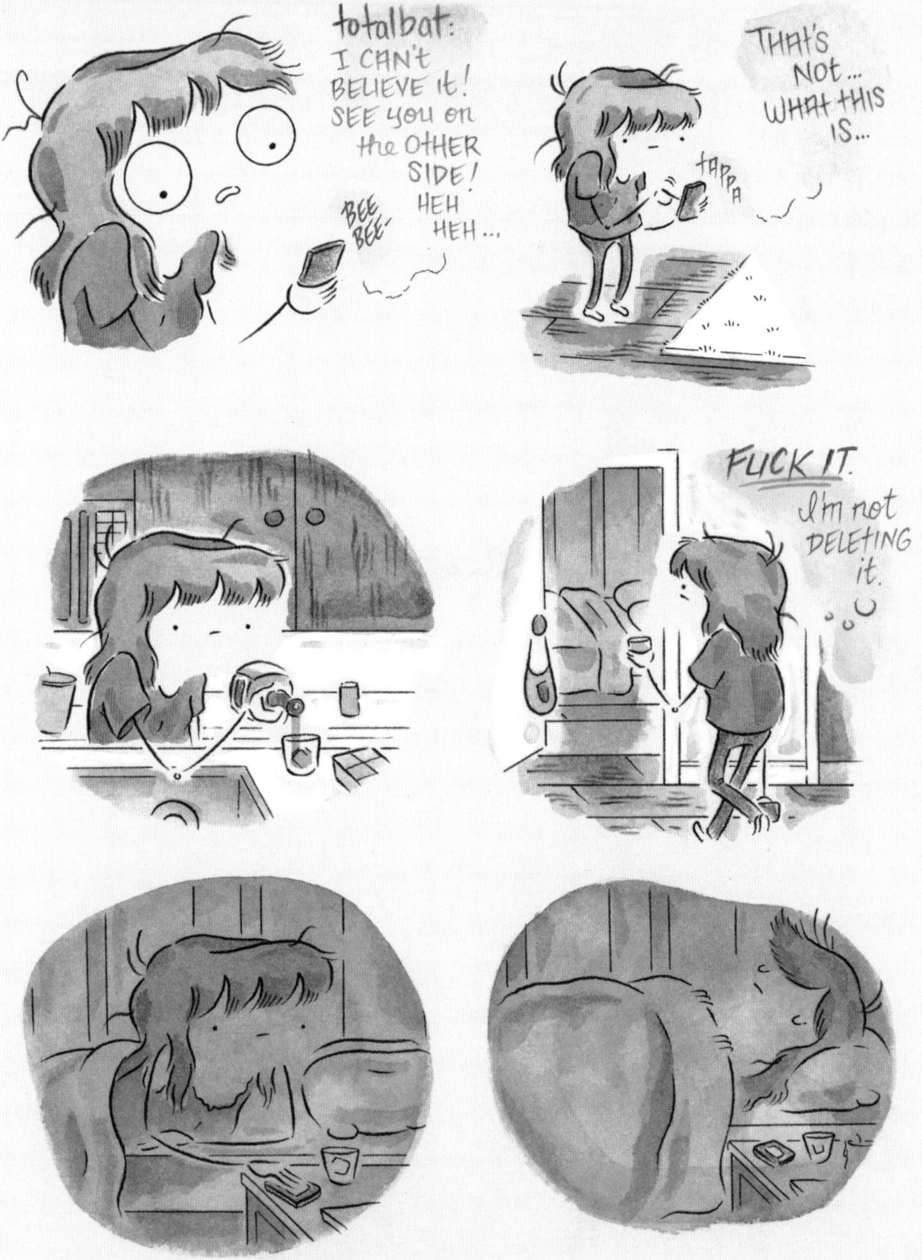
totalbat:
I CAN't BELIEVE it! SEE you on the OTHER SIDE!
BEE BEE
HEH HEH...
THAT's NOT... WHAT THIS IS...
TAPPA
FUCK IT.
I'm not DELETING it.

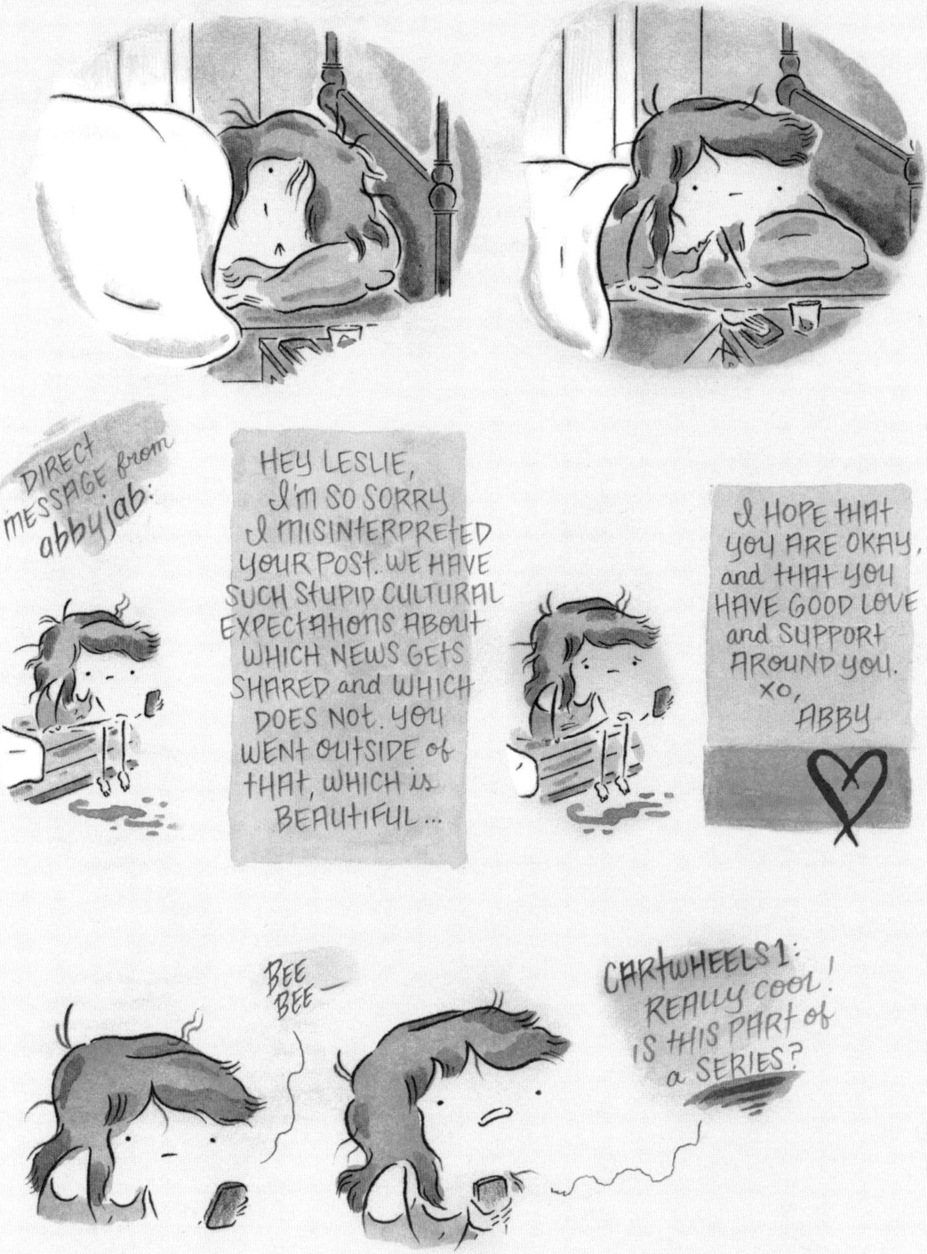
DIRECT MESSAGE from abbyjab:
HEY LESLIE, I'm SO SORRY I MISINTERPRETED YOUR POST.. WE HAVE SUCH STUPID CULTURAL EXPECTATIONS ABOUT WHICH NEWS GETS SHARED and WHICH DOES NOT. YOU WENT OUTSIDE of THAT, WHICH is BEAUTIFUL...
I HOPE THAT YOU ARE OKAY, and THAT YOU HAVE GOOD LOVE and SUPPORT AROUND YOU. XO, ABBY
BEE BEE—
CARTWHEELS1: REALLY COOL! IS THIS PART of a SERIES?

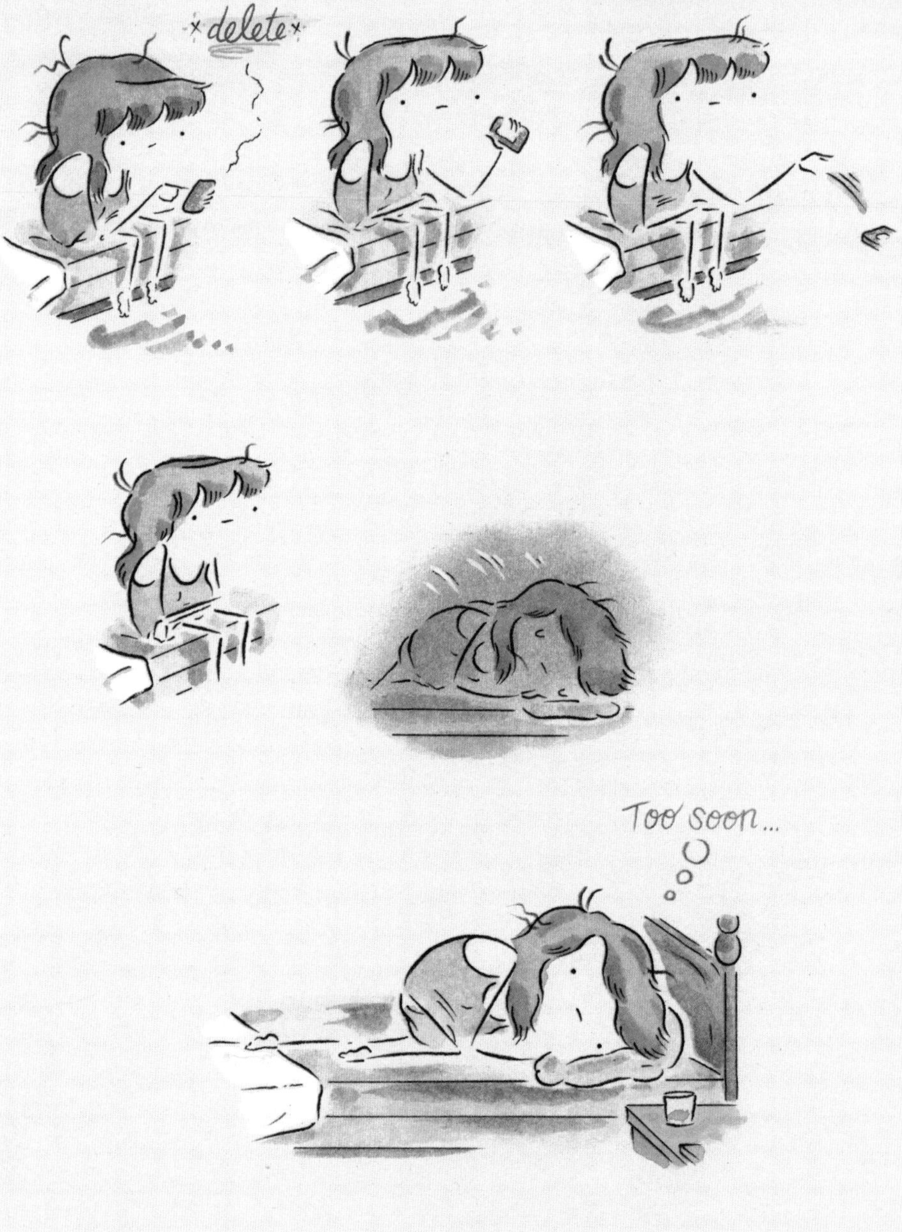
delete
Too soon...

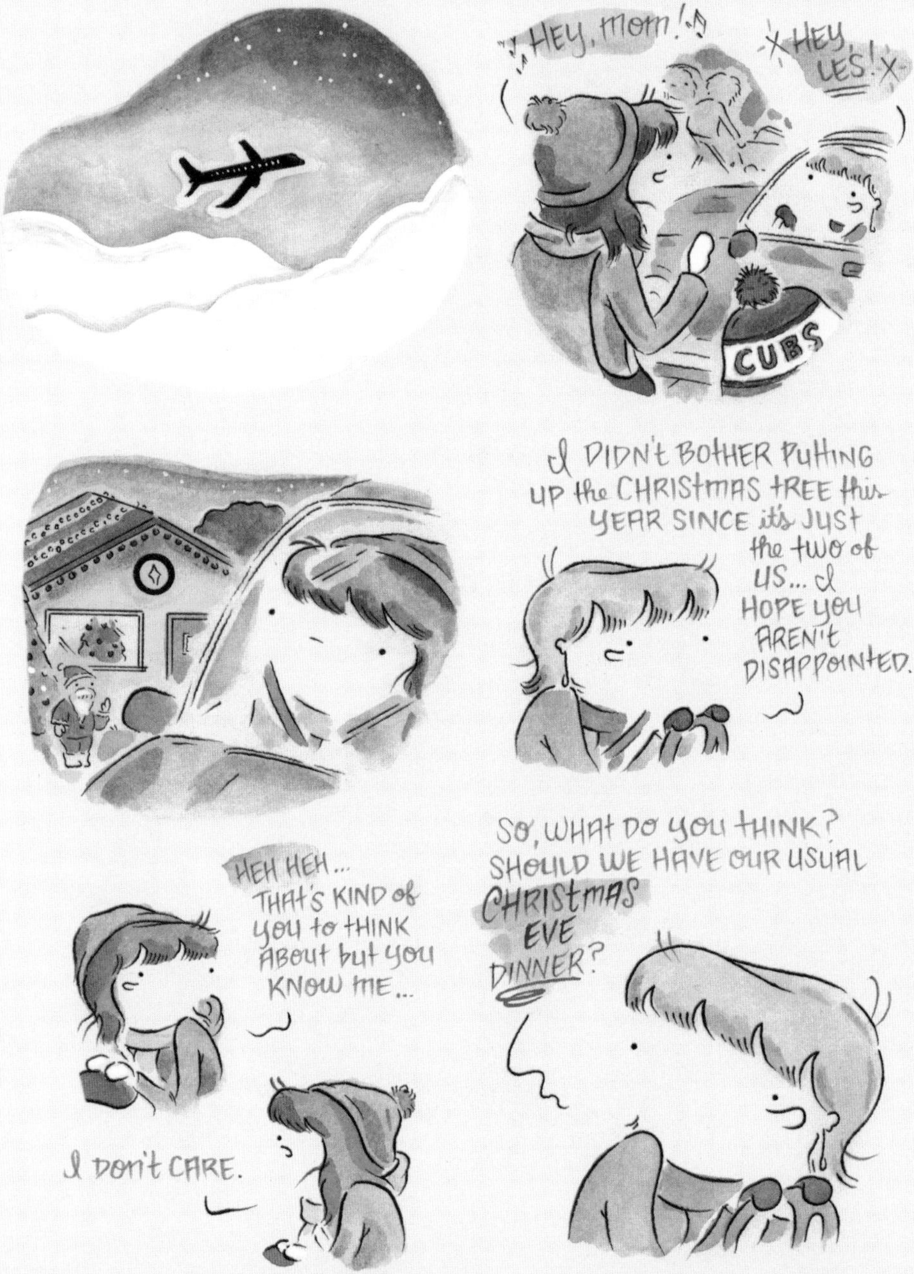
HEY, MOM!
HEY, LES!
CUBS
I DIDN'T BOTHER PUTTING UP THE CHRISTMAS TREE THIS YEAR SINCE IT'S JUST THE TWO OF US... I HOPE YOU AREN'T DISAPPOINTED.
HEH HEH... THAT'S KIND OF YOU TO THINK ABOUT BUT YOU KNOW ME...
I DON'T CARE.
SO, WHAT DO YOU THINK? SHOULD WE HAVE OUR USUAL CHRISTMAS EVE DINNER?

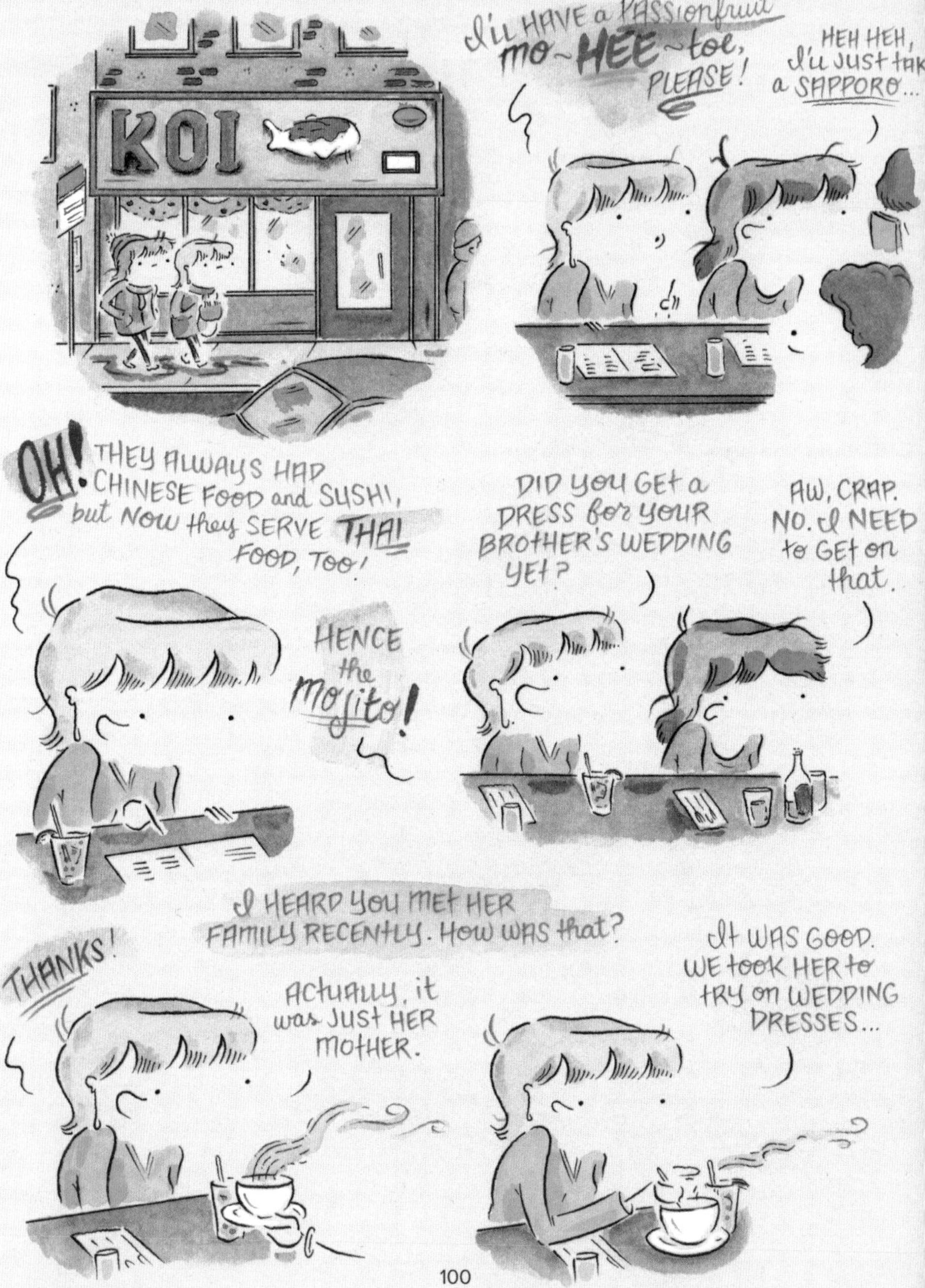
KOI
I'll HAVE a PASSionfruit mo~HEE~toe, PLEASE!
HEH HEH, I'll JUST tak a SAPPORO...
OH! THEY ALWAYS HAD CHINESE FOOD and SUSHI, but NOW they SERVE THAI FOOD, TOO!
HENCE the mojito!
DID YOU GET a DRESS for YOUR BROTHER'S WEDDING YET?
AW, CRAP. NO. I NEED to GET on that.
I HEARD YOU MET HER FAMILY RECENTLY. HOW WAS that?
THANKS!
Actually, it was JUST HER MOTHER.
It WAS GOOD. WE took HER to try on WEDDING DRESSES...

SHE WAS a REAL SPORT! SHE TRIED on at LEAST TEN!

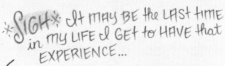 *SIGH* It may BE the LAST time in my LIFE I GET to HAVE that EXPERIENCE...

YOU GET SETTLED and I'LL MAKE US SOME TEA!

SsSLUURP!

SO, LINDA'S FRIEND is a PSYCHIC AND a TAROT CARD READER... and SHE SAID SHE SEES a BABY BOY in HER FUTURE... EXACTLY a YEAR after the WEDDING!

THAT WOULDN'T BE too SURPRISING. I BET they'll START TRYING RIGHT AWAY.

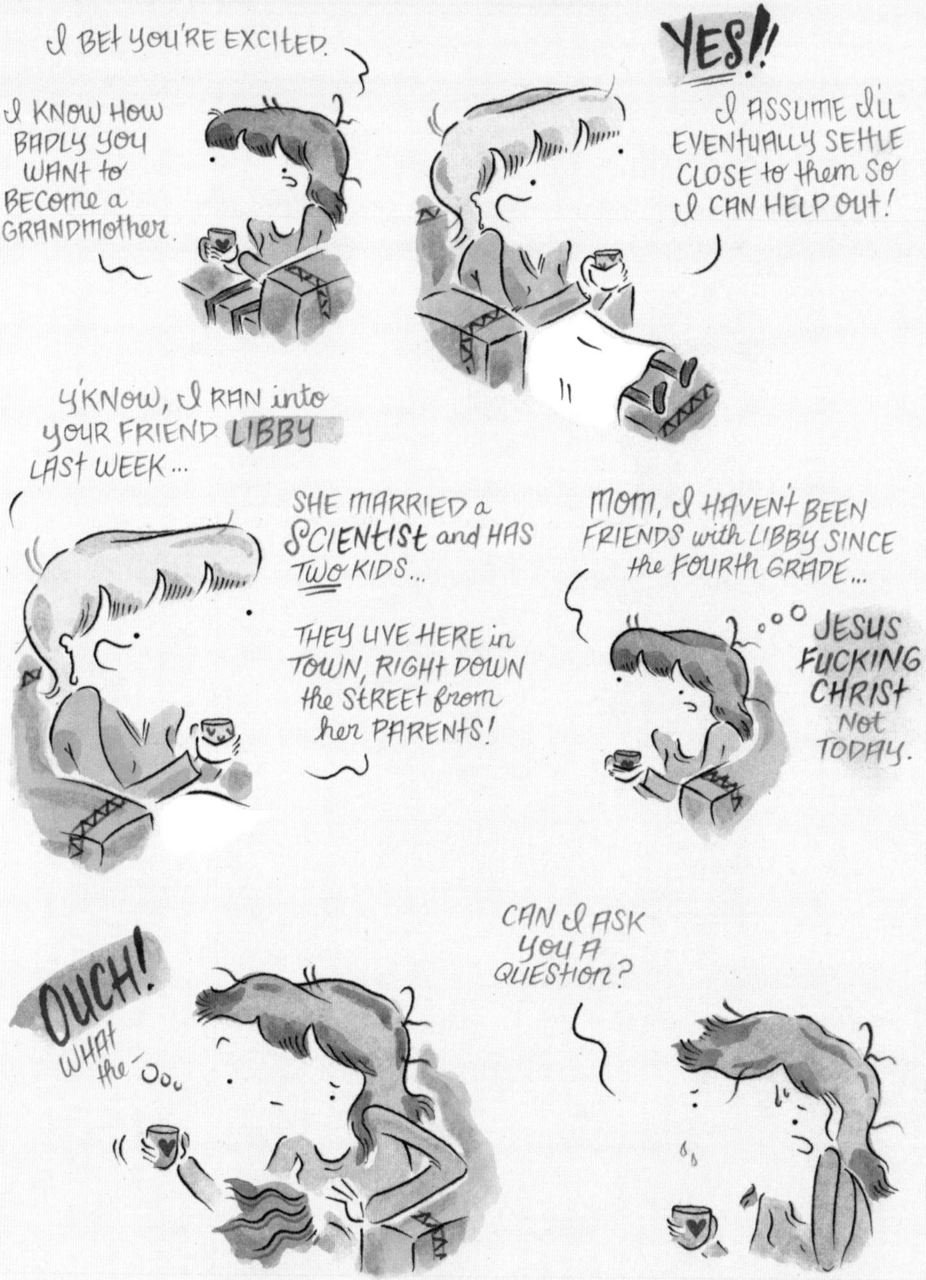
I BET YOU'RE EXCITED.
I KNOW HOW BADLY YOU WANT TO BECOME A GRANDMOTHER.
YES!!
I ASSUME I'LL EVENTUALLY SETTLE CLOSE TO THEM SO I CAN HELP OUT!
Y'KNOW, I RAN INTO YOUR FRIEND LIBBY LAST WEEK...
SHE MARRIED A SCIENTIST AND HAS TWO KIDS...
THEY LIVE HERE IN TOWN, RIGHT DOWN THE STREET FROM HER PARENTS!
MOM, I HAVEN'T BEEN FRIENDS WITH LIBBY SINCE THE FOURTH GRADE...
JESUS FUCKING CHRIST NOT TODAY.
OUCH!
WHAT THE-
CAN I ASK YOU A QUESTION?

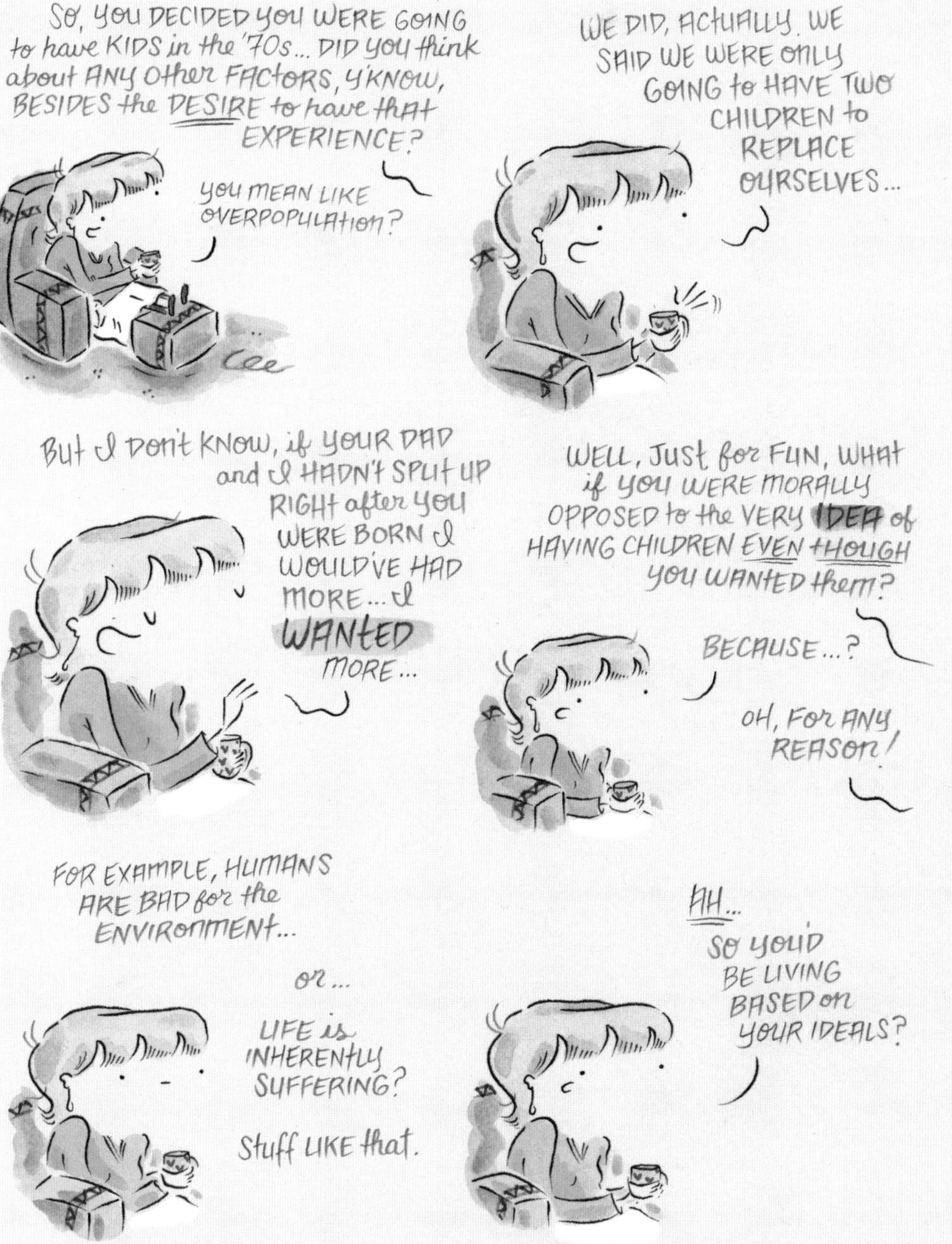
SO, YOU DECIDED YOU WERE GOING to have KIDS in the '70s... DID YOU think about ANY Other FACTORS, Y'KNOW, BESIDES the DESIRE to have that EXPERIENCE?
YOU MEAN LIKE OVERPOPULATION?
WE DID, ACTUALLY. WE SAID WE WERE ONLY GOING to HAVE TWO CHILDREN to REPLACE OURSELVES...
But I DON'T KNOW, if YOUR DAD and I HADN'T SPLIT UP RIGHT after YOU WERE BORN I WOULD'VE HAD MORE... I WANTED MORE...
WELL, JUST for FUN, WHAT if YOU WERE MORALLY OPPOSED to the VERY IDEA of HAVING CHILDREN EVEN THOUGH YOU WANTED them?
BECAUSE...?
OH, FOR ANY REASON!
FOR EXAMPLE, HUMANS ARE BAD for the ENVIRONMENT...
or...
LIFE is INHERENTLY SUFFERING?
Stuff LIKE that.
AH...
SO YOU'D BE LIVING BASED on YOUR IDEALS?

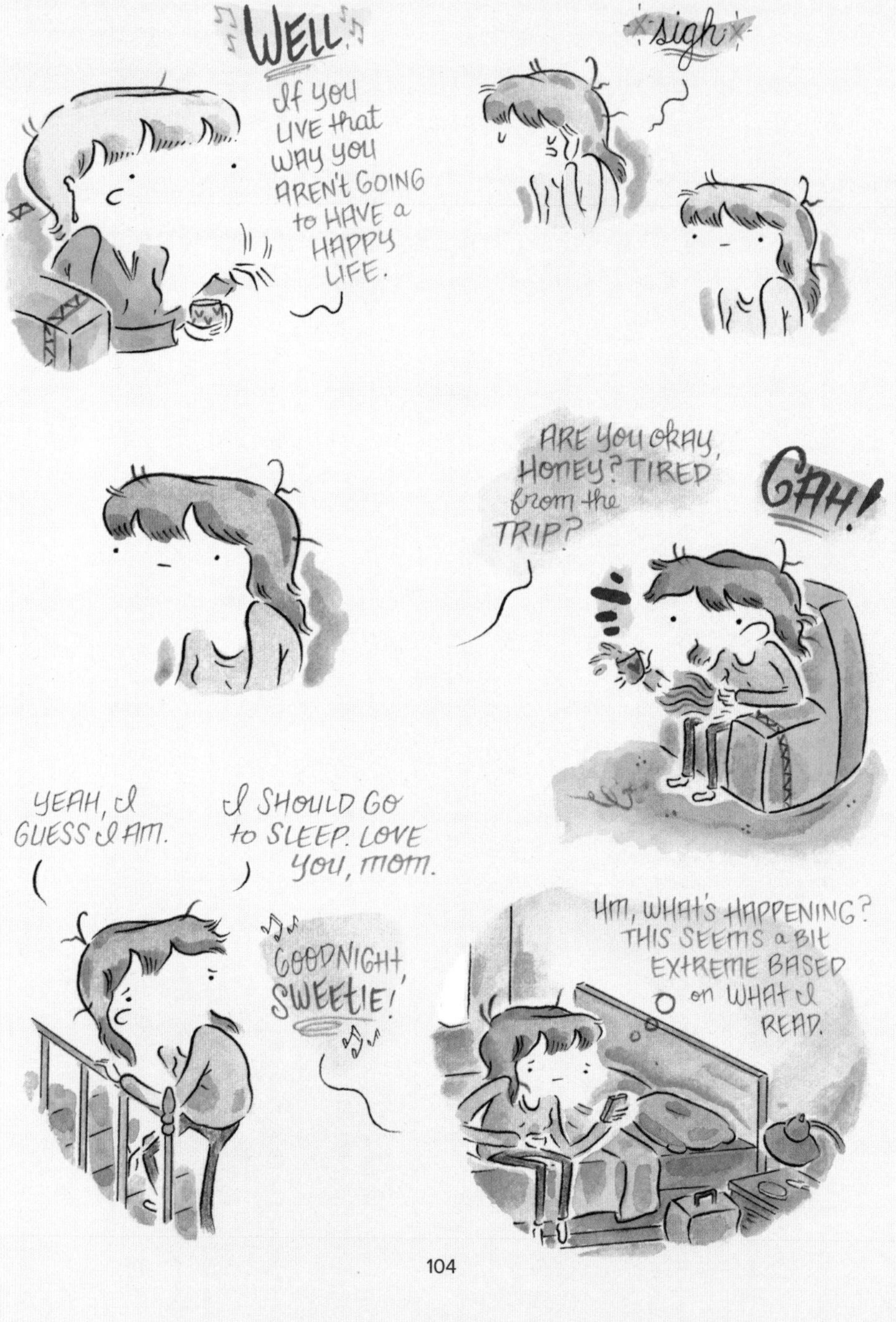
WELL
If you live that way you aren't going to have a happy life.
sigh
Are you okay, honey? Tired from the trip?
GAH!
Yeah, I guess I am.
I should go to sleep. Love you, mom.
Goodnight, sweetie!
Hm, what's happening? This seems a bit extreme based on what I read.

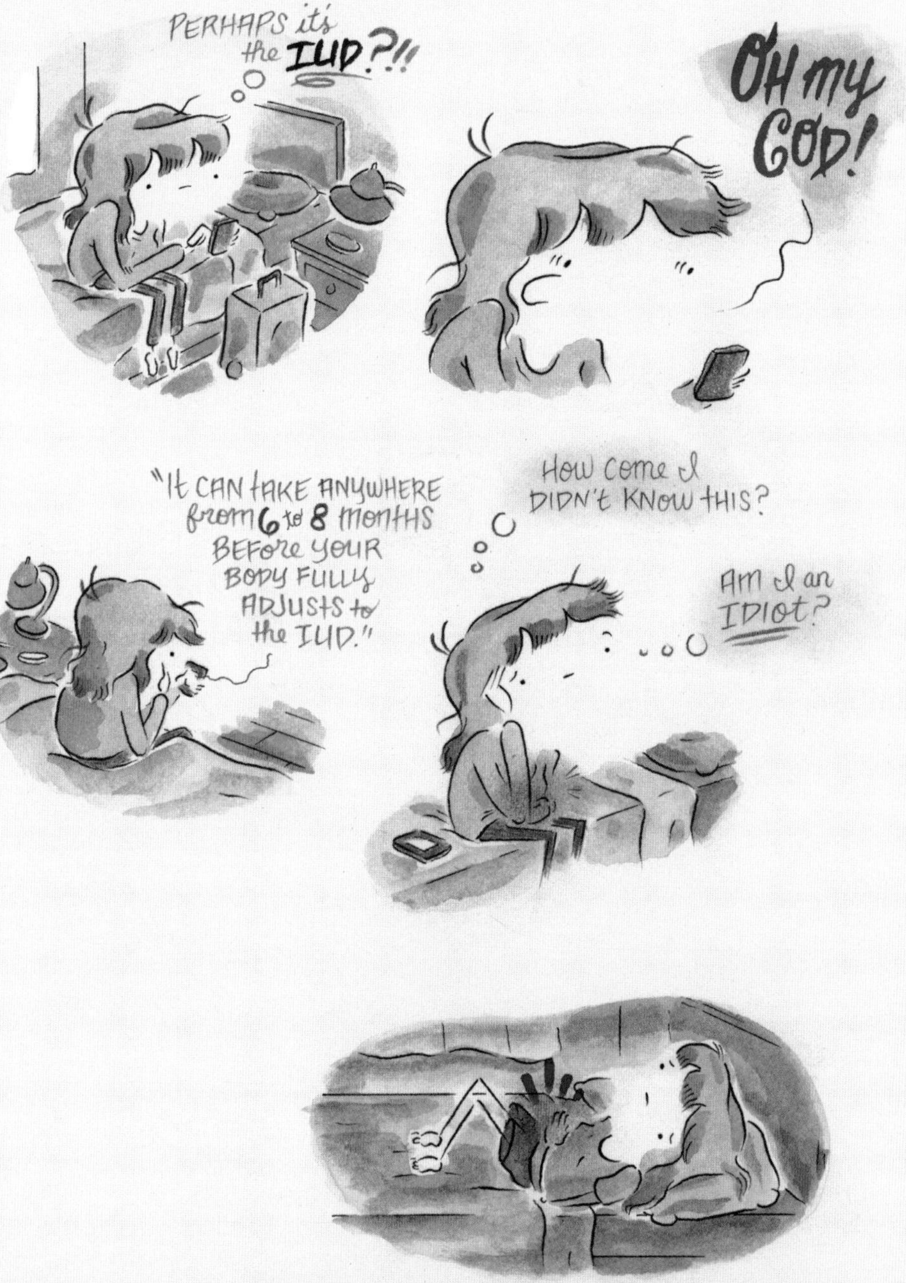
PERHAPS it's the IUD?!!
OH my GOD!
"It CAN take ANYWHERE from 6 to 8 months BEFORE YOUR BODY FULLY ADJUSTS to the IUD."
How come I DIDN'T KNOW THIS?
Am I an IDIOT?

HEY, MOM. SORRY I SLEPT SO LATE...

THAT'S OKAY! I WAS JUST DOING MY NAILS! ARE YOU HUNGRY?

WANT A BAGEL? GRAPES?

OH, AND BY THE WAY—

MERRY CHRISTMAS!!!

MERRY CHRISTMAS, MOM.

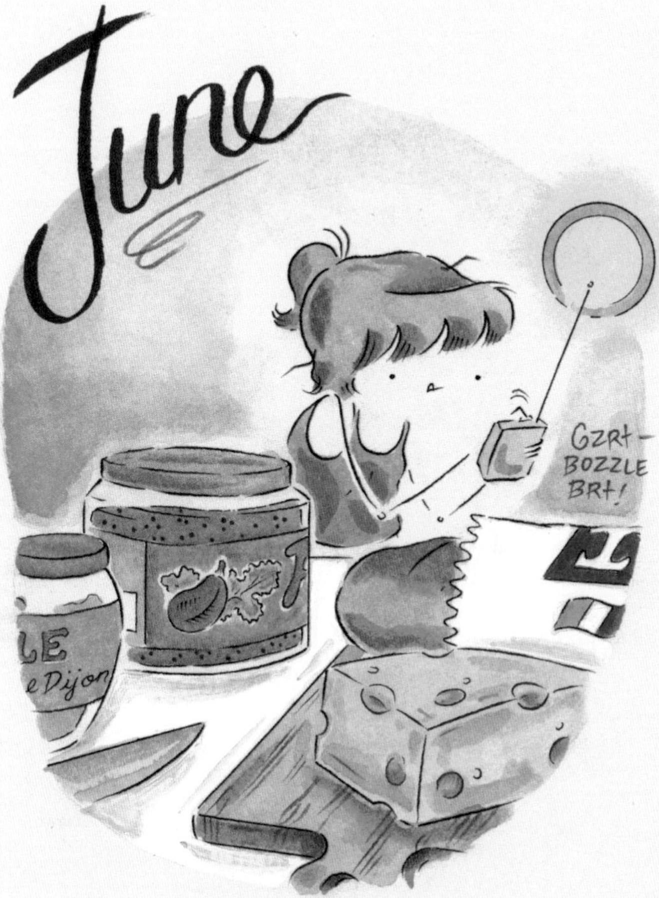
June
GZRT-
BOZZLE
BRT!
LE
e Dijon

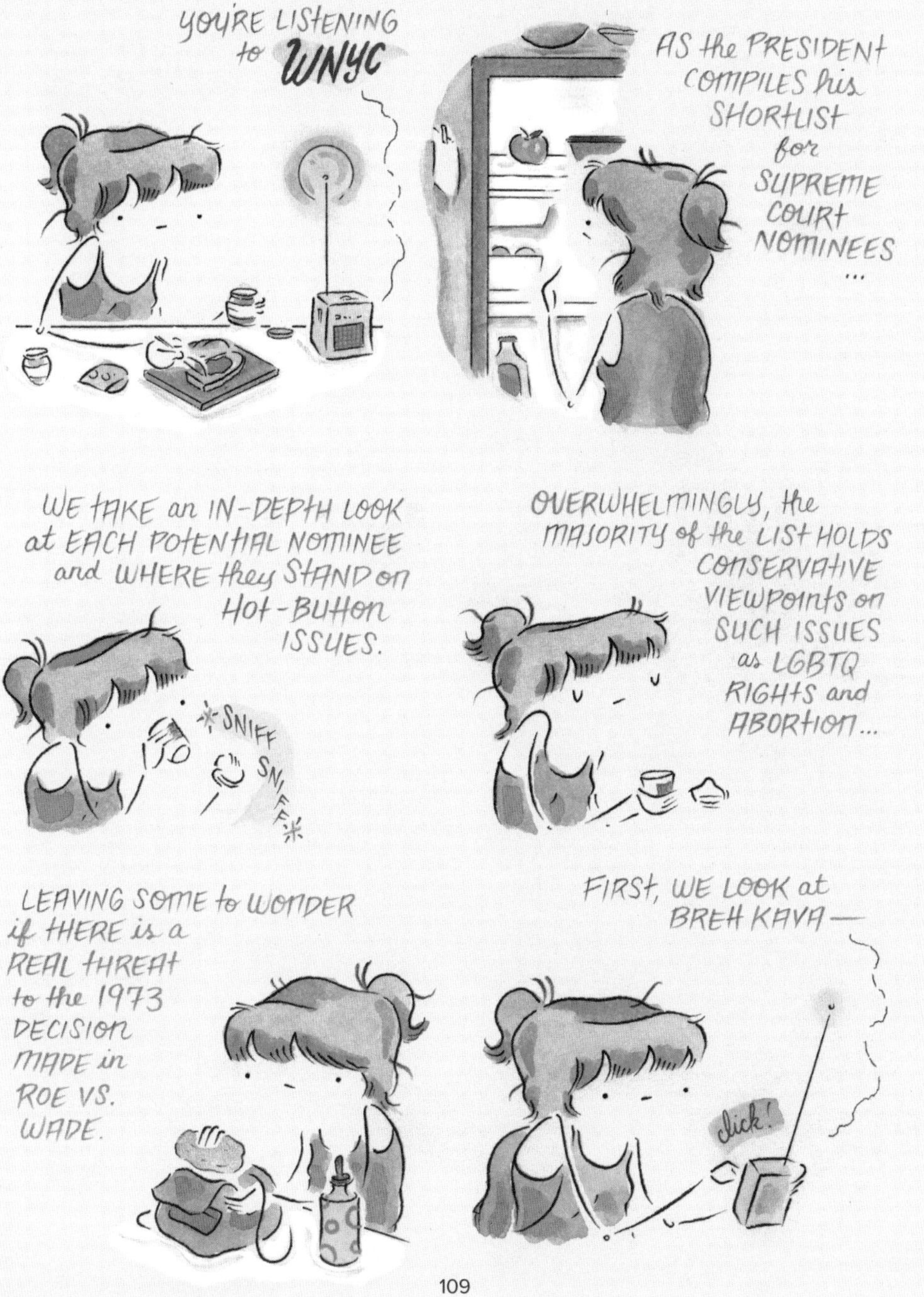
YOU'RE LISTENING to WNYC
AS the PRESIDENT COMPILES his SHORTLIST for SUPREME COURT NOMINEES ...
WE TAKE an IN-DEPTH LOOK at EACH POTENTIAL NOMINEE and WHERE they STAND on HOT-BUTTON ISSUES.
SNIFF
SNIFF
OVERWHELMINGLY, the MAJORITY of the LIST HOLDS CONSERVATIVE VIEWPOINTS on SUCH ISSUES as LGBTQ RIGHTS and ABORTION...
LEAVING SOME to WONDER if THERE is a REAL THREAT to the 1973 DECISION MADE in ROE VS. WADE.
FIRST, WE LOOK at BRETT KAVA—
click!

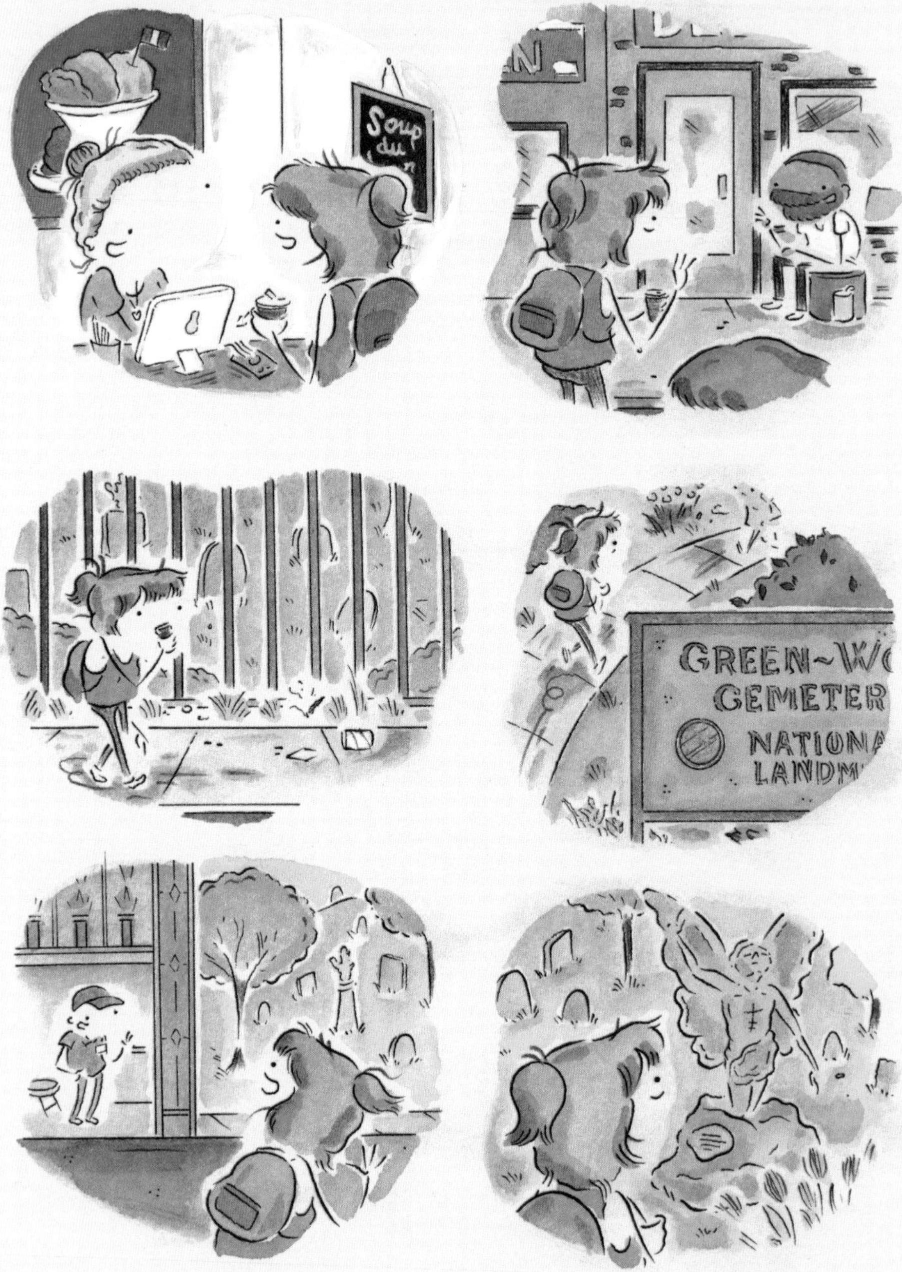
Soup
du
GREEN~W
CEMETER
NATIONA
LANDM

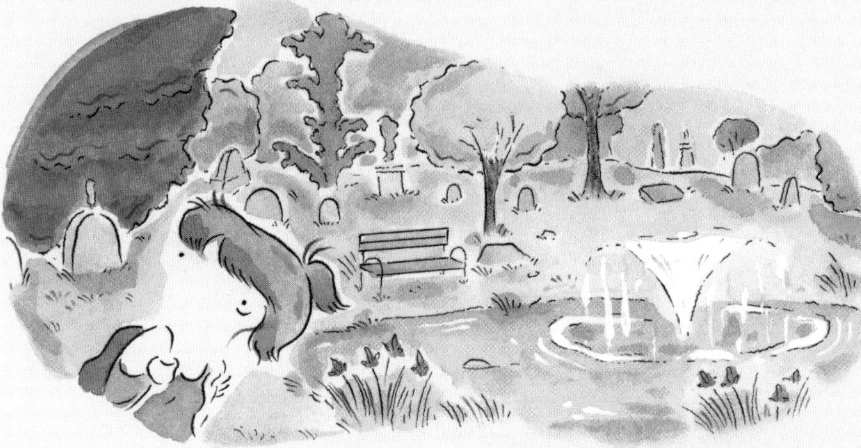

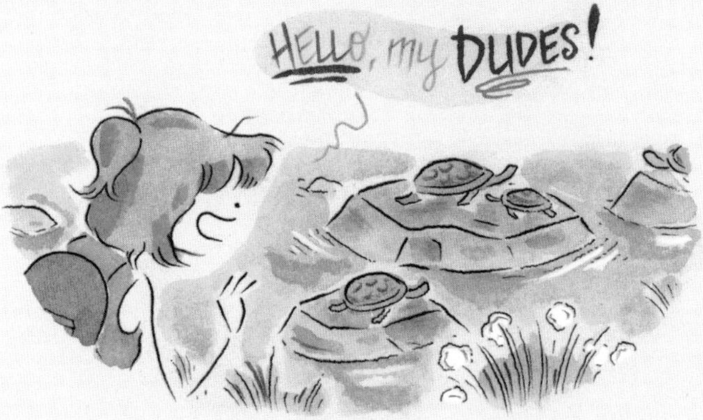
HELLO, my DUDES!

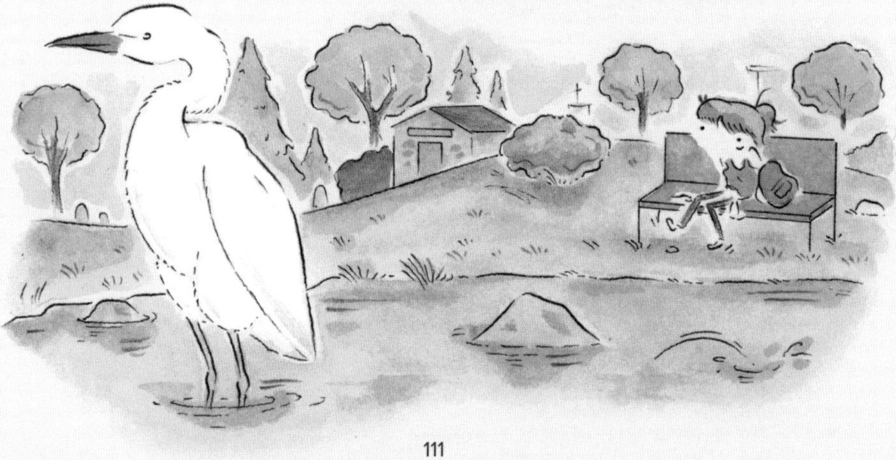

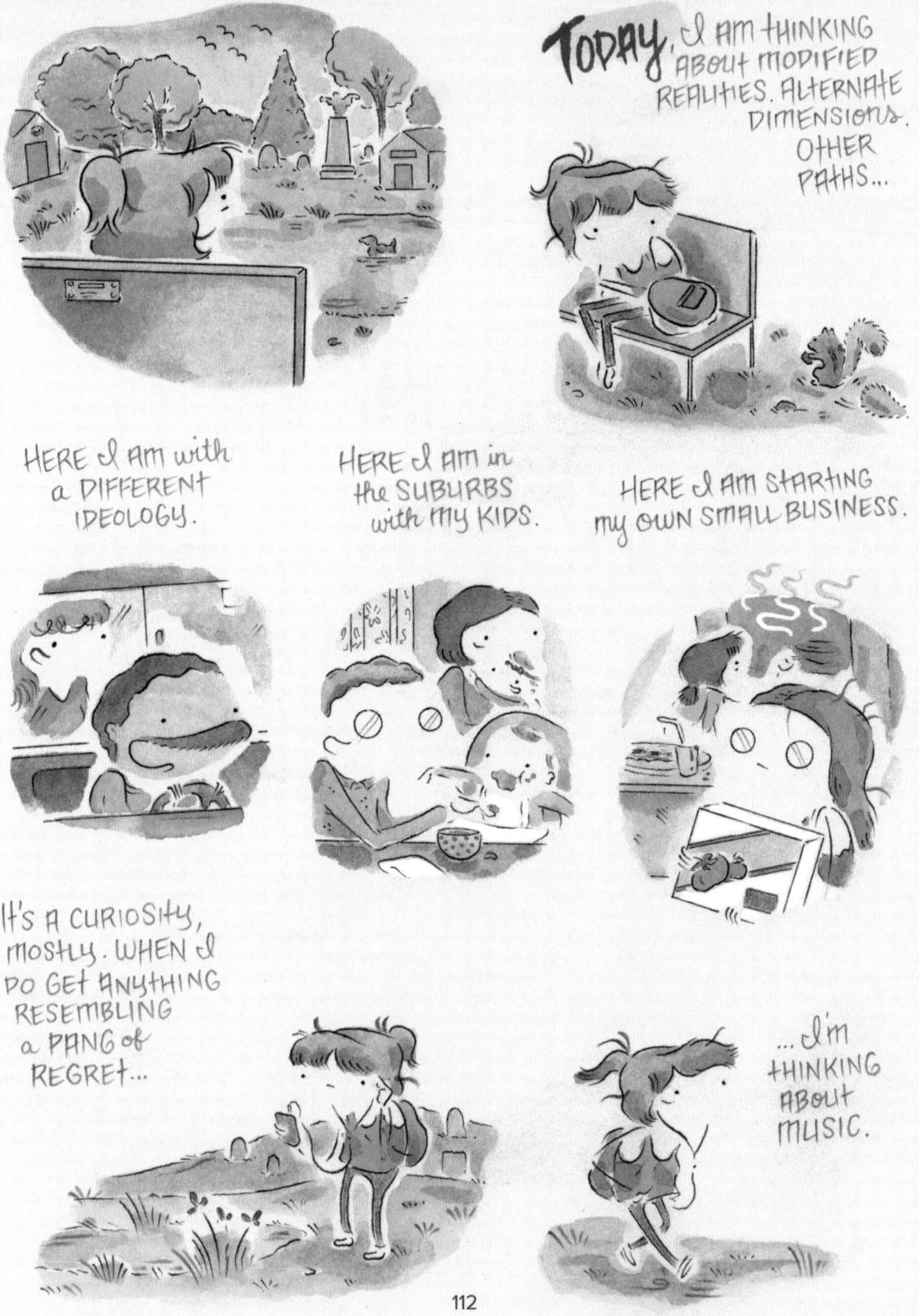
TODAY, I AM THINKING ABOUT MODIFIED REALITIES. ALTERNATE DIMENSIONS. OTHER PATHS...
HERE I AM with a DIFFERENT IDEOLOGY.
HERE I AM in the SUBURBS with MY KIDS.
HERE I AM STARTING my OWN SMALL BUSINESS.
It's A CURIOSITY, mostly. WHEN I DO GET ANYTHING RESEMBLING a PANG of REGRET...
...I'm THINKING ABOUT MUSIC.

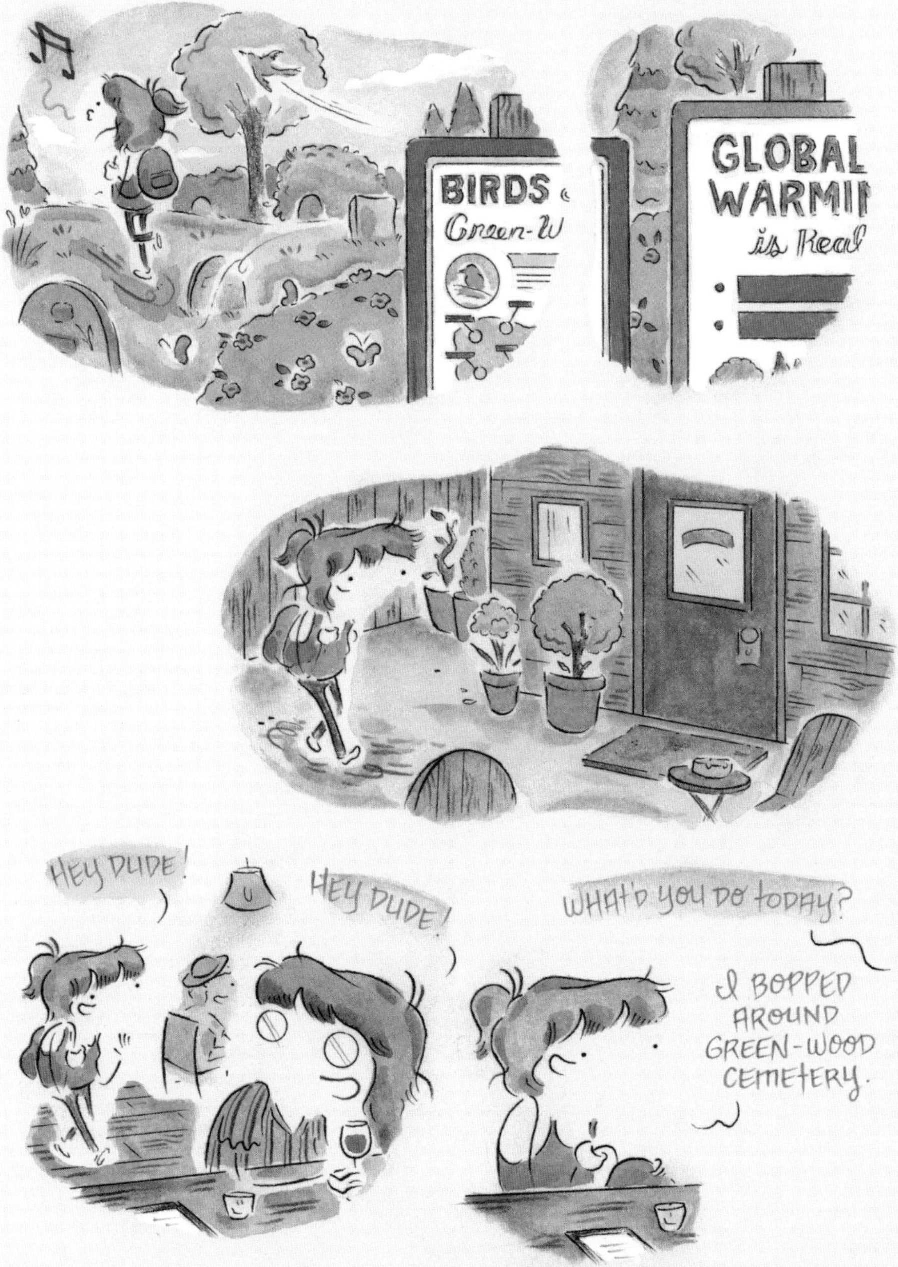
BIRDS
Green-W
GLOBAL
WARMI
is Real
HEY DUDE!
HEY DUDE!
WHAT'D YOU DO TODAY?
I BOPPED AROUND GREEN-WOOD CEMETERY.

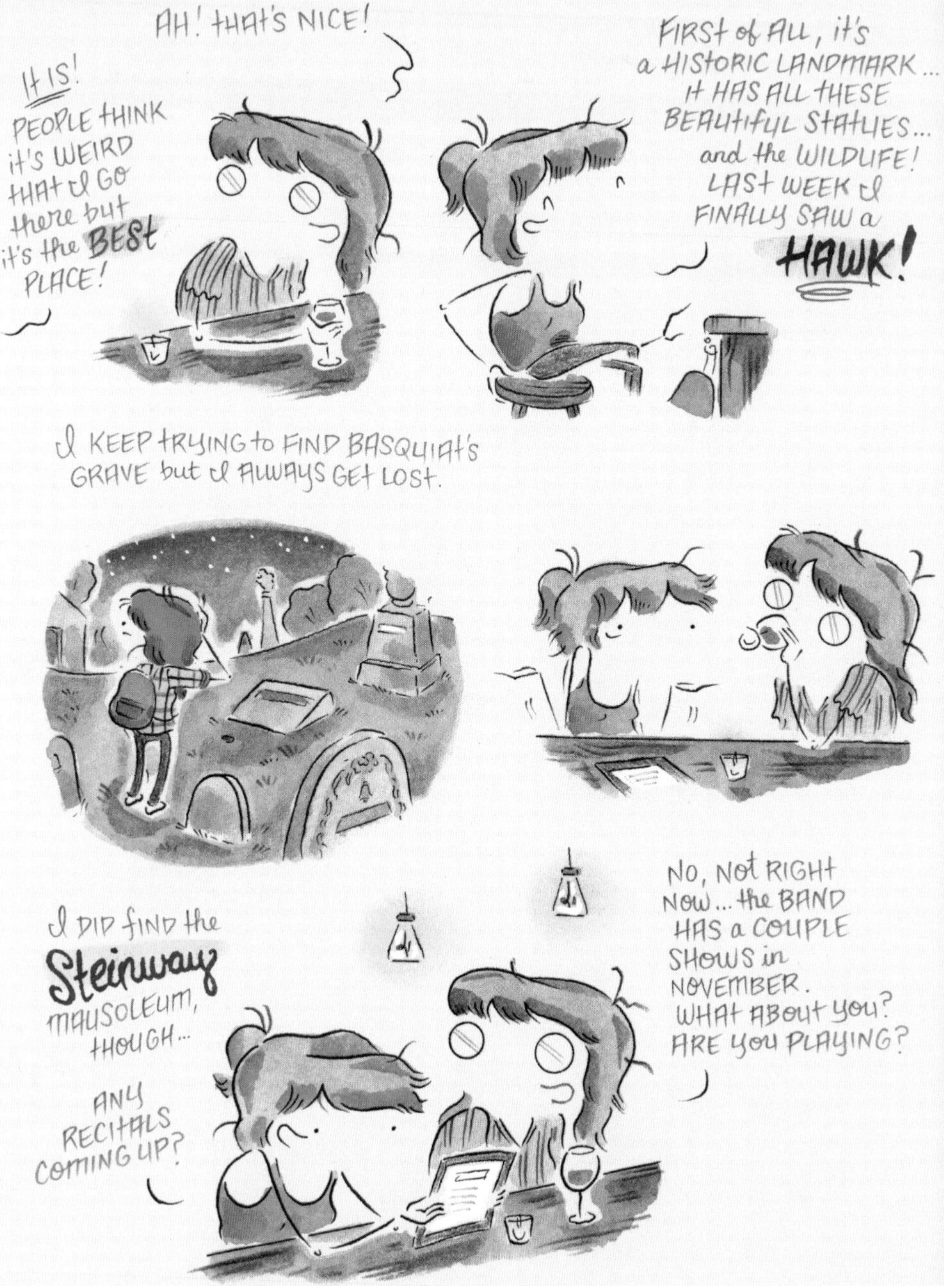
IT IS! PEOPLE THINK it's WEIRD THAT I GO there but it's the BEST PLACE!
AH! that's NICE!
FIRST of ALL, it's a HISTORIC LANDMARK... it HAS ALL THESE BEAUTIFUL STATUES... and the WILDLIFE! LAST WEEK I FINALLY SAW a HAWK!
I KEEP TRYING to FIND BASQUIAT's GRAVE but I ALWAYS GET LOST.
I DID find the Steinway MAUSOLEUM, THOUGH...
ANY RECITALS COMING UP?
NO, NOT RIGHT NOW... the BAND HAS a COUPLE SHOWS in NOVEMBER. WHAT ABOUT YOU? ARE YOU PLAYING?

JUST tinkering AROUND at Home... it's SO MUCH WORK to Put a NEW PROJECT toGETHER.

WELL, WHEN YOU DO DECIDE to, YOU'LL HAVE PLENTY of PEOPLE WHO WILL WANT to HELP YOU OUT!

OH! I HOPE I'M IN TOWN FOR YOUR SHOWS IN NOVEMBER!

MAY I HAVE a PINOT, PLEASE?

Thaaank You...

WHY? WHATCHA GOT GOIN' on?

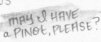

EH, MY BOYFRIEND'S DOING a EUROPEAN tour THEN, so I THOUGHT I'D HOP OVER at the END and HANG OUT for a BIT.

I'll HAVE ANOTHER, too!

If HE EVER GOES to JAPAN, I'm TOTALLY TAGGING ALONG... I'D LIKE to SEE a REAL JAPANESE GARDEN!

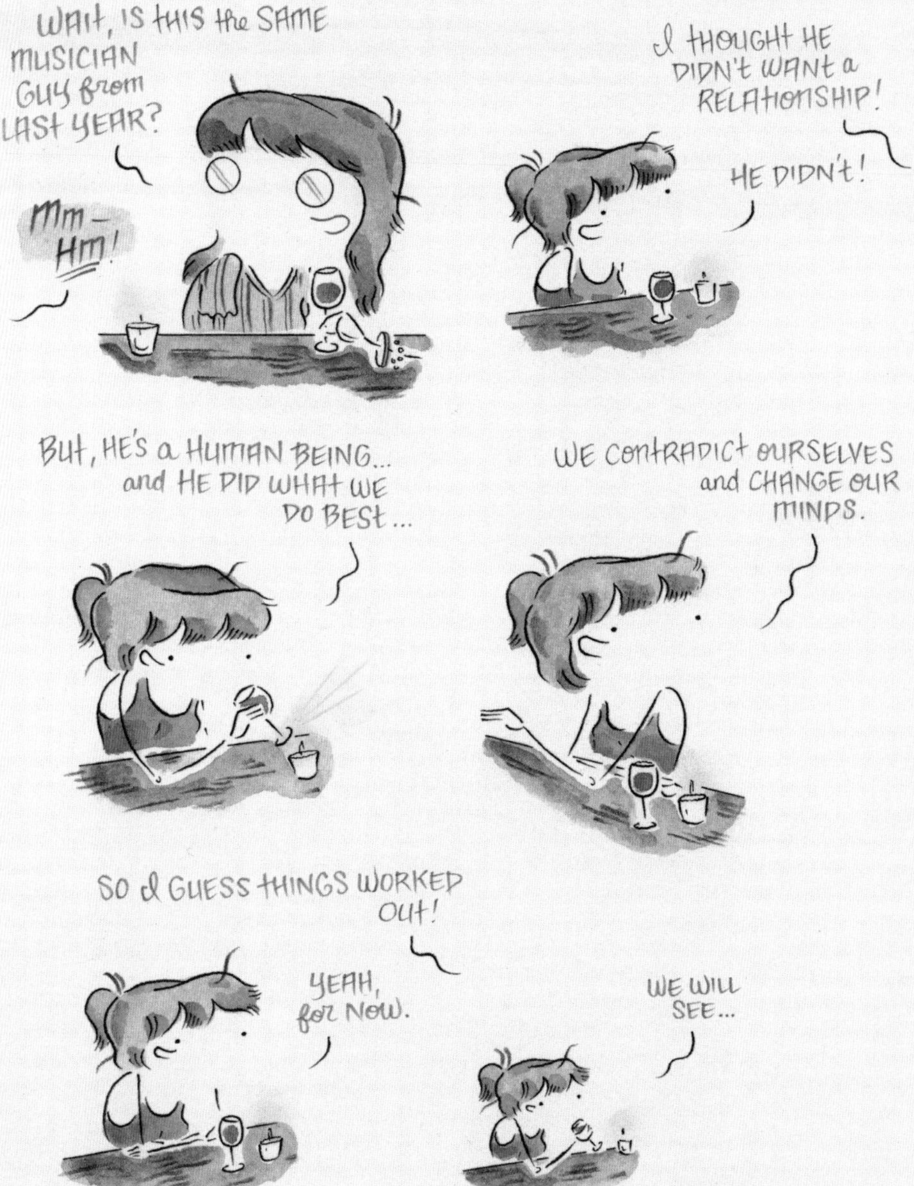
WAIT, IS THIS the SAME MUSICIAN GUY from LAST YEAR?
Mm-Hm!
I THOUGHT HE DIDN'T WANT a RELATIONSHIP!
HE DIDN'T!
But, HE'S a HUMAN BEING... and HE DID WHAT WE DO BEST...
WE CONTRADICT OURSELVES and CHANGE OUR MINDS.
SO I GUESS THINGS WORKED OUT!
YEAH, for NOW.
WE WILL SEE...

November

BEE BEE

OrBits Alert:

NORWEGIAN AIR FLIGHT 176 to GRX has been CANCELED.

PLEASE CALL NORWEGIAN AIR at (833) 200-3168 at YOUR EARLIEST CONVENIENCE to RESCHEDULE.

119

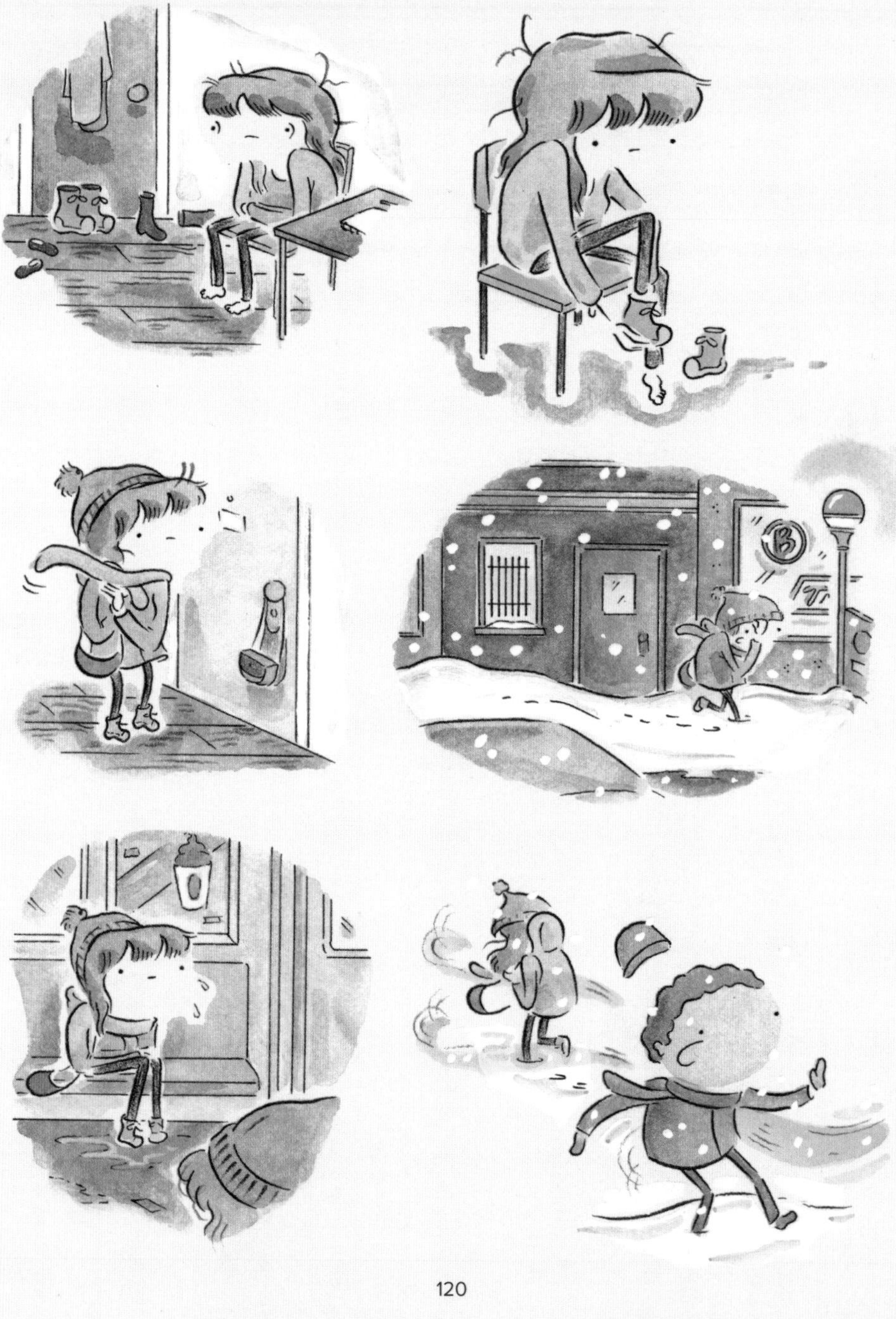

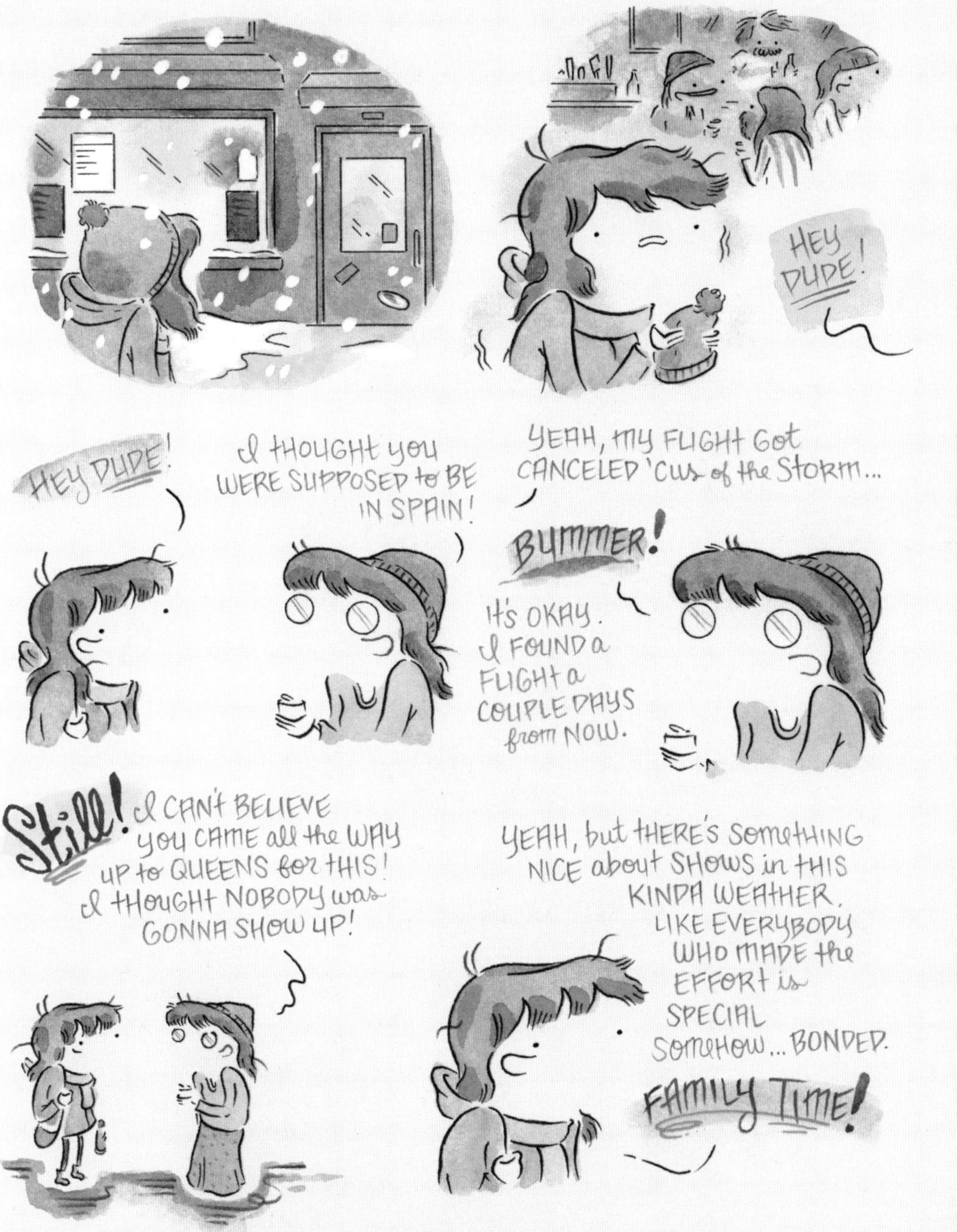
HEY DUDE!
HEY DUDE!
I THOUGHT YOU WERE SUPPOSED TO BE IN SPAIN!
YEAH, MY FLIGHT GOT CANCELED 'CUS OF THE STORM...
BUMMER!
IT'S OKAY. I FOUND A FLIGHT A COUPLE DAYS FROM NOW.
STILL! I CAN'T BELIEVE YOU CAME ALL THE WAY UP TO QUEENS FOR THIS! I THOUGHT NOBODY WAS GONNA SHOW UP!
YEAH, BUT THERE'S SOMETHING NICE ABOUT SHOWS IN THIS KINDA WEATHER. LIKE EVERYBODY WHO MADE THE EFFORT IS SPECIAL SOMEHOW... BONDED.
FAMILY TIME!

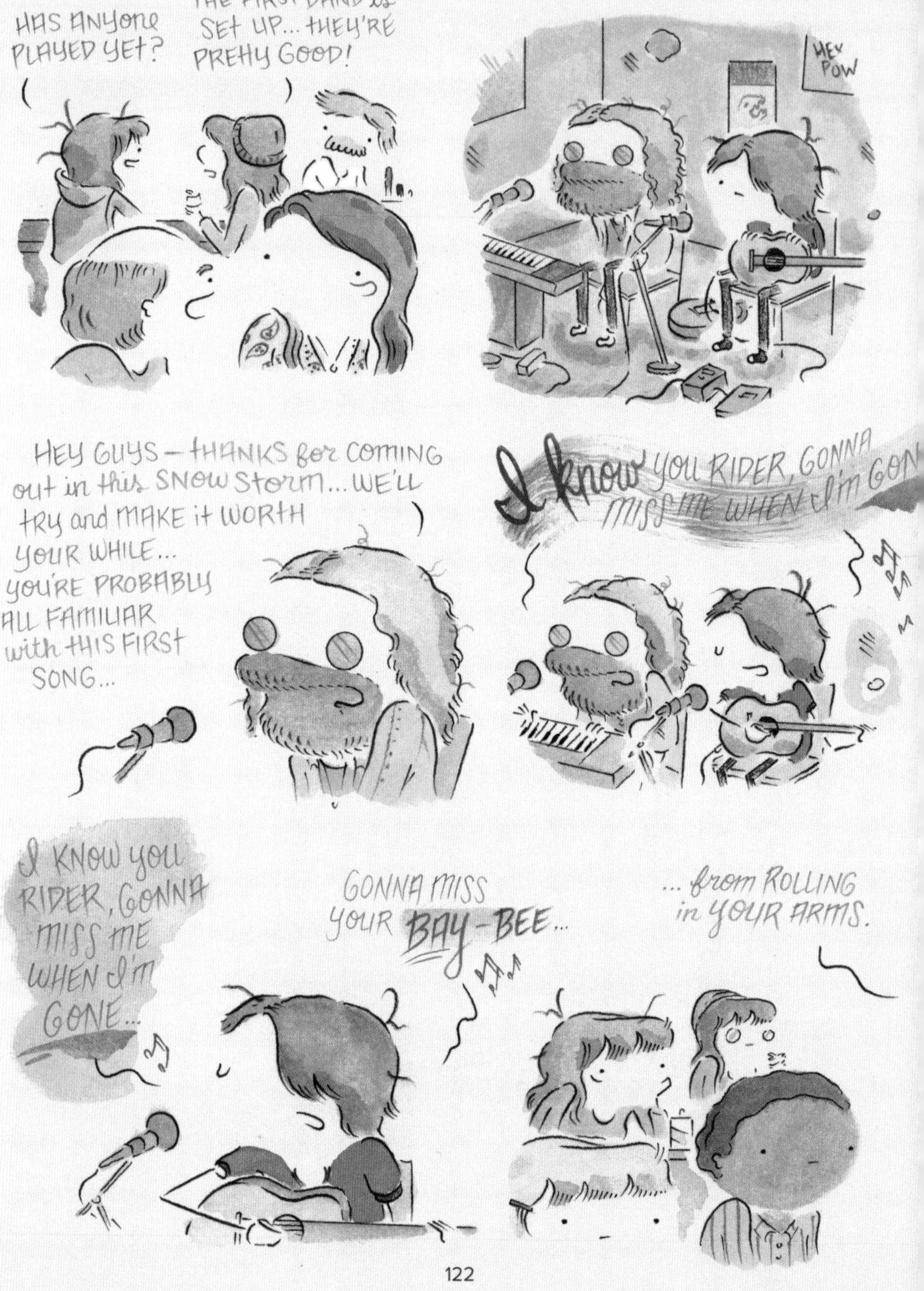
HAS ANYONE PLAYED YET?
THE FIRST BAND IS SET UP... THEY'RE PRETTY GOOD!
HEY POW
HEY GUYS — THANKS FOR COMING OUT IN THIS SNOW STORM... WE'LL TRY AND MAKE IT WORTH YOUR WHILE... YOU'RE PROBABLY ALL FAMILIAR WITH THIS FIRST SONG...
I KNOW YOU RIDER, GONNA MISS ME WHEN I'M GON
I KNOW YOU RIDER, GONNA MISS ME WHEN I'M GONE...
GONNA MISS YOUR BAY-BEE...
... FROM ROLLING IN YOUR ARMS.

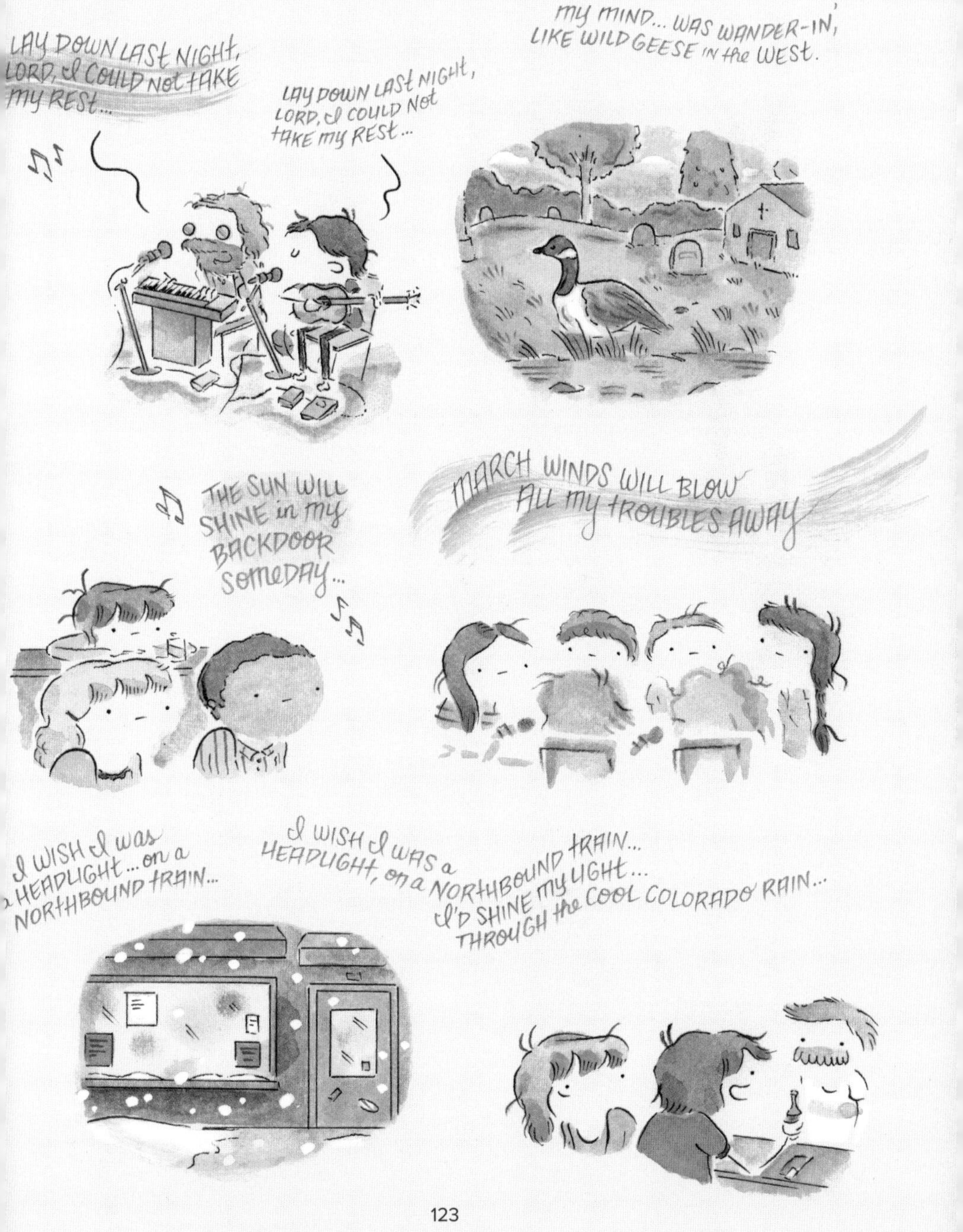
LAY DOWN LAST NIGHT, LORD, I COULD NOT TAKE MY REST...
LAY DOWN LAST NIGHT, LORD, I COULD NOT TAKE MY REST...
MY MIND... WAS WANDER-IN', LIKE WILD GEESE IN THE WEST.
THE SUN WILL SHINE IN MY BACKDOOR SOMEDAY...
MARCH WINDS WILL BLOW ALL MY TROUBLES AWAY
I WISH I WAS a HEADLIGHT... ON A NORTHBOUND TRAIN...
I WISH I WAS A HEADLIGHT, ON A NORTHBOUND TRAIN... I'D SHINE MY LIGHT... THROUGH THE COOL COLORADO RAIN...

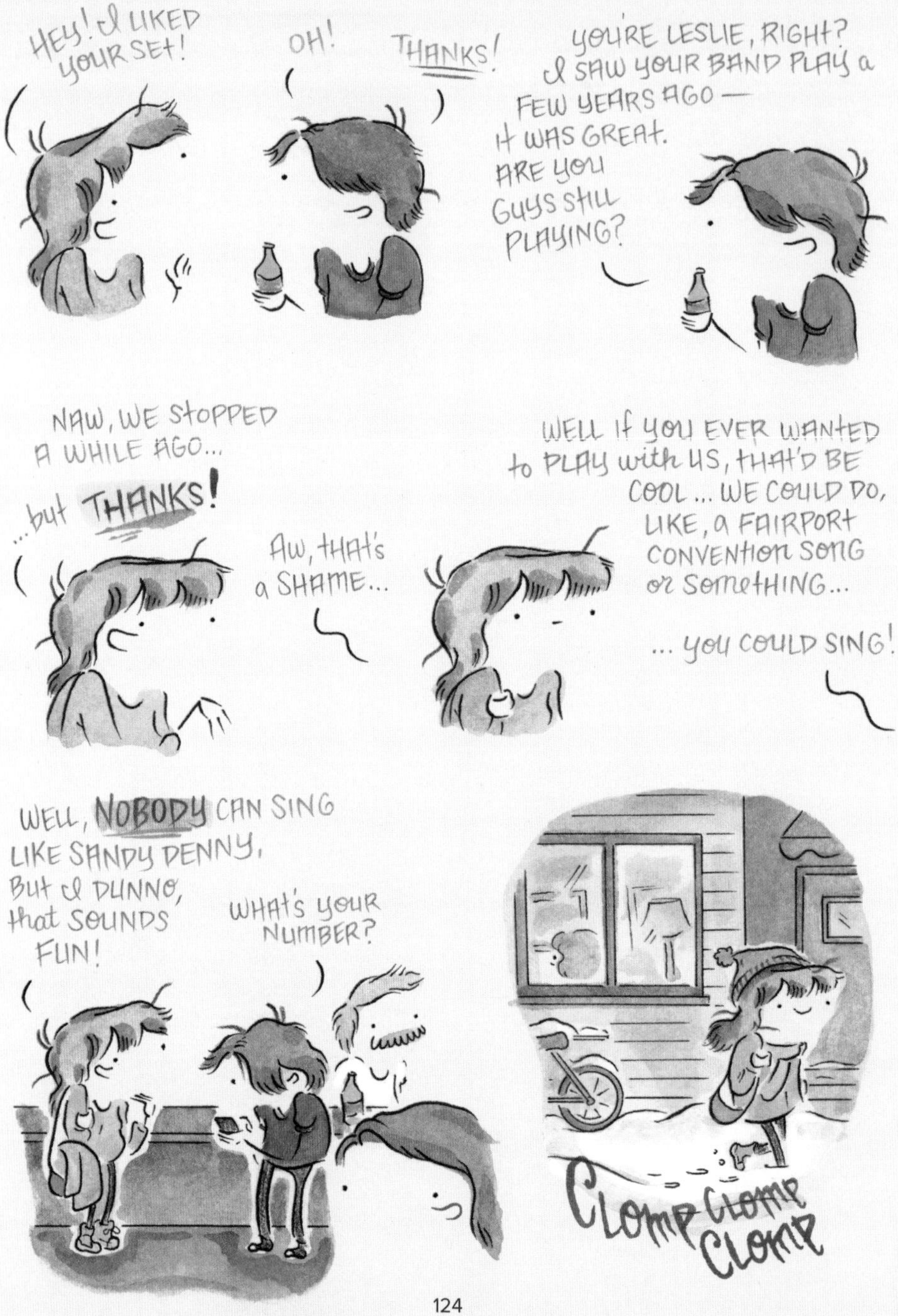
HEY! I LIKED YOUR SET!
OH!
THANKS!
YOU'RE LESLIE, RIGHT? I SAW YOUR BAND PLAY A FEW YEARS AGO — IT WAS GREAT. ARE YOU GUYS STILL PLAYING?
NAW, WE STOPPED A WHILE AGO...
...but THANKS!
Aw, THAT'S a SHAME...
WELL if YOU EVER WANTED to PLAY with US, THAT'D BE COOL... WE COULD DO, LIKE, a FAIRPORT CONVENTION SONG or SOMETHING...
... YOU COULD SING!
WELL, NOBODY CAN SING LIKE SANDY DENNY, But I DUNNO, that SOUNDS FUN!
WHAT'S YOUR NUMBER?
CLOMP CLOMP CLOMP

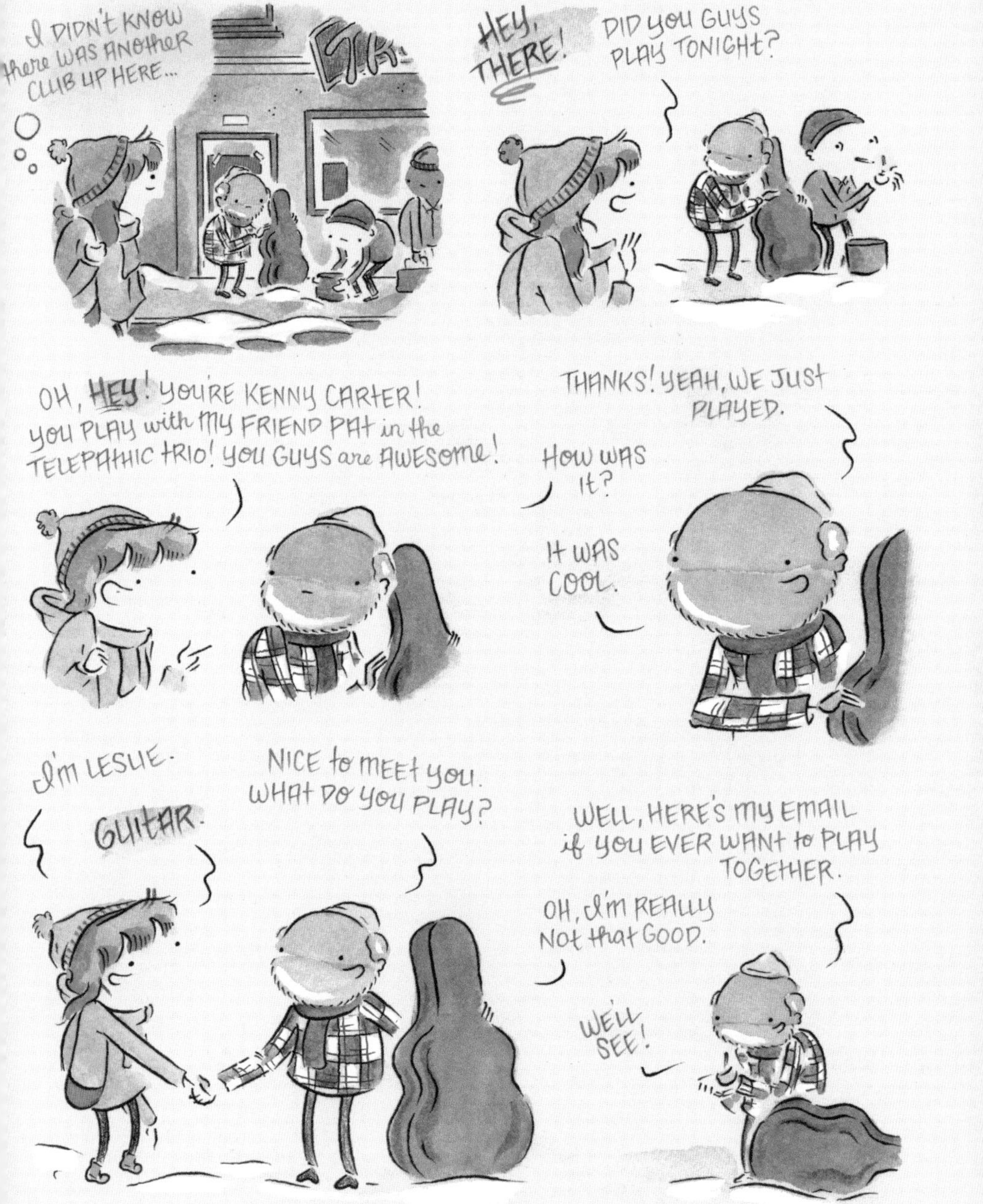
I DIDN'T KNOW there WAS ANOTHER CLUB UP HERE...
HEY, THERE!
DID YOU GUYS PLAY TONIGHT?
OH, HEY! YOU'RE KENNY CARTER! YOU PLAY with MY FRIEND PAT in the TELEPATHIC TRIO! YOU GUYS are AWESOME!
THANKS! YEAH, WE JUST PLAYED.
HOW WAS it?
It WAS COOL.
I'M LESLIE.
NICE to MEET YOU. WHAT DO YOU PLAY?
GUITAR.
WELL, HERE'S MY EMAIL if YOU EVER WANT to PLAY TOGETHER.
OH, I'M REALLY Not that GOOD.
WE'LL SEE!

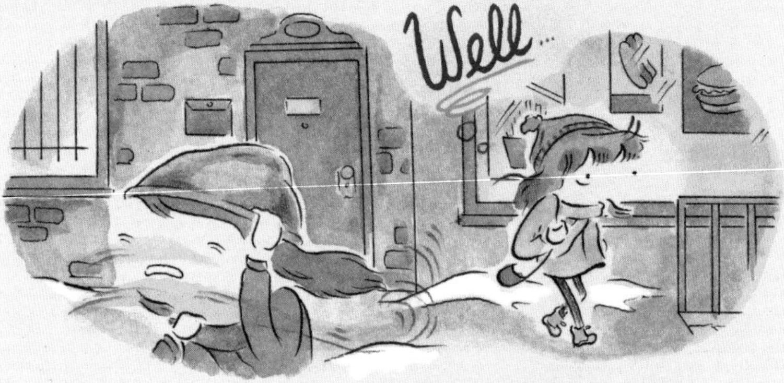
Well...

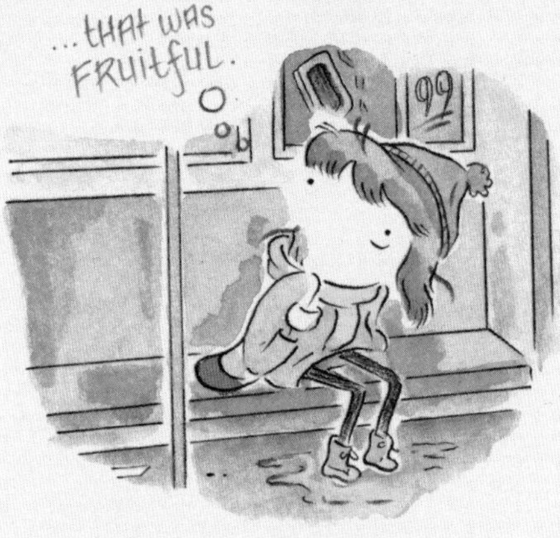
...that was FRUITFUL.
99

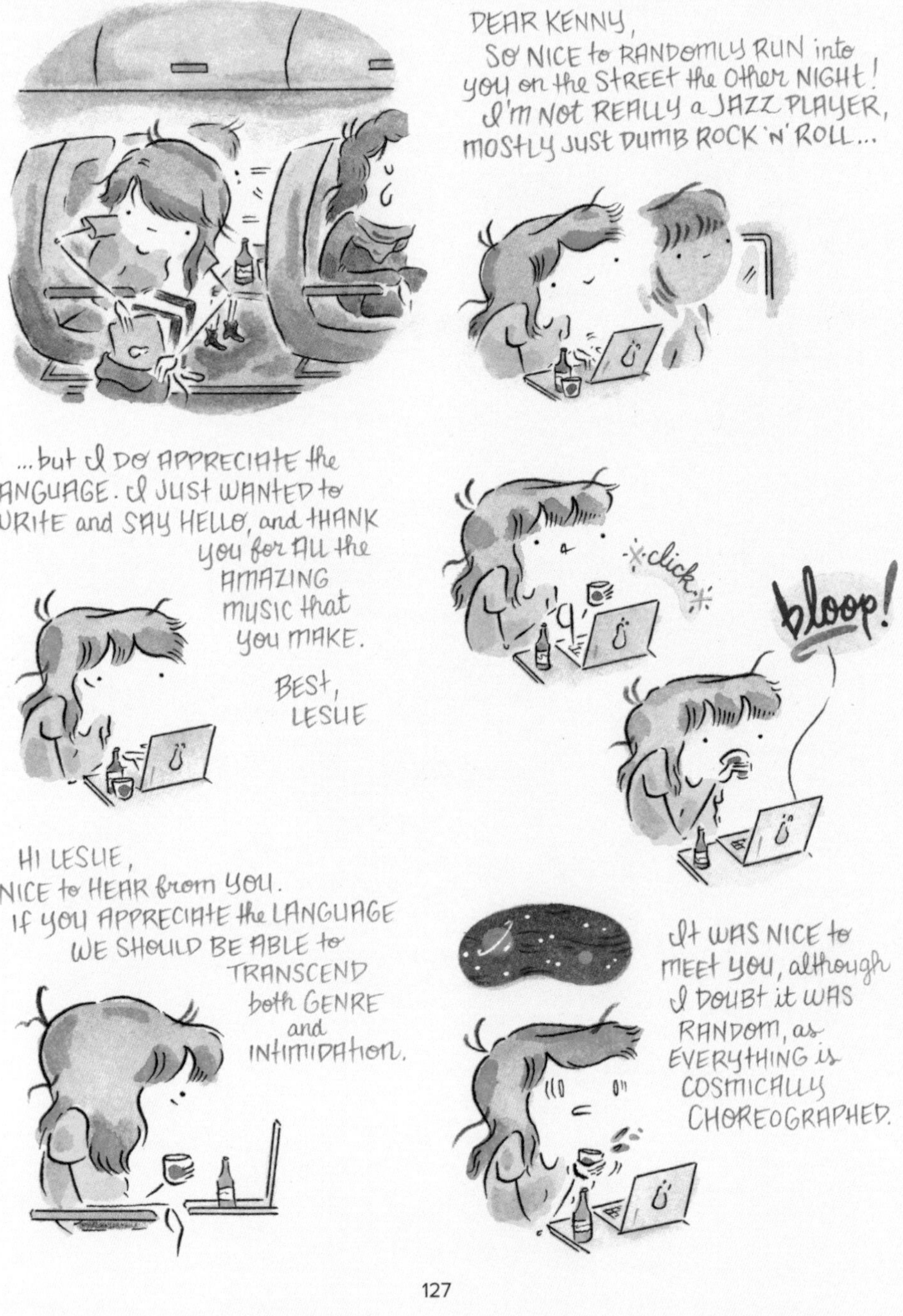
DEAR KENNY,
SO NICE to RANDOMLY RUN into YOU on the STREET the OTHER NIGHT! I'M NOT REALLY a JAZZ PLAYER, MOSTLY JUST DUMB ROCK 'N' ROLL...
...but I DO APPRECIATE the LANGUAGE. I JUST WANTED to WRITE and SAY HELLO, and THANK YOU for ALL the AMAZING MUSIC that YOU MAKE.
BEST, LESLIE
click
bloop!
HI LESLIE, NICE to HEAR from YOU. IF YOU APPRECIATE the LANGUAGE WE SHOULD BE ABLE to TRANSCEND both GENRE and INTIMIDATION.
IT WAS NICE to MEET YOU, although I DOUBT it WAS RANDOM, as EVERYTHING is COSMICALLY CHOREOGRAPHED.

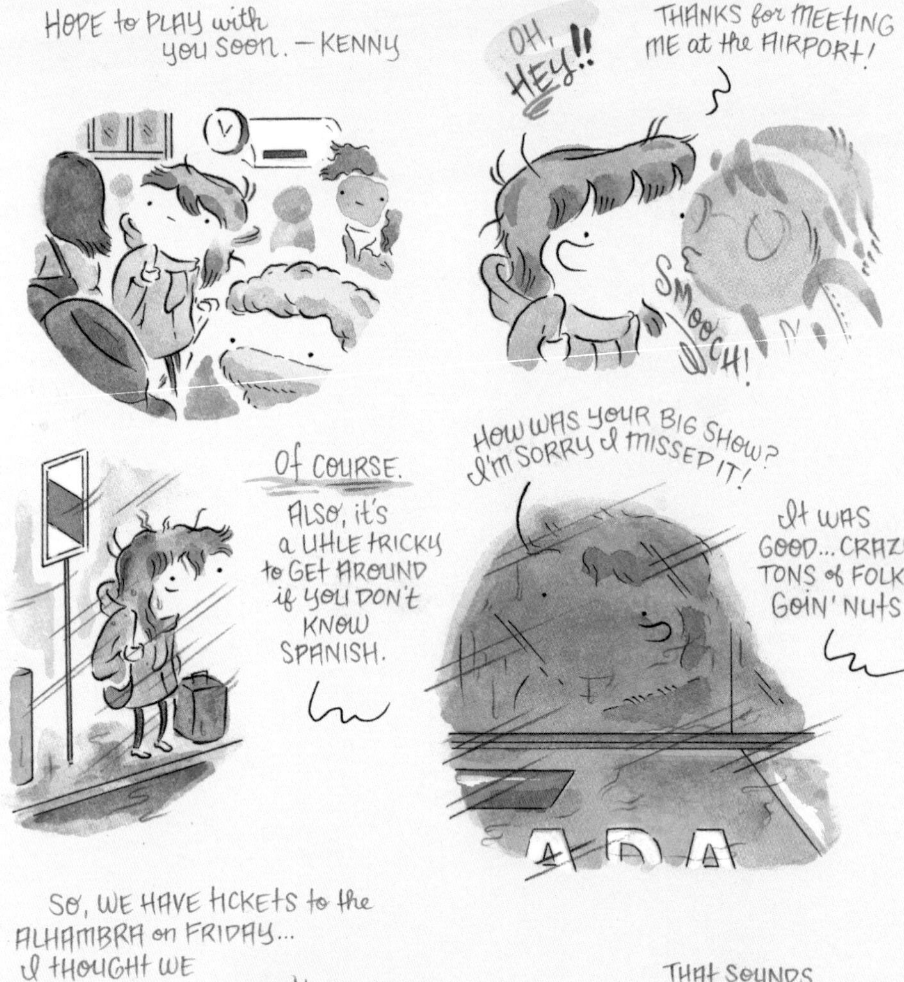
HOPE to PLAY with you soon. — KENNY
OH, HEY!!
THANKS for MEETING ME at the AIRPORT!
SMOOCH!
Of COURSE.
ALSO, it's a LITTLE TRICKY to GET AROUND if YOU DON'T KNOW SPANISH.
HOW WAS YOUR BIG SHOW? I'M SORRY I MISSED IT!
It WAS GOOD... CRAZY. TONS of FOLKS GOIN' NUTS.
SO, WE HAVE TICKETS to the ALHAMBRA on FRIDAY... I THOUGHT WE COULD JUST CHILL and RELAX until THEN?
THAT SOUNDS PERFECT.

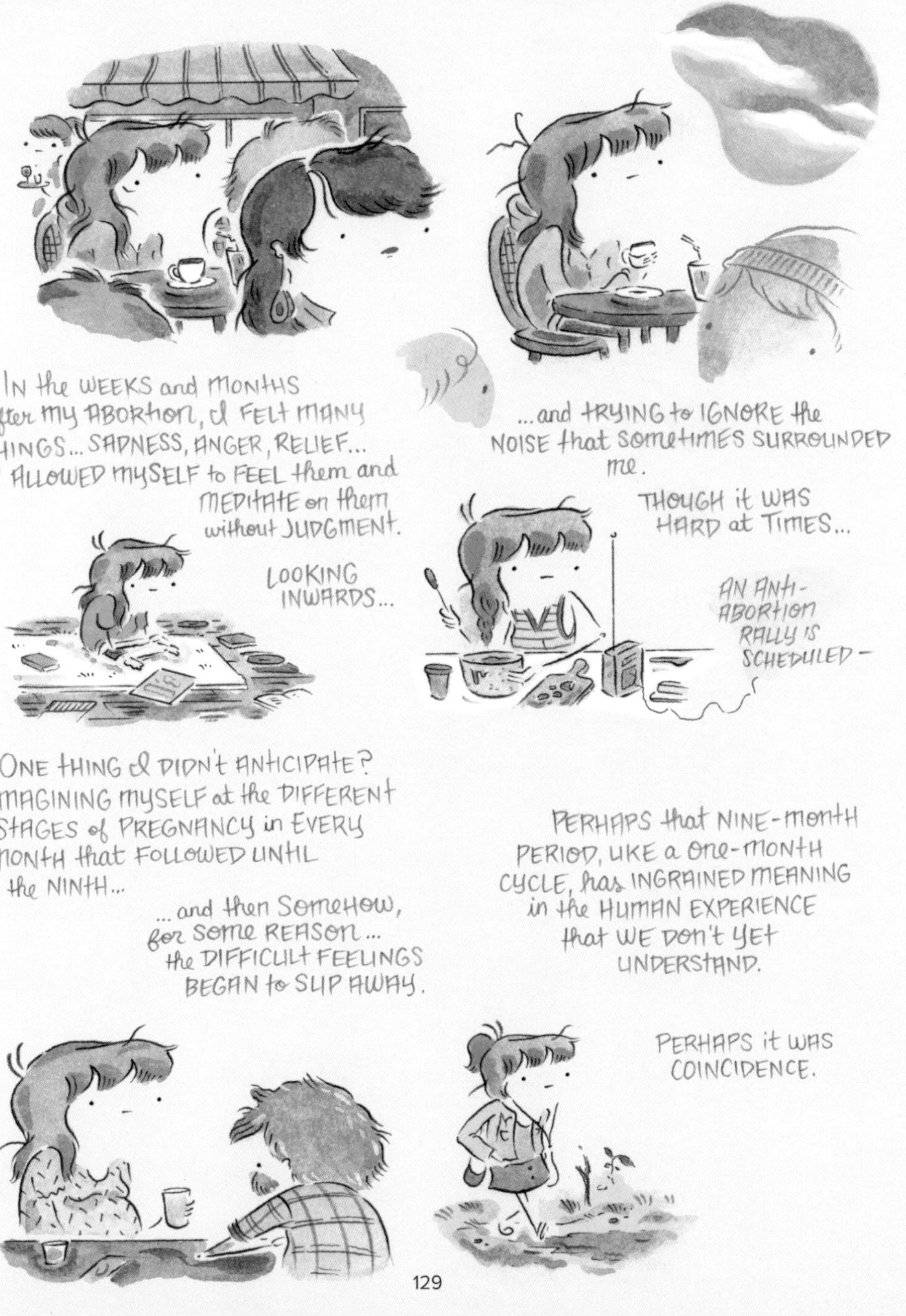
In the WEEKS and MONTHS after my ABORTION, I FELT MANY THINGS... SADNESS, ANGER, RELIEF... I ALLOWED MYSELF to FEEL them and MEDITATE on them without JUDGMENT.
...and TRYING to IGNORE the NOISE that SOMETIMES SURROUNDED me.
LOOKING INWARDS...
THOUGH it WAS HARD at TIMES...
AN ANTI-ABORTION RALLY IS SCHEDULED -
ONE THING I DIDN'T ANTICIPATE? IMAGINING MYSELF at the DIFFERENT STAGES of PREGNANCY in EVERY MONTH that FOLLOWED UNTIL the NINTH...
...and then SOMEHOW, for SOME REASON... the DIFFICULT FEELINGS BEGAN to SLIP AWAY.
PERHAPS that NINE-MONTH PERIOD, LIKE a ONE-MONTH CYCLE, has INGRAINED MEANING in the HUMAN EXPERIENCE that WE DON'T YET UNDERSTAND.
PERHAPS it WAS COINCIDENCE.

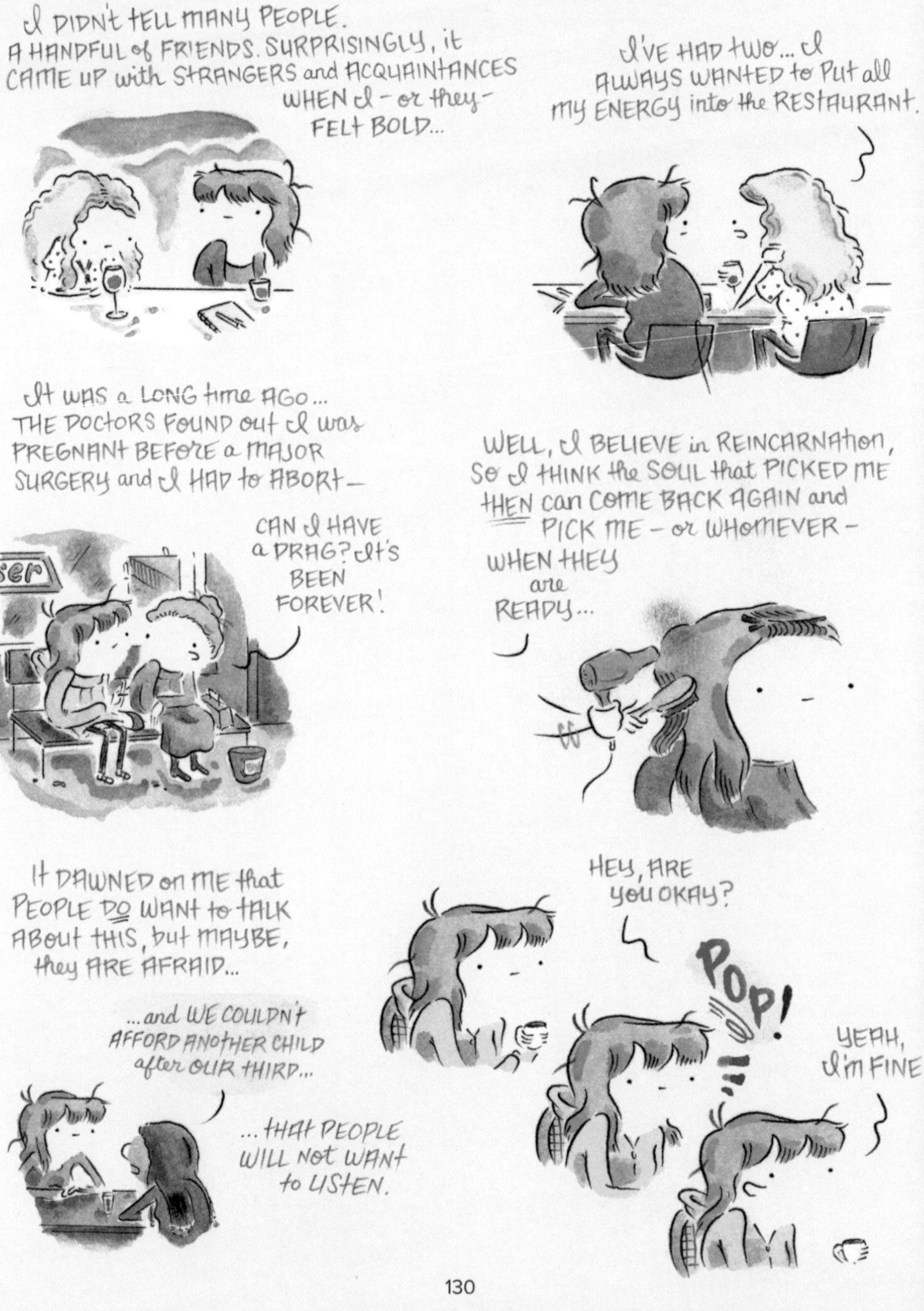
I DIDN'T TELL MANY PEOPLE.
A HANDFUL of FRIENDS. SURPRISINGLY, it CAME UP with STRANGERS and ACQUAINTANCES WHEN I – or they – FELT BOLD...
I'VE HAD TWO... I ALWAYS WANTED to PUT all MY ENERGY into the RESTAURANT.
IT WAS a LONG time AGO... THE DOCTORS FOUND out I was PREGNANT BEFORE a MAJOR SURGERY and I HAD to ABORT—
CAN I HAVE a DRAG? IT'S BEEN FOREVER!
WELL, I BELIEVE in REINCARNATION, SO I THINK the SOUL that PICKED ME THEN can COME BACK AGAIN and PICK ME – or WHOMEVER – WHEN THEY are READY...
IT DAWNED on ME that PEOPLE DO WANT to TALK ABOUT THIS, but MAYBE, they ARE AFRAID...
...and WE COULDN'T AFFORD ANOTHER CHILD after OUR THIRD...
...THAT PEOPLE WILL NOT WANT to LISTEN.
HEY, ARE YOU OKAY?
POP!
YEAH, I'M FINE.

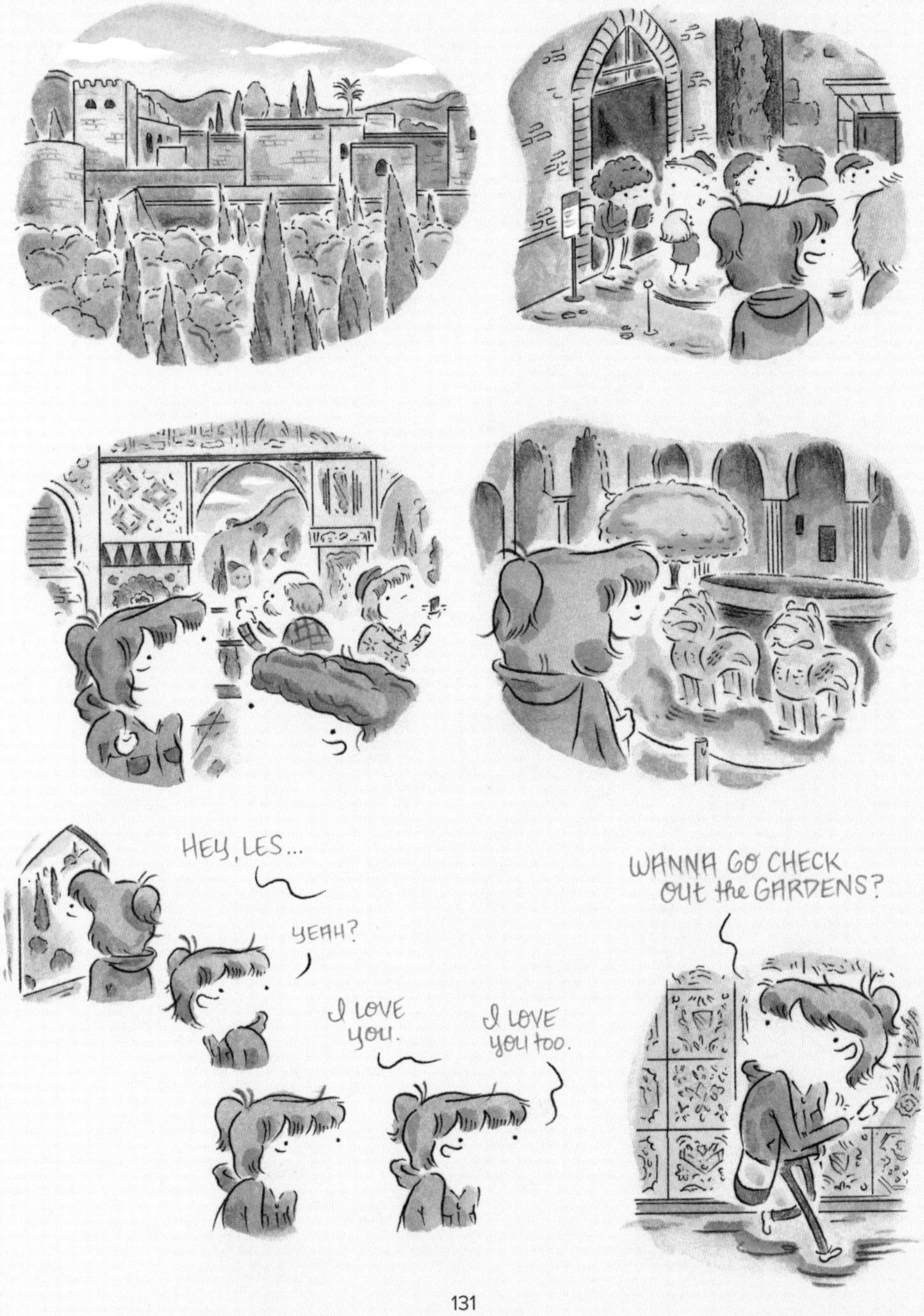
HEY, LES...
YEAH?
I LOVE YOU.
I LOVE YOU TOO.
WANNA GO CHECK OUT the GARDENS?

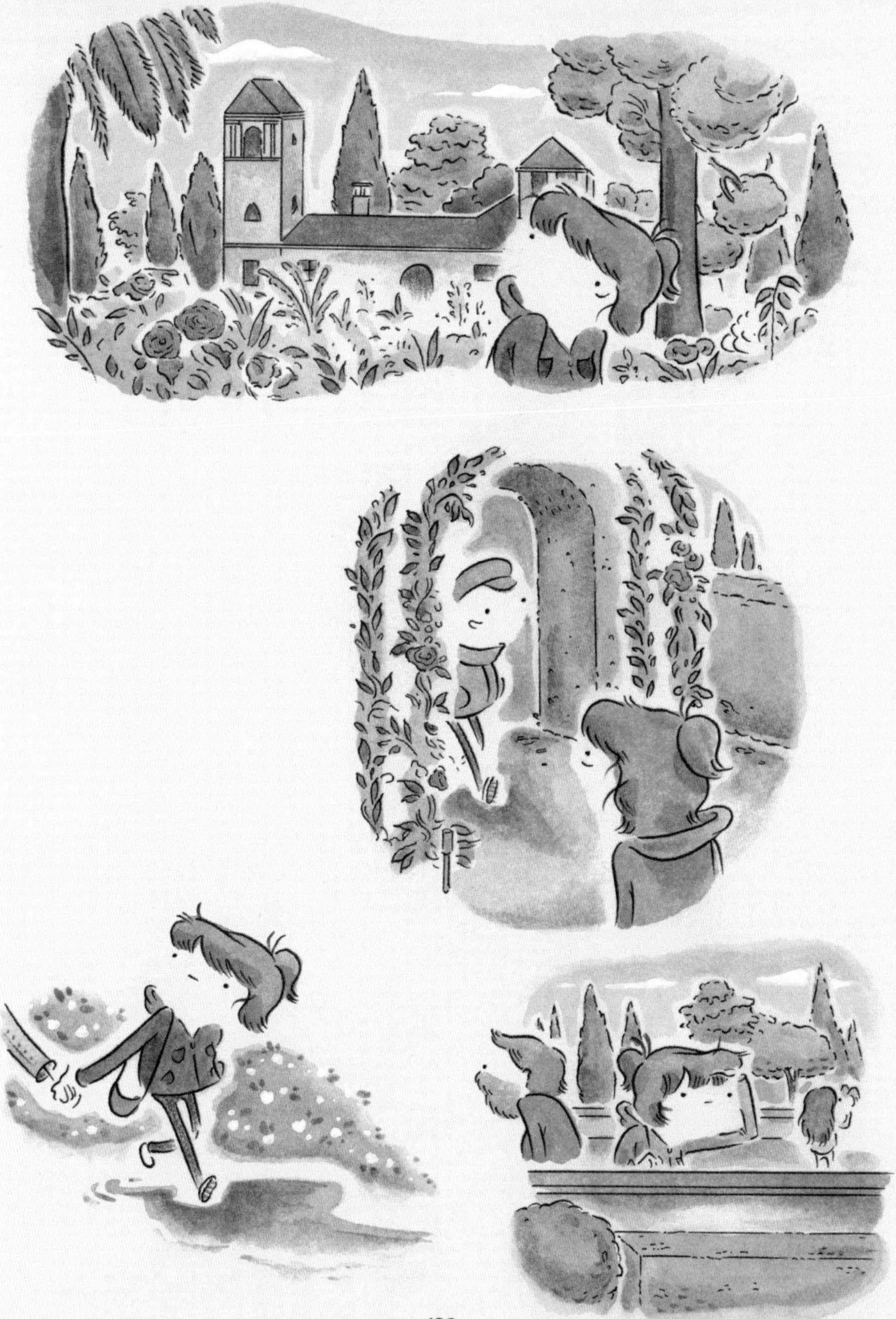

IN the DISTANCE
I SEE HEDGES that
SEEM to FORM a MAZE.

BUT WHEN
I ARRIVE
THERE, I
REALIZE I
was
MISTAKEN.

THEY are EASY
to NAVIGATE.

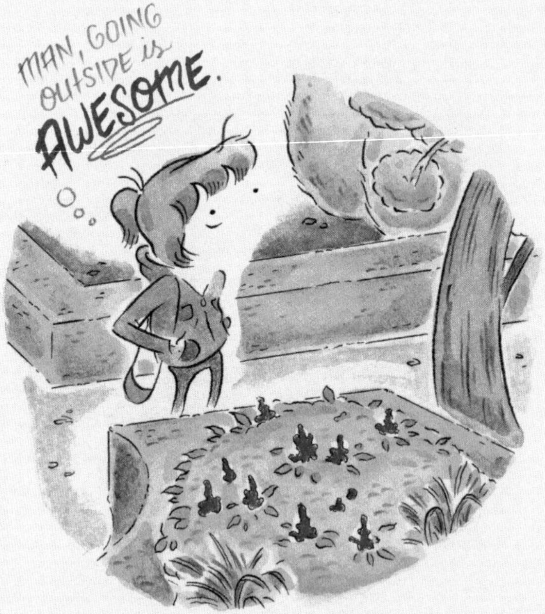
MAN, GOING OUTSIDE is AWESOME.

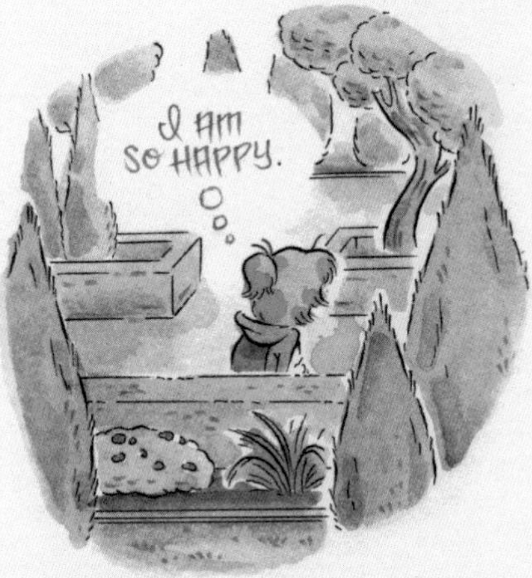
I AM
SO HAPPY.

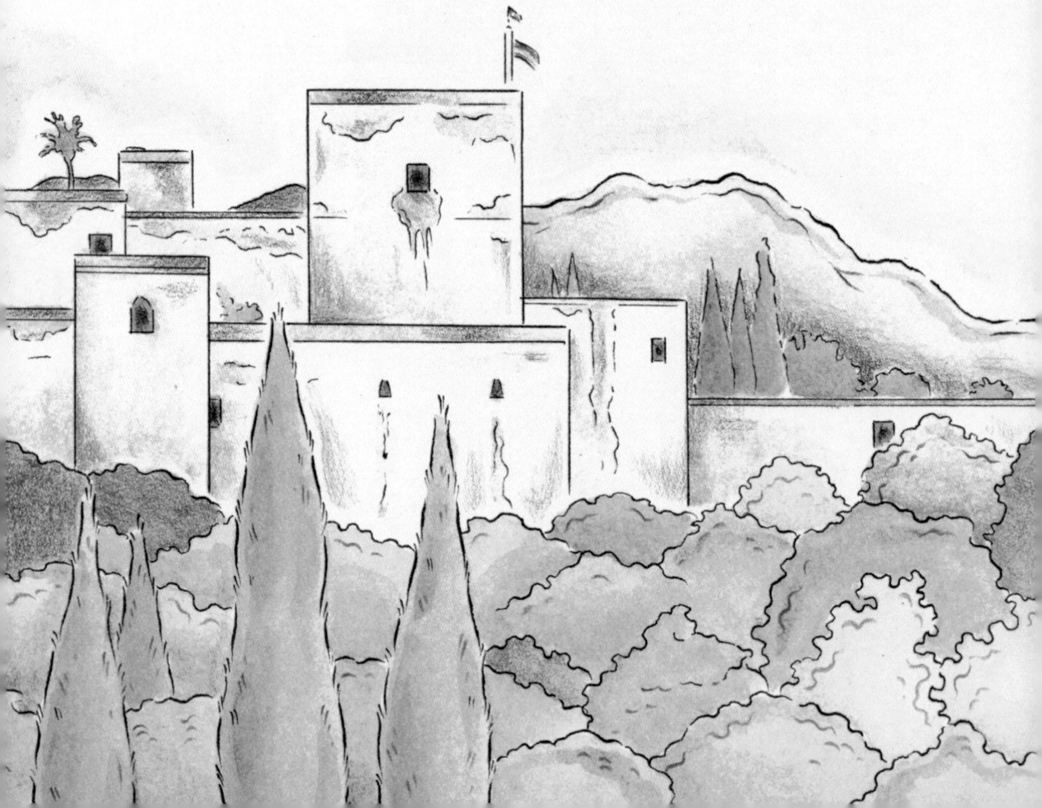

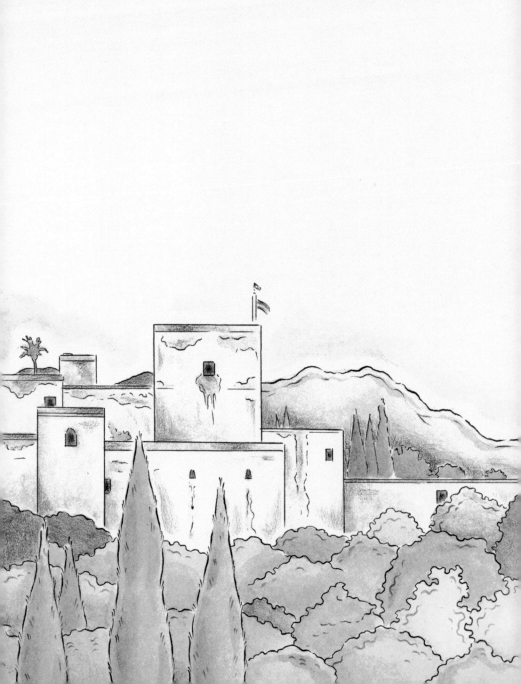

LESLIE STEIN
is the cartoonist of the *LA Times* Book
Prize Award–winning *Present*, as well as
Bright-Eyed at Midnight and the *Eye of the
Majestic Creature* series. Her diary comics
have been featured on *The New Yorker*, *Vice*,
and in the *Best American Comics* anthology.
She lives in Brooklyn, New York.